KNOCK!
KNOCK!
KNOCK!
ON WOOD

KNOCK! KNOCK! KNOCK! ON WOOD

My Life In Soul

EDDIE FLOYD
with TONY FLETCHER

BMG

KNOCK! KNOCK! KNOCK! ON WOOD:
MY LIFE IN SOUL

Book production by Adept Content Solutions.

Cover photo via Getty Images.

All interior photos from the collection of the author, except for the following:
Photo on page P4, top photo on page P5, photos on page P8, and top photo on page P10 via Getty Images. Top photo on page P9 courtesy of W. Robert Johnson.

Library of Congress Cataloging-in-Publication Data available upon request.

ISBN: 9781947026421

Published by BMG
www.bmg.com

CONTENTS

Introduction
KNOCK-KNOCK-KNOCK ON WOOD

September 5, 2017: I'm standing on the stage of the Royal Albert Hall in London, on my third day of rehearsals for a sold-out concert to take place this evening: *Stax Records: 50 Years of Soul*. Now, just to be clear off the bat, as we start this story, the famous Stax Records, which was my musical home for one of the best decades of my life, was dealing in soul *long* before 1967. Still, that was the year we "Hit the Road Stax," as we called our first visit to Europe, and that's the anniversary that the British are celebrating tonight with a live BBC broadcast. Even half a century on, people in Britain, France, Scandinavia—they still talk about that Stax/Volt tour as a major musical event, one of those revue shows that helped shift the tastes of a generation.

Only five of us who were part of that tour have made it over for the anniversary: yours truly, William Bell, and Sam Moore as featured singers, and Steve Cropper and Booker T. Jones, the two surviving members of the Stax house band, Booker T. & The M.G.'s, that was on stage for every minute of those package shows fifty years back. Just about everyone else has passed on, sadly. Al Jackson Jr., without whom my signature song would never have had its signature drum fill, was tragically murdered in 1975; his killers have never been brought to justice. His rhythm section partner in the M.G.'s, bassist Donald "Duck" Dunn, died in his sleep in Tokyo, in March 2012, after the second of two double shows with the Blues Brothers Band. He spent the last night of his life on stage with me, Cropper, and other musical friends, playing the songs he so loved, many of which he had helped make famous in the first place.

Otis Redding, who closed out the Stax/Volt Revue in 1967, left us when his private plane crashed into Lake Morona, Wisconsin, at the end of that year, taking the lives of almost all the original Bar-Kays, his young backing band at the time, with him. I was here in England at the time, and when my own plane had problems getting me home in time for Otis's funeral, I wrote a song about it: "Big Bird." A few weeks later, Otis had his biggest hit with one of the last songs he recorded, "(Sittin' On) the Dock of the Bay." Steve Cropper, who cowrote it like he did a lot of my hits too, will be playing it tonight alongside Booker, with our BBC host Jools Holland on piano and the great Sir Tom Jones on vocals. Tom and I have our own good history, but that's true of me and most people, as you'll find out if you stick around.

Me, I turned eighty years old just six weeks ago. By rights, I should have slowed down by now. And by my own standards I have: I've told everyone this is the last time they'll see me on stage in Europe. But if you are to know anything about Eddie Floyd, it's that I don't let the grass grow under my feet. For my eightieth birthday, I hosted a massive family gathering at my ranch outside Montgomery, Alabama. Brought in my children, my brothers and sisters, nieces, nephews, friends, exes. They came from all over the country: Detroit, D.C., Memphis, Atlanta, Macon, Montgomery . . . just some of the places I've called home over the years. A few weeks before the event, I drove up to Memphis to record with my friend there, Lester Snell, and a group of soul-funk musicians I've been using there for the last few years. Made a CD single called "It's My Party" and gave a copy to everyone who attended the celebration. When you reach my point of life, it's really not about selling the music no more. Took care of that a *long* time ago.

The BBC wants me to do two songs tonight out of the several hundred I've written, recorded, or performed over the decades. One of them is from my first working visit to Stax as a writer in 1965 when Cropper and I penned "634–5789 (Soulsville, U.S.A.)" for Wilson Pickett, who was coming in to cut a session for Atlantic Records the next day. Pickett and I already had history, and you'll be hearing a lot more about him in the coming pages. Tonight, I'll be singing "634–5789" with James Morrison, a young Brit whose inclusion at the Albert Hall, along with other newer artists, goes to show how soul music has carried over into future generations.

Shortly after "634–5789," Cropper and I wrote my biggest hit, at the Lorraine Motel in Memphis. A massive thunderstorm kicked in that night, and Cropper and I took inspiration from it. We figured we had something good, and we thought it would be perfect for Otis Redding. But because he never showed up to claim it, Stax put it out on me. By the summer of 1966 our record was on top of the R&B charts, and all over pop radio in ever country, so it seemed. In the years since, it's been recorded by *hundreds* of different artists, from David Bowie to Ella Fitzgerald, and in every genre you can think of: rock, country, jazz, Latin, instrumental. Disco, too: in 1979, Amii Stewart took it to the top of the charts all over the world.

So I wrote some of my biggest hits with Steve Cropper; I wrote some of my best with Booker T. Jones, from the psychedelic soul of "Big Bird" to the ballads "I've Never Found a Girl (To Love Me Like You Do)" and "California Girl." I know that the British especially worship "Big Bird." Funny to think about it now, but at the time, it was ignored. It didn't fit in with what Stax was doing; the R&B disc jockeys didn't know how to respond. And they didn't really know me over in the rock field, so I didn't get play there either. But my mind covers the universe. Always has. It seems to have worked out just fine in the long run.

I've always been a singer and performer, but I wrote hits for almost every other artist on Stax—and beyond—along the way. For Sam & Dave, for Otis, and a couple for my friend William Bell too. And I wrote my *first* hits for the one surviving person from that original Stax/Volt tour who is missing tonight: Carla Thomas. If it wasn't for Miss Carla agreeing to record two songs I wrote for her in D.C., way back in 1964–65, and making hits out of them, I would probably never have got invited in at Stax in the first place. Everything would have been different. And don't think I don't know that.

But that's why I call Stax a family, because there was nobody jealous of nobody else. It was just like: If he can do it, I can do it, and that's what we did. And we all had the freedom to do what we wanted. It's the same with every artist I've ever worked with: I'm a fan. I've always been that. We've never had any problems with the music over the years, whatever anyone tries to tell you.

So now the cameras are in place, and the director is giving me a signal. A couple of minutes back, I was sitting quietly in the wings, talking with my son Alan, who's flown over from his home in Atlanta to join me during some time off from his regular job as tour manager for Beyoncé. And we were both just chatting with Deanie Parker, who came to Stax in the early 1960s as an aspiring singer, was hired as its first secretary and publicist, and for the fifty-plus years ever since has been one of its main keepers of the faith. Deanie and I wrote some songs together, too; that's how things were back there. Anyway, there we were talking about the old times, when a young assistant from the BBC politely interrupted to remind me—again—that I was up next. You don't need to tell me to do nothing two or three times. Same with singing; almost all my hits have been captured on first or second take. I could never be a movie star, not with all the takes they have to go through. B-o-r-i-n-g.

See, many people get the wrong idea about me. You won't see me coming in kicking down the doors. I can sit in the club totally quiet, not even look like I'm getting ready to do anything, but believe me, I am. It's like, quiet was the time to be quiet. Now it's the time to do my thing. And when I do, people are often left asking, *Is that the same person?*

Same when people ask how I keep my voice in shape. I don't know! All I can tell you is that I don't rehearse when I'm not at home. I don't practice on anything—but while my running and boxing days are long behind me, I still start every morning walking a mile or two round my ranch, weights in hand. Like to stay fit. Then, when I get ready to do a show, I know the songs I'm getting ready to do, and I just split my mind off into those songs. Will I hit the note when it's time to hit it? I won't know until it's time. But I can think the note, I can think the song, I can hear the tone, the pitch, in my mind. Once I hear something in my head, it just goes over and over. I live music all the time inside my head. That's why I never stop performing, never stop writing, never stop recording. Being a soul man is for life.

My attitude is, no matter what gig I got, I do the best I can do. I call it "Take No Prisoners." I don't think I could do it any other way if I don't feel like it's real. And people call me back. I've been on the road almost all my life. And sometimes I have to stop myself and say, *Wow! Do you realize how far you've been in music and how long you've been in music, and you've still got a gig?* I've had people saying, "But you could be this, you could be that." And I say, "I'm *fine*, man. What are you talking about?" I mean look at me tonight. Eighty years old, and I'm on the stage of a sold-out Albert Hall—again—closing out a live BBC broadcast.

As you can imagine, there's a lot of stories in a life like mine. But right now, I hear the band starting up, and it's time for me to do my thing. As the horns start in on that famous riff, I prepare to Take No Prisoners: *Everybody, put your hands together, come on . . . We're gonna Knock on Wood!*

KNOCK!
KNOCK!
KNOCK!
ON WOOD

Chapter 1
ALL MONEY AIN'T FOR YOU

If you want to see the road in Montgomery, Alabama, where I grew up, you're out of luck. Mason Street, in the heart of the area known as Washington Park, was bulldozed in the 1960s and now sits right underneath the intersection of two big Expressways: I-65, which runs north to south, and I-85, which runs east to west. Used to be I knew a thousand people in a neighborhood that barely exists anymore. The main street, Holt, still stands, running near enough alongside the I-65, but it's a ghost of what it once was, back when it was full of stores and offices and churches and clubs and everything that make a neighborhood a neighborhood. There was the Carver Theater, one of the great old cinemas of the day; there was Dr. Smiley's dentist office, Pitts Drug Store,

Arrington's Sweet Shop . . . the shops have all gone, but the Carver—which my older brother Benny used to manage—remains. These days it's called Big Boyz Club, and that tells you something about how our culture has changed over the years.

Some of the local churches have survived, too, though the most famous of them are boarded up. Still, no way anyone's going to tear down the Holt Street Baptist Church. That's where 5,000 people gathered the evening of December 5, 1955, four days after Montgomery resident Rosa Parks refused to give up her seat on the bus for a white person. My grandmother was out there that night, bringing water to the crowds; nobody had seen nothing like it. Dr. Martin Luther King Jr. gave his first major speech to a crowd there. He was only twenty-five, a new pastor in town, and I guess people knew he was special because only hours earlier, he had been elected as first leader of the Montgomery Improvement Association, itself formed that evening at the Mount Zion AME church right next door. A decade later, in March 1965, just before the bulldozers came and wiped out half the 'hood, the famous civil rights march from Selma to Montgomery came right on up Holt Street and passed those two churches on its way to the state capital. Sometimes it feels like everything that moved around the country was on my goddamn block.

But before my neighborhood became famous to the rest of the world, it was just that: a neighborhood. A *thriving* neighborhood. There was no distress. No people out here in pain. Just people living. Doing what they had to do to get by and then coming home again. We lived all right, me and my mother and my grandmother and my younger brother Joe. We moved around a little when I was very small, but by the time we were on Mason Street, we had a backyard, and I had family all around me. Joe and I got on fine; when the weather was good, we'd play outside, and when the storms rolled in at night, we'd get scared and hide under the bed, where we'd knock on wood for good luck. That memory served me well over the years.

My grandfather Ben West worked as a pullman—a porter—on the trains, a coveted job for black men back then. My uncle Price West was an electrician who helped build the clock at the Union Station downtown. Another uncle, Robert West, was a bellman at the Jefferson Davis Hotel, named for the only President of the Confederate States. Robert went up to Detroit after that; you'll hear a lot more about him soon enough. Like I already said, my older brother Benny ran the Carver as well as two black theaters downtown. And so it went. There was work for everyone, and so everyone worked.

But it was the women in my family who had the major impact on me. My grandmother, Louise Williams, was a strong woman, a loving woman, a no-nonsense woman, and after marrying Ben West, whose family came from Virginia but had moved down to Montgomery, she passed those qualities on to my mother, Florence West. Florence was first married to a man by the name of Benny Horton, and they lived up in Anniston, Indiana, where my mother attended school for nursing. There they had three children: Louise, Benny Jr., and David, before they got divorced and my mother moved her family back on down to Montgomery. There she met my father, Prince Edward Floyd, who hailed from nearby Selma, and he and my mom got married in 1936, I believe. I came along on June 25, 1937, and my brother Joe was born a couple of years later.

Prince Edward—and maybe that name told me I'd have me some love from the British people down the line—had gone on up to Detroit by then and got himself a job in the steel mills there, part of the exodus of black people from the south in search of better wages and conditions in the industrial cities of the north. They called it the Great Migration. Dad was a part-time boxer, a welterweight; he trained at the Brewster-Wheeler Recreation Center in Detroit, where Joe Louis—who also moved from Alabama to Detroit between the wars—had trained on his way to becoming heavyweight champion of the world. As a little kid, Joe Louis was our idol, so I'm not really going to be thinking about my father as a boxer when we got a connection to the greatest one in history. Still, the only picture I have of my father is one that shows him in the ring, with a look in his eyes like he's fixin' to kill someone. I took up boxing myself for a short while, just before I hit my teens—until this guy hit me in the eye, and then I figured that singing was a better way to earn my keep. Not that I can't fight, but I've never gone looking for it.

I only saw my father but maybe three times in my life. I remember at four years old; that's when my mother said, "Go downstairs and see your daddy." We met again when I was twenty-five and he saw me sing in clubs in Detroit. Then all of a sudden, he's sick, and I go and I see him in the hospital and I leave, and I come back home, and next I know, he's passed. And I go back for the funeral. That's the end of it.

But my dad has been in me all my life, and still is. I've noticed other people wear the absence of a father on their shoulder like a big chip. But not Eddie, because I'm not ever going to be like everybody. That's a promise. What I told you about my father is what I know. I ain't gonna cry about it.

Besides, I got my mother, my main influence—my one influence, I might say. Especially on my music; she took me to concerts up in Detroit as a child, turned me on to everything and everyone, and when I set out on my own, she backed me all the way. As a qualified nurse, Florence was able to get work in Montgomery and in Detroit, which was partly how we were able to keep going back and forth.

Everything you hear Eddie Floyd say, any words of wisdom, all come from my mother. How to treat people, what to do. She would tell me, "Eddie, there isn't anything you can't do," though maybe there was a lot that I didn't *want* to do! In her honor, I remain the same way, and I do the same. There's never any time that she's not in my mind. And any situation that I speak of, I speak the way she did; I think that way. So a song like "Make Up Your Mind—so I can make up mine"—well, that's her way of speaking. Same with "Raise Your Hand." Or "Things Get Better." That's the way I write. They're statements of intent, of instruction, of inspiration. And I got them all from her.

There's another thing my mother used to say to me, which I never turned into a song title, though maybe I should have done: "All money ain't for you." You gotta think about that one for a minute and maybe cast back to when I was younger, when maybe I wanted more out of life than I deserved, when maybe I thought I could get real rich, real quick, and my mother would always remind me, *"Hey Eddie, all money ain't for you."* As a musician, as a singer, as a songwriter, I've carried that with me. You don't have to demand every dime that's out there to be a success—especially not by taking it from other people. You don't have to be the biggest earner to be happy. The pot is for everyone, not for just one.

After my mother and my grandmother passed on, I erected a memorial to those two wonderful women on the ranch I'd built when I moved back down to Montgomery, over by what I call the "pier," by the pond I'd dug out. Every single day I'm at home, I go down to the pier and speak to them. And in their memory, I keep their beds in a separate room: Grandma Louise's bed goes back to the 1850s, because it was *her* mother's before her. By connecting all of that to the present day, by keeping those beds in my house, I feel like I'm paying tribute to the two people who did the most for me. I wouldn't have been anything without them, so I like to keep their presence in my own life.

My first school was right on Mason Street, at one of the many neighborhood churches that don't exist no more. I'd pretty much roll out of bed, out the front door, and straight into Miss B's class, kindergarten through second grade. Elementary school for black kids like us tended to be in the church back then; we didn't have free-standing schools of our own.

Now I know a lot of people are going to want me to talk more about this, about race, about segregation, about growing up in the heart of the South, before the Civil Rights movement took hold on my very street, and at the peak of the old Jim Crow laws. But I'll tell you something now, and if it's a disappointment to you, well so be it . . . I don't go there. I don't deal with politics, period. We know there was drama down here, but what has that got to do with me singing all these songs? That's all I'm saying. I was born in this town, and all the shit happened in this town. I left this town, I went to Detroit, we did music back and forth. What else? There's always some journalist saying, "Yeah, but during that time when things was happening, did you not have a problem?" Well, maybe I did and maybe I didn't. Music's always been the thing I care about, and I leave the politics to the politicians. Don't misunderstand me, I know right from wrong, and I'll call you on it if you speak some bullshit. But I don't make it my business if you don't.

Look, we know our history down here, we know the struggles our people went through, and we have our heroes— and our heroines—as a result. We were always educated about *that*. But I know world history too. And it's very similar. So, this is America, and this is what you want me to be talking about, but it's not *just* America. Did the British not own part of America some day? Spanish too. Every country has its history of racism, every colonial power had slavery, so every country has to figure its own shit out. So for sure, Montgomery was the heart of the Old South, the birthplace of the Confederacy—but it was the birthplace of the Civil Rights movement too. You want to talk history: the British settlers came here and drove the Creek natives all the way to Oklahoma. Now, what's left of the Creeks got a piece of land down by the river where they run casino boats, just a skip-and-a-hop down from the old slave auction blocks. History's complex.

Besides, you go downtown to Montgomery nowadays, and young kids don't want to hear about the old days; it's not about that no goddamn more. There ain't no discrimination on knowledge, what people want to know. Black person and white person be looking at the same piece of history about black people and white people, just we ain't fighting each other when we looking at it! We just looking. I know the reasons things went down, you know the reasons—but it wasn't you or I. So, sure, there's always some old person who can't turn it loose; he'll make some little quote or something and spoil it, but believe me, the young kids don't want to hear that shit. Nor do I.

I would take my bike and ride into downtown when I was a kid. Used to be this little studio you could go get your photograph taken, and when I was about thirteen, that's what I did. The place was run by a black dude and it cost 25 cents; this guy had a couple of curtains that he'd open up so that it looked like there was a view outside of a window when in fact it was just a painting, and he had a little stool right there, so I put my foot up on the stool and acted cool as I could while the photo was taken. Years later I saw a photograph of Wilson Pickett's father—he came from Prattville, just outside Montgomery— and I said, "That's the same photo booth!" There weren't many around, and to have just even one photograph of yourself back then was considered a big deal. That might be why, nowadays, I take photographs of everything and everyone. I want to document all that's happening around my life.

Sometimes, in Montgomery, I'd see Hank Williams driving around in his big old Cadillac with his name on the side. Hank was a legend even then, the biggest name in country music, and he came from *our hometown*. He died young, just thirty years old, a victim of chronic pain, alcoholism, and, as often the case, some other unexplained business nobody's ever fully figured out. Around 25,000 people came out to pay tribute to him after he died on New Year's Day, 1953; they say it was the biggest event Montgomery had ever seen until then. I wasn't among them; I was "otherwise disposed" for reasons you'll find out soon enough. Still, I liked Hank's music: just because it's country don't mean black folk don't enjoy it. And just because it's soul music don't mean white people can't dig it. A good song is a good song. A good singer, same thing.

They've got a museum for Hank Williams now, downtown, and it brings a lot of people to Montgomery. There's talk of a museum for Nat King Cole too. So there should be. For many of us, he's the *real* famous musician out of Montgomery, the greater legend. Like Joe Louis, Nat was a true role model; the man always carried himself correct and proper, whatever he may have been up against. A few years back, Cole's childhood home was moved to the grounds of Alabama State University so that it could be renovated, and there's a historical marker where it once stood on Harris Way. Even though Nat and his family left Montgomery for Chicago when he was just four years old, back in 1923, the Coles remained a major name in town. Nat's nephew Ethan was a good friend of mine. Perhaps too good, as you'll find out.

Like pretty much every kid from my time, I went to church on weekends with my mother, my grandmother, and my siblings—we were part of Mount Zion, where my grandmother, Louise, was one of the main people in charge. But unlike a lot of the future soul singers who are going to pass through this book, my background was not in gospel. I didn't get my vocal chops from years of singing in the church choir.

No, I was blessed that from the earliest age—six weeks old, or so I'm told—when I was spending half my time in Detroit. My mother would take me there to stay with her brother, Robert West, and his wife, Katherine, who didn't have children of their own. Like I already mentioned, Robert moved on up to Detroit where he started a real estate business, which was important work in a city where there was not just a housing shortage as people flocked to find work, but invisible "red lines" marked where black people could buy a house. He was also a massive jazz fan, with 78s going back as far as the 1920s. And of course the great singers of the era all started out up front of one of those big jazz bands, so I got to hear the best of both worlds.

Going to Detroit from Montgomery, we'd take the train. You had to change at Cincinnati, and we'd usually stay overnight there. In the train station they used to have the Rock-Olas that played music. They actually had a screen that far back with pictures of the people who were singing the songs. Not moving pictures, just a picture that would pop up and you'd see someone . . . All the same, I used to think they were *inside* the Rock-Ola, and I'd say to my mama, "Can you give me some money so I can play the Rock-Ola and see those people?" I was just always interested in anything to do with music, no matter what.

Sometimes I still feel that way; when a great song gets to you, it's like you can see the musicians in your head, you can see the singer, and you can imagine that they're playing just for you. Music has always had a magical ability to transform me like that.

I admit I was lucky. Up in Detroit, thanks to my mother, I got to see all the greats, mostly at the Fox, which was the major black theater at the time, like the Howard was in D.C. or the Apollo was in Harlem. The concert that I always talk about, the one that I remember most vividly, the one that just cemented the magic for me, was Lena Horne, who performed with a big orchestra there, the way that used to be. Everyone's in the theater and they're talking loud, you can feel the excitement in the air, and then all of a sudden it gets quiet, and the announcement comes up: "Good evening, ladies and gentlemen, it's . . . showtime!" I get the shivers, because I know something special is about to happen, and then the lights go down—except for those that are on the curtains. The curtains open up, and you can hear the band playing, but you're not seeing them, because there's another set of curtains. Then those curtains open up, and you're *still* not seeing the band, but then the third curtains open up, and finally there they are, the orchestra in their fancy suits, swinging that special groove, and there's Lena Horne in her gown, looking like a million dollars and . . . oh wow! For me it was just unique. It was like all the glamor of Hollywood just a few feet in front of me—but with one of the greatest singers in the world instead of a film star. What more could a young boy ask for?

I knew then, if I didn't already know from the Rock-Ola in Cincinnati, that I wanted to be a singer. I wanted to be the person inside that jukebox, the person on the Fox Theater stage, the one who brought magic to the world. Over the next few years, I had enough training: it felt like I saw all the greats in Detroit with my mother. Count Basie, Ella Fitzgerald, Billy Eckstine . . . These people were icons to me, like they existed on a different level to anything I could ever imagine. And yet, fast forward just twenty-five years or so, and would you believe it, but Ella Fitzgerald is out there covering one of my songs. So is Count Basie and his Orchestra! And Billy Eckstine!

My two brothers can sing; my sister can sing and play piano. My older brother told me recently he'd had a little group for a while, and my other brother played trombone for high school, and then he sung in the choir through military. So maybe music ran in our family. But fact is, I was the only one who wanted to do something about it.

My uncle wasn't a musician himself, but he understood how music worked, because he could talk to me about a particular record, what made it so special. I didn't necessarily understand all that he's telling me, but I was hooked on his every word all the same. By the age of seven, I'd memorize a song from his record player and then set myself up in another room, call my relatives in, and perform for them, like I was on the stage.

Detroit at the start of the 1940s was booming. The city was the automobile capital of the world, and as well as all the car companies that were based in Detroit with their factories, there were the factories that produced all the stuff that the car industry was dependent on to build their Chryslers, Fords, and GMs in the first place. No outsourcing the tires to Mexico and the tire rims to Canada; all of it got made right there in Michigan.

When the USA entered the Second World War, after the bombing of Pearl Harbor in December 1941, domestic car production stopped entirely, and the factories switched over to producing aircraft, tanks, anti-aircraft guns, you name it. All of which meant there was an even bigger demand for workers, especially as many of the men folk signed up to fight. So now even *more* people came up from the South—blacks went from 4 percent of the workforce at the start of the war to 15 percent of it just three years later—and in the meantime a lot of women moved on over into jobs that had previously been considered fit only for men. You can see why my mother could get work as a nurse up there. I'm just a small kid at the time, I don't really know what's going on with the war, and my family's of an age that none of us get caught up in the actual fighting. We managed to avoid what they called the "race riots" of 1943 as well, when thirty-four people were killed, most of them black, and largely at the hands of the police and National Guard. Detroit was a home for us, and we were determined to make it our own.

So, after the war, Detroit returns to producing cars and all the things that go into them, and the workers from the South stay on, even though there's competition now for jobs with those coming back from the war. But America is prosperous, and Detroit is booming once more, and it's a proper jazz town with it. All the great groups are coming through, and some of them are picking up local musicians as they do. Dizzy Gillespie would make a habit of it. We've got our own big bands now as well, and they're attracting national attention: Paul Williams hit it big in the late 1940s with "Thirty-Five Thirty," the street number of Joe Von Battle's record shop on Hastings Street, right there at the heart of what they called Black Bottom. Battle put out records by everyone back then—characters with names like Boogie Woogie Red, One String Sam, and Detroit Count—people you could find singing on up Hastings Street itself, not just in the bars and nightclubs but on the streets at times too. Battle also released sermons by the great Reverend C. L. Franklin, pastor at the New Bethel Baptist Church just on up Hastings Street, and the father of the future Queen of Soul, Aretha; he put out Aretha's first-ever recording on one of those LPs in 1956, when she was just fourteen. I was living there myself by that point.

We also had great bluesmen in Detroit, especially John Lee
Hooker, who, like so many, moved up from the South during
the war, finding work in the factories and making a name for
himself on Hastings Street. Hooker would end up recording
for Battle, too, but first, in 1948, a label out in Los Angeles,
Modern Records, took a chance on a demo he'd made called
"Boogie Chillen," and it became the best-selling "race" record
on the *Billboard* charts the following year. After that, though, no
more "race records." *Billboard* changed the name of the chart to
"rhythm & blues," or "R&B," at the suggestion of a staff writer
by the name of Jerry Wexler. Me and that R&B chart would
get to know each other well in the years to come. Me and Jerry
Wexler, same thing.

All this helps explain why—if you're a kid from
Montgomery, Alabama, and you've fallen in love with popular
music, and you're spending half your time up in Detroit, at
almost the very heart of jazz, blues, vocal music, gospel, you
name it—then you really don't want to be spending the other
half of your time back down South. Which also explains why
it was devastating for me when my mother decided that she'd
had enough of going back and forth, and she was going to stay
settled in Montgomery, right there on Mason Street where I'd
started out. Me, I wanted none of that. I wanted to be up in the
big city. I was restless, so I started acting up. Acting up got me
into trouble. Trouble got me locked up. And getting locked up
changed my life.

Chapter 2
SENT UP

It's 1950, I'm pushing thirteen, and I'm restless, brother. I'm trying to get back to the music, back to Detroit, where it's all happening. But my mom, she's getting older, and she isn't traveling anymore. So I tried to get there myself two or three times by running away. I was trying to run all the way to Detroit. If I could have called my uncle, I'd have called him. If I could write him, I'd write him. The way I think of it is, I ain't really leaving family in Montgomery; it's not like I'm running away *from* something. It's that I'm running *to* something: Detroit.

Of course, I got no money, so I don't get very far. One time I make it forty-nine miles to Selma. Another time, I get further: all of eighty-nine miles to Birmingham. Detroit? That's another

700 miles, and here I am, only halfway up Alabama at best. And I got no money to ride the Greyhound bus there. So now what? I'll tell you what: I turn around and go back!

All right, you can tell I don't want to be here. And I'm making it obvious; I'm getting into trouble. Officially, I'm attending junior high at Loveless, just the other side of what's now the I 65 from my house. The school is named for Henry Allen Loveless, who came of age in the years after the Civil War, back at a time when the Reconstruction meant something. He owned funeral homes, a coal and wood yard, a livery stable . . . And he gave back: Loveless helped found the Dexter Avenue Baptist Church, where Dr. King ended up as pastor. He died in 1921, just before they started building Montgomery's first junior and senior high school for African Americans. They named it for the man who pushed hard for our right to that education.

But that education wasn't working out for me. I was rebelling. Like I say, restless. One day, I had a little fight with the principal, and I might have hit him, okay? And back then in that time, you didn't really do things like that! Fact, you still don't. You shouldn't.

My running partner at the time is Nat King Cole's nephew, Ethan Cole. He lives on Mason Street with me. Ethan Cole's dad is a successful man in his own right: like that old Mr. Loveless, he's got funeral homes. So anyway, me and Ethan, we get into trouble together. I'm already on the count for this incident at school, and back in that day, anybody did anything wrong, the police could pin it on you if they wanted to. They tried to say we broke into churches. We didn't break into no churches, no way; that's not me. But that's what they would do: if you got into trouble, they would put something else on you.

I don't know any other way to tell what happened next except that we were arrested, put in the county jail, held overnight, and then they ain't taking but no time to get us straight to the county courthouse the next morning. We're hauled up front, facing the judge, and then they all start talking about who did what, and before I know it, it comes down like this:

"Edward Floyd, you get three years in Mount Meigs. Ethan Cole, you can go."

My mom leaves with Mr. Cole and his son; I leave with the sheriff. But we both did the same thing!

At the time I'd never even heard of Mount Meigs. I can tell you plenty about it now, however. It was founded as the "Alabama Reform School for Juvenile Negro Law-Breakers," and it was designed for "Negro boys," under fifteen years old— like me at the time—giving "special attention to moral training so as to make (him) a self-respecting, industrious, good person."

And you know what? They weren't wrong. Even though I got locked up at the age of thirteen for three years for one count of hitting my teacher and then a bunch of trumped-up charges they threw in with it, it was the greatest thing that could have happened to me.

Mind you, that's not the way I first felt about the place. You've got to imagine the shock of it. I'm living in a real neighborhood in Montgomery, got my school nearby, my family, the church, the cinema, my friends. Sure, I'd sooner be in Detroit, but main thing is, I got some sort of freedom. And all of a sudden, I'm off in the countryside, *imprisoned* more or less, sleeping in dorms with twenty or thirty other boys who, like me, have been marked as criminals for something that may not have been a big deal if they weren't black.

Mount Meigs had four or five buildings. Three hundred kids, maybe a hundred girls and two hundred boys. But before we all get excited, the girls are in a totally different building, maybe a whole mile away. We only see them for school classes and church. And believe me, we looked forward to it!

When you arrived at Mount Meigs, you'd have to fight. And we *all* know how to fight. So I'm new, and I'm gonna be approached, and as soon as I'm approached, I know it's on. This guy comes at me, just looks at me, and starts throwing me down, but I keep getting up. And then he looks at me like he's going to kill me, but then he looks away, and . . . Bam! I take him out. And after that, we're best of friends. In fact, I still got a picture of that boy, from the day three years later when I'm getting ready to leave. Half my family comes out to greet me, and someone takes a picture, and there's this one buddy standing next to me that ain't going home: Samuel Hawkins. I left him right there. Samuel ran away one time, got as far as Birmingham. But then two or three months after he's gone, you hear the boys howl across the yard: "They got Samuel Hawkins!" And here he comes, driven back through those gates in a car. And you know the warden's going to give him some personal attention for taking off like that: he's going to get himself a beating.

That warden was named Mr. Holloway, and he lived there with his wife and two daughters. Other than them, we got us three guards. And a nurse. And two teachers, a Mr. Arthur Wilmer and a Mr. William Ford.

Now, you might think that two teachers for 300 boys is not exactly a good ratio, not if they want to fulfil their remit to give us a "common school education." But of course education back then for black kids meant being trained for the fields and the factory. And that's basically what it was: three days a week out in the fields, picking cotton in the summer, or cutting trees in the winter, the guard just sitting there under a tree all day. They didn't really have nothing for you to do: they couldn't have made but five dollars off that cotton we picked. And then just two days in school. And at the weekend: two days doing nothing! We're laying up Saturday and Sunday, though of course Sunday we go to church.

Now, at that church, they got a choir. And me, I can sing. I've been singing in front of people since I was seven years old. And Mr. Wilmer, he knows some of that. But he only really knows because, soon after I arrive with the sheriff, I decide I don't want to be at Mount Meigs, and I break out of there. Kids would do that. It wasn't hard. It wasn't like they had the big-ass gates and fences like they do now. They just know they're going to get you back. 'Cause where you gonna go? You ain't got no cars, you're just walking. That kid Samuel Hawkins, who got to Birmingham, he was the exception.

I actually left twice. I got all the way to Montgomery twice. The first time I go to where my older brother lives. Man, he looked shocked to see me. He told me to sit and watch a movie and wait. And then he called my mom, and then I guess one of them called Mount Meigs. So when my brother takes me back to my mother's house, Mr. Holloway is there. He says, "Come on, let's go, you know you gotta go back." And he's right, I got no choice; there's no way of getting around it. I mean, for my mom, it wasn't like she agreed I should be in there, but she figured that once I was locked up, I had to do my time and hopefully come out of it a better person.

Once I was back inside, I got a beating, like I expected. To mark you as a runaway then they put me in white or red, instead of the usual khakis, and they took your shoes, so now you're working in the fields with no shoes. They figure that's to stop you from running away again. Ha! Didn't stop me. I was off again as soon as I had some footwear back. And same thing happened all over again: I get home, Warden Holloway come around and take me back, I get a whooping, labeled a "rabbit" for running away, and marked by wearing different clothing.

Now, at this point, I could have gone *real bad*. I could have kept fighting the system, and although they'd have had to let me out of Mount Meigs eventually, I might as easily have just been transferred to the big house. So, when I get taken back in the second time after running away, they have a proper conversation with my mom. What can they do about me? Is there anything I'm interested in? Is there anything I really care about?

And the answer is obvious. It's music. I want to sing. And so, out of the 300 kids that are in there, Mr. Arthur Wilmer makes a point of taking an interest in me. He takes me into the choir. Up until then, I'd just been fooling around with my voice—dreaming of singing, really. But Mr. Wilmer, he taught me harmony. He taught me the different parts of the choir: bass, alto, first tenor, second tenor, soprano, contralto. I would sing them all, even the contralto. That's the way I write songs too, with all the voices in mind, because I can hear any part of the music. In fact, I wrote my first songs in there at Mount Meigs, not even thinking about recording them yet. And that's thanks to the lessons I had with Mr. Wilmer. He taught me how to hold my notes, how to fit in alongside other singers, raise my voice high or low to match the tone and the key, where to put in the emphasis, all that good stuff.

On Sundays at church we're singing hymns and spirituals and gospel. And we're getting good, and I'm really enjoying this. And I'm focused on it, too: I don't have the distractions I had back in Montgomery. I mean, I'm still locked up. I'm still down South. Detroit's still a long ways away. But at least I'm singing every day.

Some Sundays they'd bring in a group from a local college to sing for us, which was wonderful because it gave us something to aspire to. And some other Sundays—well, once a month— we'd get the chance to sing somewhere other than at the Mount Meigs church. In fact, my mom got to see me sing one time with the choir because they brought us to the Holt Street Baptist Church, of all places, right at the end of my road. We came by bus, and for just a few seconds, I can see my house across the road; I just can't *go* there. Once we're in the church, I look out from the choir. My mom is there, my family is there, church members are there. We sing for them, get back on the bus, go back out. I don't even get to speak to any of them.

I only got to see my mother but once a month: you were allowed just one visitor every first Sunday. My mother never missed. Never. I know it's not much, but there's a lot of 'em boys who didn't even have a mother; I was grateful for what I had. My mother would bring me a big box each month, a care package. There'd be a few of the boys looking for some of it—and sometimes I'd share it and sometimes I'd have to fight to hold onto it.

They had a band at Mount Meigs as well as the choir, and the band had a piano. Fact, first time I'd ever seen anyone my age behind a piano was another inmate, playing "Blue Moon." I heard him, and I was like, *Whoah? What is that?* I mean, I knew the song, I'd just never seen anyone play it before. It was a revelation.

After a couple of years in Mount Meigs, I've settled down. I'm no longer looking to run away. And I'm enjoying my time in the choir; I'm feeling like a real singer. I don't think I would have ever been the singer I became—and probably not the writer, either—without that training while "inside." And so, every chance I've ever had in life, I've been sure to give public thanks to Mr. Wilmer and Mr. Ford for having that faith in me. For the first several years after I got out, any time I was back in Montgomery, I'd go back there to see them. When I had my very first record, I took a copy to them just to show them I had recorded something. And they spoke of me all the way through life; I guess they held me up as a positive example. I got a lot to thank them for. I mean it when I say that getting sent there was the best goddamn thing ever happened to me. And that's why, when someone asks where I went to school, I always answer: "The University of Mount Meigs."

Chapter 3
BABY, THAT'S IT

I get out of Mount Meigs in late 1953 to find my uncle Robert West and his wife Catherine at the family house on Mason Street; they're visiting. This turns out to be just as well, because after a few days, they take me back to Detroit to live with them. Come to think of it, it's possible that had been arranged with my mother already, that they'd figured there was no point in me staying in Montgomery, where I might just get in trouble again, when it was so obvious I wanted to be living up in Detroit with the music. Either way, I wasn't about to complain. Obviously, I was going to miss my mother and grandmother, especially as I'd seen so little of them these last few years, but I was sixteen. It wasn't like there was a lot of schools nearby that could prepare me for college—and not a lot of money to pay for college if they did. The jobs paid better in the North, and there was the chance to make something there from my love of music. So off I went with Robert and Catherine, to their house just off Euclid Avenue, around 12th and 14th Streets, a little west of Hastings Street and the Black Bottom neighborhood and just a few blocks north of West Grand Boulevard, which would become a prominent musical Detroit address in the years to come.

Music had changed a lot while I'd been away. When I was a small kid, first going up in Detroit with my mother, the popular singers had been people like the Ink Spots and the Mills Brothers, Nat King Cole and the new sensation Frank Sinatra . . . what you might call "formal" vocal singing. But things started shifting in the years right after the war. The Ravens, a new "bird group" from New York City, combined falsetto tenor vocals with the deep bass of Jimmy Ricks and scored big, not just with standards like "Ol' Man River" and "Silent Night," but also more bluesy tunes like "Write Me a Letter" and "Bye Bye Baby Blues." The Orioles, out of Baltimore, named for the Maryland state bird, had a number-one hit, "Tell Me So," featuring the beautiful lead tenor of Sonny Til. Louis Jordan, of course, was tearing it up with the "jump" music of his Tympany Five, occasionally bringing in Ella to sing lead with him—they'd first worked together in Chick Webb's big band. And, as I already mentioned, John Lee Hooker was bringing Southern blues to the national charts from the streets of Detroit. You can understand from all of this why people started talking about this music by a different name—rhythm & blues, or R&B for short.

Then, during the three years I spent in Mount Meigs, it was like all the strands of music that had gone into R&B *really* mixed themselves up together, all getting down and dirty with each other, so that what came out of the melting pot was something

much firmer, but also fresher. From New York City, Billy Ward
and his Dominos introduced the stirring gospel-trained voice of
Clyde McPhatter with "Do Something for Me," "That's What
You're Doing To Me," and the raucous "Have Mercy Baby,"
although some might say their *real* memorable hit was "Sixty
Minute Man," sung by Bill Brown in one of the deepest bass
voices ever. The Clovers, out of D.C., brought a tough, blues-
based backing group into their session for "Don't You Know I
Love You" and that topped the charts too. The Clovers were
on a new label called Atlantic, which also released what some
said was an "answer record" to "Sixty Minute Man" by the
jazz-blues belter Ruth Brown, called "5–10–15 Hours"; it had
a piano dancing its way through the verses and a blaring sax
accompanying the chorus, and that too leaped to number one.
Down in North Carolina, a gospel group called The Royal Sons
Quintet changed their name to the "5" Royales as they made
what may have seemed like a brave decision for some people,
perhaps even foolish—to switch from sacred to secular lyrics,
but it paid off when "Baby Don't Do It" became one of the big
hits of 1953.

That was the year Clyde McPhatter quit the Dominos, signed
to Atlantic, and started a new group with friends from his old
Harlem gospel days: the Drifters came flying out of the gate
with the unforgettable "Money Honey" just before I came out
the prison gates. McPhatter's place in the Dominos was taken by
a young singer from Detroit called Jackie Wilson. On his first
real big hit with the Dominos, "Rags to Riches," you could tell
he had been raised singing gospel. And again, 1953: from my
hometown of Montgomery, Willie Mae "Big Mama" Thornton
hit number one with a rocker called "Hound Dog."

When I got to Detroit at the end of that year, the big news
out of the Motor City was a group called the Midnighters.

They'd just changed their name from the Royals, to avoid confusion with the group I mentioned down in North Carolina. And, funny enough, before *that*, the Royals were briefly called the Four Falcons. Somehow, Johnny Otis, a Greek American bandleader who'd produced "Hound Dog," found his way to seeing the Royals and got them signed to Federal Records. The Royals brought in Hank Ballard—another Alabama boy raised on gospel but still working the Ford assembly line at the time— for the lead vocals on a song called "Get It." That was about as tough as anything you'd heard at the time from a vocal group, which, judging by the way things were going, probably only helped it on its way to the Top 10.

It was after "Get It" that the Royals changed their name to the Midnighters and, in the spring of 1954, just as I was settling in on Euclid Avenue, they released a song called "Work with Me, Annie," which left nothing to the imagination. In fact, a lot of radio stations banned it. "Annie" went to number one all the same; that's how music was moving back then. Detroit was hardly lacking for talent, but it was the Midnighters who put the city firmly on the rhythm & blues map.

Now, I'll be honest with you. Maybe there's a part of me that would like to claim I knew everything that was going on at the time, saw all these acts perform in the clubs, owned their records, and played them all night long to learn my chops, but that's not the case. When I get to Detroit, I'm just sixteen years old. I've only been able to look at girls, not make out with them. Barely been able to listen to music that's not part of Mr. Wilmer's curriculum. Got no experience stepping foot in clubs, let alone having a drink at the bar. And my uncle's taste, fine though it may be, is largely based on blues, jazz, and the great singers; he's not cutting a rug to "Work with Me, Annie" or "Hound Dog."

I'm not looking to head right down that path of dirty rhythm & blues either. No, the first artist that I wanted to sing like, and *tried* to sing like, was Johnny Ace. To this day, he's the one who most reminds me of that time and that era, all the way back. Johnny Ace came from Memphis, and touring with Big Mama Thornton brought him to the attention of Johnny Otis, who produced the song "Please Forgive Me" with his own orchestra. The one that *really* got me, though, followed a little later. It was released at the start of 1955, a week after Johnny Ace accidentally shot himself dead backstage in Houston on Christmas Eve. "Pledging My Love" proved to be bigger than any hit he'd ever had while he was alive. *Forever my darling, I will be true.* I admit, I fell for that song as hard as any other. I can rock, there's no doubt about it, but I love the ballads.

That love of ballads is one reason I was especially taken by a Detroit group that was a major influence on just about everything and everyone that followed in Motor City: Nolan Strong and the Diablos. From the outset, the Diablos had something most vocal groups did not—except for the Royals/Midnighters, so maybe this was a Detroit thing—and that was a guitarist. It gave them a connection to the instrumental side of rhythm & blues, and it also gave them an edge, like in the physical sense. Plus, it meant that when they went into Detroit's Fortune studio to record some demos in 1954, they weren't just another group of street-corner singing hopefuls; they were a proper *band*. Fortune was your classic mom-and-pop operation: a small stand-alone brick structure, a one-track studio, no real distribution or business plan, but lots of enthusiasm and hands-on control. Other than Joe Von Battle on Hastings Street, they were pretty much the only game in town. Acts would come by to record, knowing there was a fair chance the Browns would put the music out on wax if it was anything better than bad.

Nolan Strong and the Diablos were considerably better than that. They'd go into that room at Fortune and get these amazing echo sounds just from being in the room together. Listen to their single "The Wind" and tell me you don't hear the future Smokey Robinson in there. That song is a bona fide classic of the era, and it had a massive impact on the singing scene in Detroit in particular.

Now, my uncle knew I could sing. He certainly knew I *wanted* to sing. So he took me to a teacher in Detroit, a German music teacher, light opera or something, who of course tried to get me doing the scales and all. I tried it my way in turn, and he came back to my uncle saying, "Well, he'll never sing opera, but I can teach him voice control," and he did. When I chose to sing it from the top of my voice, from my throat *up here*, the teacher would hit me in the solar plexus *down here* and say, "*This is where you bring it up.*" It was painful, but it worked!

Meantime, I go out to get a job. I find one quickly enough at the J.L. Hudson's department store on Woodward Avenue. That place was amazing. It occupied twenty-five *floors* of retail, with eight more stories used for storage and support, all of which made it the tallest department store in the world, second in square footage only to Macy's in New York. When the building was demolished in 1998, they said it was the tallest building ever brought down by controlled explosives. As you can imagine, Detroit was booming like crazy if it could support a store this large, and that meant there was always going to be jobs available there, for black and white people alike. You couldn't run a store that big with segregation.

My job is at Hudson's jewelry store, though most of the time they've got me in the stock room. And this is where I find myself alongside a guy called Bob Manardo. He's much the same age as me, and we're both into all the music that's happening. I'm telling him I'm a singer, and he says, "I got a buddy and we sing together." So I tell him, "I got a buddy and we sing together too," which was true enough: I had this friend, Arnett Robinson, I'd met in the neighborhood, and we'd been harmonizing when we could. Thing is, Arnett and I were both lead tenors, but Bob, he fitted in just below us in the vocal range, and the friend he brought along, Tom Shetler, was more of a baritone. So now, we got a little bit of *range*. Which means we have ourselves a group.

It never occurred to me at the time that I was doing something special here, but fact is, me and Arnett were black, and Bob and Tom were white. You'll have heard a lot about race in Detroit, and it's true that blacks and whites lived mostly separate lives in separate neighborhoods, but Bob and I weren't thinking about that when we talked about putting a group together. Perhaps if I'd been hung up on race like a lot of people, I wouldn't have wanted to ask a white guy to sing with me. But I *wasn't* thinking about color: I was just thinking about the music. As it turns out, we were one of the first integrated vocal groups in all of America.

My uncle's totally cool about this as well. Soon as I tell him that I think I've got a group, he takes us in, and we practice in the basement at the house. We'd moved by then, from the place near West Grand up to a house on Keystone, near 7 Mile Road and Ryan Road. From the beginning, we were fortunate because of my uncle's involvement. He was more than just a music fan: with his real estate office, he was already a business man, and it was like he'd been cultivating me ever since I was a little kid, waiting for his opportunity in the music world. He could see, feel, and hear all the musical action taking place on the Detroit streets, he could sense that something new was happening and, like me, he wanted to be a part of it. Soon enough, he sold his real estate office and turned it into a recording business, Silhouette Records. He didn't even wait around for the Falcons to be ready; he released his first record by a group called the Classmates late in 1955.

But back to our group. We weren't happy with just the four members. To really make an impression, we knew we needed a bass singer, someone in the style of Jimmy Ricks or Bill Brown. My uncle and I went out and started actively looking for one, hitting the nightclubs in the process. And soon enough, we found Willie Schofield at a club called the Gold Coast. The place had a good PA system, and Willie's voice came booming over the auditorium, drowning out the rest of his group, which was in the Drifters mode.

"They approached me after the show," Willie recalls. "Eddie said, 'I never heard a bass like that . . . we got a group we'd like you to hear.' I said, 'No, I got a group.' But they were so persistent that I finally said yes, figuring that when I actually saw the group at least then I could say no. When I did get to meet them, they didn't sound nowhere near as good as the group I was with, but there was just something about Eddie and Arnett, and those two white guys, and they said those magic words: 'If you sign with us, we'll get you into nightclubs and make you some money.' I said, '*Money?*'"

Willie was younger than the rest of us, by a couple of years, and he was still attending Eastern High. But he had these sideburns, which made him look older than he was, and of course that deep voice of his made him sound older than he was too. With Schofield on bass, we figured we had a real group. All we needed was a name, and it was Arnett who came up with the Falcons. The "bird group" craze that had started back with the Ravens and the Orioles was still in full flow, and it turned out there were groups called the Falcons all over the country: even the Midnighters had traded in that name originally. But, hey, in 1955, we were the only Falcons we knew of—at least in Motor City.

By now, that group scene was exploding. Everywhere you looked, every time you turned on the radio, there was another new group, another amazing ballad, and maybe something a little harder than that too. You had the Crows and the Chords out of New York, and people were calling those guys rock 'n' roll, but I have to be honest, it was two groups out of Los Angeles, the Platters and especially the Penguins—with "Earth Angel"—that did it for me. That music just sent me sideways; it was the sweetest sound you could imagine.

Still, it was Frankie Lymon and The Teenagers that broke the floodgates. "Why Do Fools Fall in Love," which hit in early '56, was the record everything had been leading up towards. In many ways, that was the start of it all.

Almost overnight, "Why Do Fools Fall in Love" was parked at number one, and in the wake of the Teenagers' success, it seemed like every teenager in the country thought they were good enough to make a record. Many of them tried, and most of them failed, for the simple reason that they couldn't sing. The Falcons could sing already, but my uncle Robert West wasn't taking no chances. He wanted to make sure we could *really* sing, so he hired us a vocal coach, a guy called Bob Hamilton.

Willie Schofield calls Hamilton "a genius with the harmonies." We weren't used to someone who could, as Willie puts it, "just look off into space and then say, 'Okay, I want you to go here, and sing this,' and pick it out on the piano." Bob got our harmonies in place, beyond the obvious notes that every other group on the block would be aiming for. He knew what he was doing, for sure: years later, he cowrote the hit "(Just Like) Romeo and Juliet."

Meantime, we worked to get ourselves some shows, and my uncle bought us some suits so that we could look the part as well: he was one of the best-dressed men that I knew, and no way he was going to let *us* look anything less than stars. We managed to get on the bill at the 509, a supper club at Woodward and Congress, which was a big deal. Blacks weren't allowed in there, except as employees—or performers—and most of the audience came down from over the border in Canada. We made a good impression, and that was encouraging.

Willie remembers me having "a beautiful voice" on numbers like "The Nearness of You," an old Glenn Miller song that was back on the radio as a duet between Ella Fitzgerald and Louis Armstrong. I'd sing songs by Nat King Cole and the Platters too. That's all we were basically doing at first. To some extent I was the leader at this point, because I was the person who put the group together. But it was more like, if *you* sung a song, you led that one. If *he* sung one, he led it. All of us were trying to write songs as we went along, and in the spring of 1956, after Frankie Lymon went to number one, my uncle figured we were good enough to make a record—or that the timing was right to make a record. Or, most likely, both.

Still, he didn't want to release us on his own label, Silhouette. He was still learning the ropes when it came to production, promotion, and distribution, and he thought the Falcons had something that made it worth our trying to start at the top. So he drove us all the way to Chicago to audition for Mercury Records there.

To do so, he had us dress up in our suits. He wanted everyone to be total and correct, figured we'd look more like a group if we were smart and professional. Thing is, this was not nighttime, on stage, but daytime, on the streets of Chicago. We had to walk through the streets of downtown Chicago to the Mercury office, and everyone's making fun of us as we go. We're embarrassed.

We get to the office, and my uncle introduces himself and ourselves—the Falcons—to the woman sitting there, and he says, "We've come to audition."

"Do you have an appointment?" she replies.

"No."

"Did you know that we do our auditions in New York City?" she now asks.

"Um, no."

"Wait here a minute."

Then this guy who was the A&R Director at Mercury, a big shot, came out and looked at us, and he said, "Well, maybe I'll listen." He had probably thought we'd be an all-black group, and once he could see we were a mixed group, that aroused his curiosity. So he took us back into his office, and he had his piano there. We started singing this modern harmony, and all of a sudden, he said the magic words:

"I'm gonna sign you guys."

The whole episode was like something out of the movies!

We went back to Chicago in September and recorded four songs at the Mercury studios there—with Willie Dixon as producer and band leader. Willie Dixon was a legend in Chicago; after moving there from Mississippi twenty years earlier, he'd put together a group, the Big Three Trio, which he led on his double bass. When Chess Records opened up in the late 1940s, Dixon went to work for them as songwriter, producer, and arranger. He wrote "Hoochie Coochie Man" for Muddy Waters and "My Babe" for Little Walter. Willie Dixon was a seriously big name in blues, and even if we didn't listen to so much of that music ourselves, we knew to respect the man in the studio. Come to think of it, he was such a great songwriter that it was a miracle that we were allowed to sing our own songs.

I wish I could remember more about that first session, but you have to allow it's over sixty years ago now! We did what we were told, we sung our best, Dixon conducted the band, and a few weeks later, Mercury releases our first single: "Baby, That's It" featuring Eddy Floyd, as they misspelled my name on the label, singing lead. It's a decent little record, got a good syncopated rocking groove as you'd expect with Dixon running the show, a wailing sax solo in the middle like all the new rock 'n' roll songs featured, and then an equally loud electric guitar solo as a bonus, and the words and melody aren't bad either. I can say all that because I wrote the song too.

On the label, though, "Baby, That's It" is credited to "Eddie *and* Rachael Floyd." Who's Rachael, I hear you ask? Well, she's a girl about my age, and she's my wife. She lived down the street from my uncle, and we started dating, and one thing led to another until, at the age of just eighteen, I found out I was going to be a father. Before I know it, we've got us a family going: me, Rachel and little Edward Lee Floyd Junior, the first of three children we'd have together. Life is moving quickly for me, make no mistake. And Rachael was at all the rehearsals, because in the early days we're always doing everything together.

But the song was not a hit. It sold so poorly that Mercury never released the other songs we recorded that day. I'm not even sure the tapes still exist. The single itself is impossible to find. Let me know if you come across a copy!

Still, having a contract with Mercury helped the Falcons get lots of shows in Detroit, and we became one of the more popular groups on the scene. The Diablos and the Midnighters would come watch us perform, which was respect of the highest order. It was good times all around.

There's one photograph from that period that I treasure. It shows the five of us Falcons on stage together, the audience pushing up close, and you can just about make out the call letters of the local AM station CKLW, which was sponsoring the show. We look like babies up there, we so damn young! But Uncle Sam didn't think we were babies, because it wasn't long after that Bob Manardo got his draft papers. Bob was pretty excited about the prospect—so much so that he got Tom to enlist with him. The two of them tried to convince the rest of us to sign up, too, but we knew better than that. Singing might only have been of passing interest to them, but for me, at least, it was everything. Ain't no way I'm going to risk dying for my country when I'm dying to make music instead.

Chapter 4
YOU'RE SO FINE

Bob and Tom's departure into the army could have been the end of the Falcons. But instead, it's where the story really starts—because my uncle Robert West has got the bug like I've got the bug, and before I know it, he's found a replacement. He's got Joe Stubbs to join us, and Joe's voice will more than do the job for two.

Now, if the name Stubbs sounds halfway familiar to you, it's probably because you're thinking of Joe's older brother, Levi Stubbs, who sang lead on all those amazing hits by the Four Tops in the years to come. Back in the late 1950s, the Four Tops were known as the Four Aims, and they were on the same supper club circuit as the Falcons. We considered them our big brothers. They looked perfect; they moved perfect. And Levi could

37

sing, ain't no doubt about that. But so could Joe. Fact, Joe was something of a sensation already: he'd got his name in the paper from going up to Canada to perform with the Five Dollars, had recently cut a single with The Fabulous Four, and was still only fifteen! He had a high tenor that was either graceful or powerful depending on the song's needs. He could float his way around a single note, but he could also shout it like the best of the gospel singers. Getting Joe to join the Falcons was a serious move.

Even better, Joe brought over the guitarist from the Fabulous Four, Lance Finnie. This is important because, like I already said, the guitar is what helps separate the Midnighters and the Diablos from all the other vocal groups in Detroit. And if we want to do not just the ballads that I love but the "rough and tough," as I call it, we need that energy. Willie and I are super excited by the changes, but Arnett has something else on his mind, and no sooner has my uncle gotten pictures taken of the new lineup than he quits. Okay, better tear up them photos; let's find someone else!

My uncle puts an ad in the paper, a whole number of people respond, we go down and audition them all, and when it comes to casting our votes, we all go for this guy Bonnie—or "Mack"—Rice. Mack came to us with experience. He'd released a couple of singles with a group called the Five Scalders—so-named because they were "hot"—and he'd just returned from his own two-year stint in the Army, where he'd put together a group called the Bobaliers. Bonnie could write songs: he proved that enough in the years to come. And he had a slightly different musical taste: with Mack, we could stretch out into country and blues. His experience meant he knew more about being in a group than us, and he wasn't the kind to take any bullshit from anyone, even though he was a gentle man at heart. He had leadership skills, and he put all of us together. Mack and I hit it off immediately. It was Mack who gave me the nickname

"Green Tree," a reference, I believe, to the fact I've always managed to make out all right for myself. I don't think I worked but six months at that jewelry store, and it's the only job that I can recall my whole life—except for my actual career, of course!

So now we got a new lineup, but given that Mercury has soured on us, my uncle decided to put out our records himself. We went into Detroit's one independent studio of quality: United Sound, down on Second Avenue—it's still standing, by the way—and recorded a *real* raw song called "Sent Up," which Lance Finnie had written while in the Fabulous Four. Mack Rice sang lead. Perhaps because the lyrics dealt with some pretty bad behavior, we backed it up with a ballad called "Can This Be Christmas," the first of many times I got to sing about my favorite holiday of the year. Robert put those songs out at the end of 1957 on Silhouette, one of the last R&B singles you'll find on old 78 rpm shellac, anywhere. To this day it's the only release on Silhouette that people can tell you anything about; the rest of the acts on that label were never heard of again.

We went into the Fortune studios for a couple of recordings as well, and then my uncle set up a new label, Kudo, along with a disc jockey from WJR, and released a single written and produced for us by our music coach Bob Hamilton, "This Heart of Mine," with me singing lead again. It didn't go anywhere at the time, but it stirred the interest of Chess Records back out in Chicago, who had us re-record it along with a number of other songs. But then they decided not to release them! Some people might have been knocked back by this, but not my uncle. He hired us as the backing group for a single he was putting out with Joltin' Joe Howard, the breakthrough disc jockey on Detroit's brand-new WCHB, supposedly the first black-financed radio station in all of the USA. Robert already knew how to keep in favor with the influential radio personalities.

The local music scene was jumping harder and faster than ever by this point. Detroit had a new star in Little Willie John, who'd come out of the Jeffries Houses, got noticed by Dizzy Gillespie after winning the talent show at the Paradise Theater, toured with Paul Williams, came to the attention of that man Johnny Otis, and quickly landed a massive R&B smash with his first single for Cincinnati's King label, "All Around the World," before following it up with the legendary "Fever." Little Willie managed all this while still a teenager, which gave those of us with similar ambitions some serious hope. Meantime, Jackie Wilson left the Dominos—he'd found it wasn't that easy to fill the shoes of the mighty Clyde McPhatter—and came back to town to try his luck as a solo artist. His first single, "Reet Petite," rightly made some noise, but it was the follow-up, "To Be Loved," that hit the charts big-time. Both were cowritten by Berry Gordy.

And this is where things in Detroit get *real* interesting. Berry Gordy was in his late twenties, several years younger than my uncle but older than all of us groups. After trying his hands in the boxing ring and, so they say, representing some available women, he'd figured on the exploding music business as his best path to success. As a songwriter, it was evident from what he'd already achieved with Jackie Wilson that he had talent. But he hadn't yet figured out the process of producing, promoting, releasing, and distributing records. So he started hanging out with my uncle. The same period that we put out our single on Kudo, my uncle released one by a promising local singer called Marv Johnson, and another by Brian Holland; Gordy wrote the B-side for that one. And while my uncle was getting ready to record his first girl group, the Primettes—Diana Ross, Mary Wilson, Betty McGlown, and Florence Ballard—Berry was getting involved with a local act called the Miracles, fronted by a gifted singer and writer, Smokey Robinson. We shared rehearsal rooms with both the Miracles and the Four Tops—as the Four Aims were now calling themselves—over at the Northwestern Rec Center; everyone knew everybody. Gordy sold his first production with the Miracles, "Got A Job," to a New York label run by George Goldner, the guy who'd discovered Frankie Lymon. But it was obvious he had plans of his own and that he was learning from my uncle how to go about things—and, you might say, how *not* to go about them too. Because to be honest, often as my uncle got us in the studio, we were never quite sure what label we were singing for, at which studio, and under exactly what name.

Things finally clicked for the Falcons when my uncle hooked us up with Sax Kari, for yet another label he'd set up, Flick. Sax Kari is one of those names now lost in the mists of time, and that's a shame because he was a talented multi-instrumentalist, big band leader, writer, producer, arranger . . . you name it, Sax did it. He was about forty years old already by the time my uncle suggested he produce a song that Lance Finnie and Willie Schofield had written together called "You're So Fine." Willie recalls writing it real quick—in half an hour or so. Sometimes that's the way it goes. He also remembers trying me out on lead vocals, and then Mack—"but when we heard Joe singing it, that was *it*. That's when we thought we had something."

Hey, we were not competing with each other in the Falcons. If a song sounded better on Joe, let him sing it. Mack Rice, same way, we know his style, we know what he's capable of doing. We would open up on stage with Mack doing bluesy stuff like "Blueberry Hill." And everyone was always happy to have Eddie sing the ballads. I loved the whole doo-wop sound; that's why I stayed in that area over the years and still refer back to it. Thing is, there weren't many groups around like us that had three lead singers—as well as a great bass. So we made the most of it.

We recorded "You're So Fine"—along with a ballad of mine called "Goddess of Angels"—at a studio owned by another of the main disc jockeys in town, "Senator" Bristoe Bryant, who had an R&B show called "Bristoe's Place" on WJLB. The studio was in a basement on East Alexandrine, underneath the record store Music City, and the session was pretty chaotic. The bass player didn't show up, so Sax Kari—as well as playing the sax solo in the middle—tuned a guitar down. Everyone thought it was a kazoo; it had such a funny sound. We didn't think much of it, but when the record came out, everyone else was like, "What is *that?*" It was a unique sound, and maybe if he hadn't done that, well, who knows?

The other thing I really remember about that session was recording the vocals, late at night, in the bathroom! It was because of the echo you could get in there. The band was playing on the other side of the wall, and you could hear them. You had to: we had no headsets! It was just one mic in one room and another in the other. When the groove is good and the song is singing, that's all you need.

One other thing about that session: Berry Gordy was there, supposedly checking out Bristoe Bryant's equipment. "He stuck his head in, between takes," recalls Willie, "and said 'Man, you got a smash.' I said, 'A smash? *OK Berry . . .* '; I felt we'd recorded some other things that were better, stronger, but you never knew."

Indeed, you never knew. Listening back all these years later, you can hear "You're So Fine" as the hit it turned out to be, thanks to Joe's sweeping tenor, Schofield's busy bass vocal, the piano and guitar going chink-chink-chink, and Sax's great solo. The record sounds real busy, and although it doesn't have polish, you know everyone involved with it is a professional.

But although we thought we had something with the song, we never talked about "making it." We talked about the songs we were recording, and we knew we were a group and trying to record, but it wasn't no big wish that "we got one now and it's going to be a big hit." We didn't speak about songs being big hits and all of that. It was still an unproven time.

Now, just as we're making "You're So Fine," Marv Johnson switches labels. It didn't seem any big deal; artists would bounce from one company to another all the time. But this move was part of history all the same, because Marv goes over to Berry Gordy, who writes a song with him called "Come to Me," brings him down to United to record it, and launches Tamla Records with it. Of course, none of us knew at the time that Tamla would become perhaps the biggest label of the coming decade, but still, Berry and Marv do a good enough job that Johnson's record *also* starts getting a lot of local play; it's R&B, but it's more of a pop record than "You're So Fine," and maybe that tells you something about how Berry is thinking from the beginning. The major label United Artists hears these two independent Detroit singles, decides they like the sound, licenses one from my uncle Robert West and the other from Berry Gordy, re-releases them both on UnArt, and puts us out on a promotional tour together.

A lot of people date the whole Motown thing—and Detroit soul music with it—from the 1960s, which is understandable. But it was in the spring of 1959 that the Falcons and Marv Johnson headed off around the country together playing record hops, visiting radio stations, and watching our singles climb the charts. "Come to Me" went Top Ten R&B for Johnson, which was big news in Detroit and good news for Berry Gordy. But "You're So Fine" went higher. And higher. It was only kept off the number-one spot by Lloyd Price's "Personality" and then the Drifters' "There Goes My Baby," the song that introduced Ben E. King to the world. Along the way, "You're So Fine" even crossed over into the pop Top 20. Not bad for a song we recorded around a commode at 3 a.m.!

We're in the big time, and so is Berry Gordy. And even though he's got the more polished record, there's got to be something he truly loves about our sound, because he does buy the recording console from Bristoe Bryant, and he moves it to the office and recording studio he sets up over on West Grand Boulevard. This will be the home of Tamla-Motown, a label that will change the course of popular music. And give Gordy credit for the fact that he already believed as much, because almost immediately, he hung a sign out front that read "Hitsville USA."

A few years later, I'd have a response to that! But right now, thanks to "You're So Fine," the Falcons are getting to play the Apollo, the Uptown, the Howard, and all the great black American theaters. The competition at these venues is tough, and it wasn't like we were a choreography group: two steps here, one hand there, look up to your right and do a spin. We did it more based on feel. What we had was that depth of singing, and that always got us across. Most of these shows are "revue" style, lots of acts on them doing just two or three songs each. The one that I'll always remember was down in Chattanooga, Tennessee, on June 10. It was promoted by Henry Wynn, and when he labeled it "Supersonic Attractions of '59," the man was not lying. Top of the bill: Sam Cooke *and* Jackie Wilson, the two greatest solo singers of their time. And that night, they were even. Just as good as each other in their own way. Sam Cooke had had more hits; he had that whole gospel thing from being in the Soul Stirrers, and when he took the stage, the girls fell out like you'd never heard nor seen. But still, wasn't anyone who could sing like Jackie Wilson. Hank Ballard and the Midnighters were listed on that show as well, though I don't recall them playing. Marv Johnson was out there with us, of course. Jesse Belvin was definitely outstanding whether or not you know of him. And the act that I really remember blowing me away that night was the Pips, with a woman named Gladys Knight up front; hardly anyone had heard of them back then, and it would be a few years before that would change. When it did, it was thanks to Berry Gordy.

That night in Chattanooga, Sam Cooke heard us and was impressed. He was already a fan of "You're So Fine," and he liked how Joe's voice had that gospel thing going. He said, "I got a song that I think you guys could do." That was all we thought of it at the time, but Sam soon proved good to his word.

Thanks to "You're So Fine" we got on American Bandstand, twice, one of those times right alongside Annette Funicello! That was the thing about having a hit like that: it made us a big name on the R&B circuit, which was what we came from, but the pop crossover brought us into a lot of other peoples' homes as well. It was on American Bandstand that we get to meet a group called the Fiestas, who had a single out at the same time called "So Fine," and which was almost as big a hit as ours. For a while we'd been running scared that people would get the two records confused to the point that it damaged us, but fortunately that was never the case.

Things are looking good. We're all about twenty years old, and we're performing on some of the biggest stages in America. We've got our own station wagon, good suits, money in our pockets, and girls at our feet. Most important of all, we've made a great record, and people have heard it. And bought it.

But now we're with United Artists, and they want us to do things their way. All of a sudden we're sent to New York City, and we're doing the songs with Don Costa and his Orchestra. Don was a big shot already—he'd arrange Frank Sinatra's "My Way" down the line—and also the A&R Director at United Artists, so what he says, goes. He gets us in a plush studio, and the backing vocals are all of a sudden being sung by girls, not just us fellas, and Don has got the parts written out for them.

We would sit at the house and rehearse for three or four weeks, the same part, and here some girls walk in, just for half an hour, pick up the charts, and they can do it. So we were introduced to that part of the music world too. All right, so they do it *that* way. The songs sounded great—we had another hit of sorts with "The Teacher"—but it wasn't the total style of what we were doing.

Because we've got hits, Chess Records decides to finally release the songs that weren't good enough to put out only a year ago, and one of them, "Just for Your Love," is a hit as well. My uncle figures in this case there's no reason for him not to keep putting out records by us on Flick. That's the way the business was in those days: you get a hit record, suddenly everyone's releasing songs on you that you barely remember recording. Probably hasn't changed none either. The one thing consistent about all these releases was that they featured Joe Stubbs on lead. For me, he was the main singer in all the years of that group. A couple of years back, I accepted an award for the group and told the people in Detroit as much: my preference was always for Joe Stubbs as lead singer for the Falcons.

I need to state that because of what happened next. Willie remembers people whispering in Joe's ear: "You don't need those guys. . . . The group should be called Joe Stubbs and the Falcons."

Now to be fair to Joe, this kind of thing wasn't uncommon. It was round this time that the Midnighters became Hank Ballard and the Midnighters—and everyone knew it wasn't the Teenagers, but Frankie Lymon *and* the Teenagers—and maybe that's what Joe was looking at. But the Falcons weren't like those other acts. We were a *group*. We had three people who could sing lead, and even if I was happy to have Joe up front on the singles, it wasn't like he was going to do the ballads or the songs that Mack Rice could sing. And the rest of us could all write, too, including Lance; we'd proved as much from the beginning. Meantime, Willie is off finding artists of his own to write for and produce. Joe was the only one in the Falcons who *didn't* write songs.

Now, I'd have been happy to find a way to keep Joe in the group; we had something special going together for sure. Joe wouldn't sing anything that he couldn't make complete. But he would be stretching out when you didn't want him stretching out, and I think it may have been that all-or-nothing aspect to his personality that caused him to quit. We had a tour coming up booked for us by the Shaw Agency, which was a big deal back then, and I guess we told Joe either he went out with us as just the Falcons or he didn't come out with us at all. And being young and full of himself, he chose to stay home.

That gave us three weeks to find ourselves a new lead singer. And he'd better be good, because you know those audiences out there won't take no second-rate singer passing himself off as the guy who sung our hit records. There was only one person properly considered for the job. It was a young gospel singer that Schofield had recently come across—on his way back from a doctor's appointment of all things—and taken under his wing.

His name was Wilson Pickett.

Chapter 5
I FOUND A LOVE

I don't need y'all. Those, ladies and gentlemen, were the first
words I recall out of Wilson Pickett's mouth the day that
Schofield brought him to meet the rest of the Falcons. That was
Pickett for you, man. Brazen. Confident. Cocksure. Fiercely
good-looking, fiercely competitive, crazy as a fox, knew what
he wanted and knew how to get it. He'd come to Schofield
as a solo artist, and he planned on continuing as a solo artist.
The Falcons was just something he was going to pass through
for as long as it was good for him. And believe me, it *was* good
for him. Pickett might have said he didn't need us, but look at
the reality of this particular situation: he was unknown when
he came to the Falcons, and when he left us, he was a star, and

it was the Falcons who helped make him one. Wilson Pickett had talent like you couldn't believe; he also had destructive tendencies that got in the way of that talent.

But Pickett was my man. I had more adventures with him, more run-ins with him, more good times and bad, than almost anyone else in this story. We went our own ways, but we kept finding our ways back to each other. He tested my patience more than once, but I was always happy to see him. Our lives were endlessly entangled. We were close.

Wilson Pickett was four years younger than me—which means he was still a teenager when he came to the Falcons that summer of 1960—and, like me, he'd spent his childhood back and forth between Alabama and Detroit, moving up for good at the age of fifteen. Pickett came from the town right next door to Montgomery, little place called Prattville. He always put it out that he'd come up hard, picking cotton on the farm, getting whooped by his mom, sleeping out in the woods, arguing with the white man, but the way I saw it, those plantation days were over. I mean, I had a few years on him, and I couldn't see Prattville being quite as backwoods as he made out. But hey, I didn't go out to Prattville, and maybe he didn't come into Montgomery.

Where Pickett really differed from the rest of us, once Joe Stubbs left, was in his singing. Pickett was pure gospel—a straight up Baptist church shouter. He had a voice that could carry across a field, and we knew he'd already put it to good use singing with the Violinaires, one of the big gospel groups up in Detroit at the time. Makes it seem strange that the song Schofield heard him singing on a porch, on his way back from a doctor's appointment nearby, was "The Sky Is Crying," an Elmore James number, but that tells you there were few people in Detroit sticking to just one style of music. Pickett may have come up through the church, may have been given all those warnings about people like us doing the "devil's music,"

but he knew which way the wind was blowing, all right. Only had
to look at how Sam Cooke was doing to figure that one out. The
gospel scene was full of shouters like Pickett, but in R&B, rock 'n'
roll, doo wop—whatever you want to call it—his kind of voice was
still rare. What Pickett brought to us was *soul*, that's for sure.

Years down the line, Pickett was dismissive of the sound of
the Falcons at the time that he joined. "I call it corny music," he
told a writer from the *New York Times*. "Pop pop doo-doo-da-
doo. I couldn't relate to that."

Well, fair enough, if he was talking about those Don Costa
productions. But hey, he'd hardly been with us a month or two
when he found himself right in that same situation. Sam Cooke
had come good on giving us a song, called "Pow! You're in
Love," and when we went around the group, it was Pickett's
voice that suited it best, same way it would have been Stubbs's
if he was still with us. Back we go to New York, to the big
United Artists studios, and Pickett steps up to the plate; he's
got to be thrilled at thinking that this is his introduction to the
big time, singing a song exclusively given to his new group by
Sam Cooke. Except that it *isn't* his introduction to the big time:
"Pow! You're in Love" doesn't do nothing for us; Pickett's first
lead vocal never gets heard much outside the record company
and the few radio stations that give it the time of day. And when
you listen to it, that's understandable: the song is not on the
level you'd expect from the great Sam Cooke and, as a result,
the delivery is not what you'd expect from the future Wilson
Pickett. When it doesn't sell, United Artists figure they've done
all they can for the Falcons, that we've had our one big hit, a
couple of close calls for follow-ups, but now we're messing with
the lineup and all and that we're done.

We've been through this before, of course. And by now,
we've got a much better name than when Mercury let us go

after just the one single. I mean, the bookings don't stop, and why would they? We can cut it live. We're one of the big groups out there. So that's what we continue to do. At first Pickett is struggling to fit in—he's not used to screaming girls tugging at his feet while having to pull off some basic stage moves—but soon enough he's hollering away and, as much as I miss Joe, the Falcons remain something special. We're making our living doing this, and for the most part, we're loving it.

One night, we're doing a show in Dayton, Ohio, and we meet this group from there called Robert Ward and the Ohio Untouchables, who are playing behind us, and Pickett's got this song he's working on, based on an old Pentecostal hymn called "Yes Lord," so I was told. The Untouchables are playing the little riff to it—Robert Ward was one hell of a guitarist, which is why he got the group named for him—and Pickett finished writing the song "I Found a Love," there and then, that night. It was immense; you could tell from the start. We called my uncle in Detroit and told him we had a song, and he came on over, and then, well, what's the nearest studio? King Records, which had James Brown at that time, over in Cincinnati. So, *let's go.*

What we came out with that night was something truly special. Nothing like what the Falcons had done in the past: nothing much like *anyone* had done in the past. Screaming and shouting like he was at Sunday service, Pickett brought full-throttle gospel to his song; with those electric guitar licks and the confidence that came from being a tight, hard-working live band, Robert Ward and the Untouchables brought the rock 'n' roll. And the rest of us Falcons, being that we knew what we were doing too, we brought that whole rhythm & blues vocal sound, right down to the bass singing. Put it all together and . . . well, a lot of people consider "I Found a Love" to be one of the first true soul records. We didn't call it that at the time, but nobody ever does;

the term only comes along later. It's like I don't remember many people calling doo-wop by that term back in the 1950s.

My uncle has *no* doubts about "I Found a Love," and he launches yet another new record label, Lu Pine, with it. (And if you're confused about all these Robert West labels, well so were we, but it tended to be the case back then that a small business man would have a lot of different imprints: it was one way to get around the "payola" scandal where a radio station couldn't be seen to play too many songs by one company. Besides, you might have a partner in one label and fall out with him and want to do the next release on your own. Could be easier to start a new label than dissolve the old partnership.) Immediately, his phone starts ringing. "I Found a Love" is raw, all right, but the radio stations don't mind it one little bit; it's like with "You're So Fine," when we recorded the vocals in a bathroom, and got us a number-two record. "I Found a Love" benefited from the King Studios setup, but this was not your Don Costa production, not by a million miles: it's like Pickett's voice is trying to blow whatever speakers you're listening through. Soon enough, "I Found a Love" is selling so well that Atlantic Records comes along. They take over the distribution, and hey, here we go again—the Falcons have got themselves another Top 10 hit. *If* that's what you care about. What mattered to me was not so much that the song went somewhere but that it never went away. To this day, people still talk about it, still play it, still revere it. That's the kind of success I care about.

With Pickett at the helm, back we go on tour, back to the big theaters. We're a star attraction once again. Still, nobody gets top billing over James Brown. I mean, some people might call the Falcons "the world's first Soul group," but *everyone* knows James Brown is the Godfather of Soul. And amazing as "I Found a Love" may be, his "Please, Please, Please" came first by a good four years. Plus of course, James has that live show like nobody can imitate, and the man can *dance*. Which is more than can be said for most of us Falcons.

So we're touring with James Brown now, and he gets to know about us; Pickett makes sure of that. I remember a show in Baltimore, would have been at the Royal Theater. The Valentinos would have been on the bill as I remember—that was the Womack brothers as they were known then, including young Bobby, just hitting big with "Lookin' for a Love." But we got "I *Found a* Love"—we're done lookin' for it!—and when Pickett sings it, he's doing it in a gospel feel. It's a ballad, and it makes the girls move: makes them scream in fact, like they would for James Brown. James's people run to his dressing room and tell him, "You got to come out and hear this guy Pickett singing." He was impressed, all right. Fact, he was a little upset because it probably seemed that Pickett was trying to sing like him, but it was a totally different song. And Pickett's voice was *way* more powerful. I mean, on that particular song, it really was powerful. But still we were doing it gospel. We were still doing the dancing in the rest of the set, but that particular song, Pickett would sing it in a gospel feel, and it would automatically make the people react, in a gospel way. It was like they were at church.

Touring in those days was hard work. There wasn't anything glamorous about it. We had a new station wagon my uncle bought us, and it was up to us to get to each show on time. Still was an era when we had to know where we could and couldn't stop, where we could and couldn't eat, where we could and couldn't stay. And at times, we risked our lives just by driving. This one time, we blew a tire . . . One minute we're on the road, next we found ourselves over in a ditch, almost upside down. The back end of the station wagon went down in a hole, and we went down in the van; the vehicle was left facing up like a rocket. It wasn't like a really violent type of thing: the way it happened, we were able to get out of the van, call back to Detroit, and tell my uncle. And he gets out on the road and comes to sort it out for us. That's the one time it happened, but Pickett would tell that story like it happened to us every day.

That first time on tour together we played Atlanta, and the next show was Baton Rouge. There was a little narrow highway led down through Alabama. If we're going to be on that highway, I'm definitely going to stop in at Montgomery and say hello to my family. Pickett says, "You're from Montgomery? I'm from Prattville." I had no idea. We'd never talked about that. So I stopped in and saw my mom for fifteen minutes, and we stopped and saw his mom and his grandmother. We surprised both of them! I was in a position where I could travel down to Montgomery on my own when I had time, so my mom and grandmother knew how well I was doing with the Falcons, and besides, my mom's brother was our manager. Sadly though, we never did get to play in Montgomery.

The show down in Baton Rouge featured another guy who had a hit record out. His name was William Bell, and the song in question was this beautiful ballad he'd written, "You Don't Miss Your Water." It was out on this little label from Memphis, William's hometown, called Stax, and it was creating a lot of action down south. If "I Found a Love" was the heavy side of a music they were going to start calling soul, with Pickett screaming through it the way he did, then "You Don't Miss Your Water" was the tender side of it, the heartbreak that comes at the end of it all. William Bell and Wilson Pickett were both gospel through and through, but there were different ways of bringing that church music to the concert hall. The playing on "You Don't Miss Your Water" was amazing as well; the piano was by Marvell Thomas, and the organ came from Booker T. Jones.

Along with William, these were people I was going to spend some of the best years of my life with. I just didn't know it yet.

That night in Baton Rouge, William Bell went on first. As he remembers things, it was a big old theater building converted into a nightclub. William came off into the dressing room, started toweling off his sweat, and we went on right behind him. "They got halfway through their first song," William recalls, "and we heard this big explosion. Someone had come into the club and shot a shotgun up in the air, looking for his woman and another man. The Falcons came running off stage and crowded right into the dressing room while I'm still getting changed! That was our initial meeting."

Those were the times, brother! Could never quite know what was going to happen at one of your shows. And what happens next to the Falcons is no less confusing. Pickett, like I said, figured himself as a solo artist from the start, and that's the main reason we never even got a photograph taken with him; it's not like it ever felt like we had a permanent thing going. So he's continuing to perform on his own, and right around the time "I Found a Love" takes off, he releases his own single on a little label called Correc-Tone, started by a local numbers runner who figured he could make even more profit out of records. Meantime, of course, Atlantic wants us to follow up "I Found a Love," so they get the group back in the King studio with Pickett and the Ohio Untouchables—who later became the Ohio Players, just so you know. But Atlantic *also* has us recording down in New Orleans with the great Harold Battiste as producer, and Pickett wasn't on those sessions. Nor was Willie Schofield, who didn't like to tour. We got a guy called Ben Knight in from another group my uncle had signed to one of his labels, the Tornados. Meantime, Schofield is getting more into production alongside my uncle, and they're bringing in the Falcons to sing backing for some of these singers—among them, Betty Lavett (as her name was originally spelled), who makes her debut on Lu Pine. But none of these singles are hits, not even the Falcons ones. And we're no longer in the studio together at the same time for the same records. Band members are coming and going. Mack is cutting some tracks, I'm cutting some tracks, and Willie's cutting tracks on other people—and then Willie gets his draft papers round this time, and he's out of the picture completely.

The way I remember it is this: we went to the Apollo to do a show, and we were coming back to Detroit, through Ohio, and we heard Wilson Pickett on the radio. But this is not Wilson Pickett singing as the Falcons, this is Wilson Pickett singing as Wilson Pickett. It's his solo single. *Oh.* We got about 700 miles left together on the road to figure *that* one out! The next show was going to be about two weeks later—in D.C., at the Howard. Some of us meet up, and we drive over to Wilson Pickett's house. And Pickett comes out, but instead of getting in our car, he goes to the car in front of us! He says, "I'm going to do a record hop in Chicago."

I guess that it's. He's going on his own? Well I'm going on *my* own.

And that's how the Falcons, the world's first Soul group, broke up. Right there, in the streets of Detroit, each of us going our separate ways—and just about all of us making good on it too.

Chapter 6
MAKE UP YOUR MIND

After the Falcons broke up, I moved to D.C. Detroit had been my home on and off since I was a baby, my permanent residence for the last ten years or so, and it had been good to me. But at this point, in 1963, the music scene of Detroit is all about Berry Gordy and Tamla-Motown. It's wonderful to see the acts that we grew up alongside, as friends and neighbors—the Miracles, the Supremes, the Four Tops, the Temptations, and more— topping the pop charts all over the world. Motown is the Sound of Young America, and there's great pride to be taken in it. But it means there's not much room in Detroit for others. If the Falcons are going to be no more, then it's time to move on.

This is a major step in my life, not just for professional reasons but for personal ones too. My marriage to Rachael has resulted in two more children—Anthony and Cheryl joining Eddie Junior. I've got a family and a responsibility towards them. I've taken it seriously and been the best father and husband that I can. But I know that the life I have here in Detroit is not everything it's capable of being, and if I want to do right by my kids, I need to do right by myself, make a real success of myself. It's a tough decision and not one I take lightly. But it's something I have to do. I'm glad to say that not only did Rachael and I stay close friends, but my relationship with my children has been solid throughout. Eddie Jr. was only the first of them to graduate college.

As for why I chose D.C., I just liked it better than the other big cities on the east coast. Way more than New York. I've *never* liked New York City. Too crowded, too dirty, too rude, too many different languages, way too fast and way too much stress. D.C. was more exciting musically than the other cities in the east. Plus, D.C. was perfectly located. You could get anywhere from there: Atlanta, Florida, Boston, Louisville, Memphis, the Carolinas, Alabama, even New York if you had to! And there was plenty of music happening for sure. The Howard Theater was at the center of it all, but all around that area from 7th Street to 14th Street was full of clubs. There was no shortage of work and no lack of good musicians to play with. Billy Stewart, one of the early great soul voices, was from D.C. There were groups like the Carltons—with this amazing young guitarist, Charles "Skip" Pitts—and what had become the second version of Chicago's Moonglows, which original member Harvey Fuqua had pulled together from D.C.'s own Marquees.

Fuqua ended up keeping only Marvin Gaye from that new Moonglows, moving on up to Detroit, where each of them married one of the Gordy sisters. That left the other Marquees-turned-Moonglows back in D.C., among them their founder, Chester Simmons. He and I had met in Detroit, and given that both our groups had broken up and I'd decided to move to his home city, it made sense for us to partner. Chester had been a driver for Bo Diddley, the great guitar gunslinger of early rock 'n' roll, the man who gave his name to a whole sound and rhythm, paved the way for the Rolling Stones among others, and who was one of the most famous of all the musicians based out of D.C.; he'd moved there in the late '50s for similar reasons I did now, namely that it was in the middle of everything, musically and geographically. Bo Diddley had a studio at his house on Rhode Island Avenue, number 2614, where he liked to stay busy producing sessions for local acts, and Chester Simmons, who was still very much Bo's friend, arranged one for me so I could record my first solo single.

Bo Diddley did more than just engineer the session, though. He played guitar on it as well. That's him you can clearly hear at the start of both songs—"Will I Be the One" and "Set My Soul on Fire." His famous twang helped distinguish those cuts from a lot of the other rhythm & blues music that was coming out at the time. Bo was a nice man. He had three or four houses—he wasn't hurting—but he took care of everybody back during that time. It was a pleasure to work with him. Years later, I'd be out on the road with him, and he'd tell everyone within earshot, "I'm the one that started him." Well, yes and no. I mean, it's not like I hadn't seen the big time with the Falcons, but to be fair, I didn't yet have a name as a solo artist.

I hadn't set my sights on one either. My main concern with moving to D.C. was to push myself. A lot of talented people had been involved with the Falcons, and I'd stopped putting myself to the front of the group; I'd let others take the lead vocals in the studio, let others compose the songs. By moving to D.C., I would get a chance to find out how good I was on my own or with new partners like Chester. By doing my own session in a different city, with a completely new set of musicians, I could see what I was capable of as a writer, a singer, a producer even.

I was pleased with the results, especially the up-tempo "Set My Soul on Fire," which had a groove to it like nothing I'd been involved with before. I sent the tapes back to my uncle in Detroit, and he put them out on Lu Pine. Just because the Falcons had broken up didn't mean he was going to slow down his business activities. Our breakup didn't even stop him managing a group called the Falcons! Robert West just approached another act—the Fabulous Playboys—and convinced them to change their name so they could get on bigger stages, release more records, and presumably make more money. Mack Rice stayed around in Detroit to help with the transition, and Lance Finnie continued to play guitar for these new Falcons, who released a whole bunch of records through the 1960s, though none of them as big as "You're So Fine" or "I Found a Love." Willie Schofield, after his stint in the Army, stayed away from singing and touring but worked with my uncle on records by Benny McCain, Betty Lavett, the Ohio Untouchables, and others. My uncle also put out a single on Joe Stubbs round this time and launched Mack Rice's solo career with a couple of 45s too.

In early 1964, Lu Pine put out another pair of my own songs, "I'll Be Home" and "A Deed to Your Heart," which we recorded at Edgewood Studios on K Street in downtown D.C., the main studio in town. The first of those songs, a ballad, took off on the beach circuit, which is what we call the club scene as you go further down the coast from D.C. One of Mack's solo singles on Lu Pine, a dance record he called "The Whip," got some action as well—Atlantic was distributing the label, which helped—and given that Mack and I were like brothers, we promoted them together. I sang "I'll Be Home" all the way from Washington to Key West. A lot of people aren't familiar with this whole beach music thing, but it was—and remains—something real impressive. In the Carolinas, especially Myrtle Beach, or in Virginia, you'd have a whole row of clubs up by the boardwalks; people would flock to them once the sun went down. They had their own taste in music, and I was always a part of that. I still am. The beach circuit was really where I started making my own name, and I return to it to this day.

My uncle Robert West had been such an important part of my early life, but his involvement in the Detroit music scene ended unpleasantly. The way it's most commonly told, he got into some kind of an argument with Herman Griffin, the ex-husband and manager of Mary Wells, Motown's first female star. This was about 1964, just after I'd left town and right after Mary famously left the label. Mary was supposedly at the meeting as well. Robert later told people that all he knew was that one moment he was talking, and he suddenly ended up on the floor, shot through the eye. There was lots of speculation about what really went down, but I wasn't there, and nobody was ever charged with a crime that I know of.

Fortunately, my uncle lived—all the way to 1983, by which time he was just about seventy years old—but he wasn't ever going to be the same after that experience, and about as soon as he was able, he and Catherine packed their bags and moved to Las Vegas. He continued releasing records on Lu Pine from out west, through a P.O. Box address, but most of them were reissues from the stockpile of music he'd built over the previous ten years. To this day, tracks come out on the Falcons that I had no idea existed. The last set I heard about managed to compile *four* CDs worth of various Falcons and Robert West recordings. We never see any money from these releases, but I figure there can't be that many people looking to buy a four-CD box set on the Falcons, and putting together such a package can't come cheap either. It's good to know people still care. And I appreciate that Robert West has finally received some of the credit he deserves for all that he did for the Detroit music scene.

One day in D.C., shortly after I get there, Chester tells me about a guy he's just met, a disc jockey on WUST by the name of Alvertis Isbell—or Al Bell, as everyone calls him—who's looking to start a label. Chester figures the three of us should do it together and says that he's recommended me to Bell. Turned out to be about the most important introduction of my life.

Al was younger than me by three years, but he hadn't wasted a single one of them. He'd been born in rural Arkansas and managed to get himself to college in Little Rock, where he prepared for a life in the ministry at a Bible college. But then he earned his degree in political science at a different college instead, all while getting himself established on a black-oriented radio station. He wouldn't have been your normal disc jockey though. First thing I learned about Mr. Alvertis Isbell—other than that he always dresses formal, with a kerchief in his top jacket pocket, like a proper businessman—was that he'll speak in a spiritual way, and he means every word of it. Like this:

> The only authentic music art form in America comes from the African American culture. That's because of the slave history. We couldn't talk to each other, so we had to learn how to sing to each other. We got in church 'cause they wouldn't let us congregate. When we got in church, we started singing about the higher being, and sang about our culture and our environment and our ethics and all of that in our songs, and they were called spiritual songs. And out of those spiritual songs came what we call blues and jazz.

From college, Alvertis Isbell's combination of spiritual and political calling saw him go to work with Dr. Martin Luther King's Southern Christian Leadership Conference in Georgia. He eventually split from Dr. King over differences in how to secure the advancement of the black race in America, and Al moved on to host the morning shift at WLOK in Memphis. There he became popular by talking *with* the music, not over it; by being calm, not frantic. What he did was to take his twin education— political science and Bible study—and apply it to music.

"I realized I can't sing, can't dance, none of that," he recalls. "But if I took a piece of music and I liked it, I would listen to it twenty or thirty times, until I knew every lyric that was in the songs, so I would know the story of what the artist was talking about. Then I would listen to what all the musicians were doing—even the mistakes, because I realized that what was a mistake often felt good! Once I learned all of that then it put me in position as a personality jock; I knew exactly where I could go in. I had to be sure that whatever I said or did, I could say 'Oww!' and not step on the lyrics or any of the music, because I had too much respect for the music as an art form. In doing all of that, I realized it *was* an art. And our industry was not talking about it then—or now—as an art form, which blows my mind.

"I also learned to listen to what other people said about music, particularly the females. Because the females would tell me more than males, because they were more emotional. I would hear a piece of music that I liked and thought would work for my audience, but I'd also have done my research on the music that people would like in my area, just from going to the beauty salons, the barbershops, the pool halls. I had a mentor who said: wherever you find a juke box, where blacks are listening to music, you know they *want* to hear that music because they haven't been *paid* to listen to that music. So that lets you know . . ."

WLOK was the big time. Memphis is the capital of the mid-South, on the southwestern corner of Tennessee, right where it meets Mississippi and Arkansas, and not much of a journey from Alabama either. That also makes it the crossroads on your way out of the *Deep* South. Over the years, plenty of people on their way up north so liked what they heard, felt, and saw there in Memphis—on Beale Street and in the churches and juke joints all 'round the city—that they never completed their journey, just stayed in Memphis and added to the city's musical melting pot. Memphis was where W. C. Handy came from Alabama to perfect the 12-bar blues, just to give one example. As the decades went by, it continued to attract the best musicians from the worlds of gospel, country, hillbilly, and R&B. Over on Union Avenue, where Howlin' Wolf, B.B. King, and Little Milton recorded in the early 1950s at the studio owned by a man named Sam Phillips, those influences got mixed up together to the point that people started calling the result rock 'n' roll.

Sam Phillips went on to become famous as the man who discovered Elvis Presley, along with Jerry Lee Lewis, Carl Perkins, Johnny Cash, and Roy Orbison, but ask those who know about it, and many will say the first rock 'n' roll record of all was "Rocket 88" by Jackie Brenston and his Delta Cats, recorded at Phillips's studio back in 1951, long before the white kids started coming through the door. "Rocket 88" had Ike Turner on piano, and a fuzzy electric guitar; the story goes that the amplifier fell off the top of the car on the group's way to the studio, and they didn't have time to fix it. Sometimes, luck comes your way just when you think your day's gone bad!

Sun wasn't the only game in Memphis for long. In 1957 two labels were established that would have a major impact on my kind of music. There was Hi Records, launched by Quinton Claunch and some other producers who'd previously been working at Sun; its records were mostly cut at Royal Studios, which belonged to bandleader Willie Mitchell, who'd release what seemed like a single a month on Hi through much of the 60s. Hi became the home of Al Green, Ann Peebles, Otis Clay, and many more of the truly great soul singers.

The other label was the one we came to know as Stax. It was set up by a part-time fiddle player and full-time banker called Jim Stewart in his little garage label way outside of Memphis. He first called the company Satellite—'57 was the year the Soviets launched the Sputnik—and didn't get into the R&B scene until he was turned on to it by a hotshot young guitarist and gambler by the name of "Chips" Moman. Stewart only got properly going on his label after being introduced to Rufus Thomas, the man who gave Sun Records its first hit with "Bear Cat," an answer record to Big Mama Thornton's "Hound Dog." Rufus had a popular afternoon show on WDIA, the major black music station in town. When he teamed up with his then seventeen-year-old daughter Carla, he gave Satellite *its* first hit, too: "'Cause I Love You," in 1960. I remember that record well: you couldn't ignore it, especially the sweet *sweet* voice of young Carla.

By then, Jim Stewart had got his older sister, Estelle Axton, a former teacher now working at a bank, on board. They mortgaged her house to buy a big mono tape recorder, which they moved in to an old cinema building at 926 East McLemore in the middle of residential Memphis. The recording studio was located in the sloping theater, and Axton set up shop—literally, selling records—in the concession stand out on the street. Soon enough they changed the label's name from Satellite to Stax, merging the initial letters of their last names as was common practice back then.

Estelle's son Packy Axton, a sax player, had an integrated nightclub band going, the Mar-Keys—no small thing in a segregated city like Memphis—and, in 1961, they recorded an

infectious instrumental, "Last Night," that just clicked with
the times. The Mar-Keys toured all over the country behind
that hit, and when they returned to Memphis, some of them
stuck around the Stax studio as its house band: among them,
the young guitarist Steve Cropper, who quickly became Jim
Stewart's right-hand man; an experienced rhythm section,
bassist Lewie Steinberg and drummer Al Jackson Jr.; and a
teenage musical prodigy by the name of Booker T. Jones.
Booker could play sax, but it was the studio's Hammond M3
organ that he sat at when he recorded "Green Onions" alongside
Cropper, Steinberg, and Jackson. That instrumental went to
the top of the charts, or near enough, all round the world,
influencing a whole new generation of musicians to instrumental
R&B/soul, and putting Stax firmly on the international map.

My life was about to be changed by Stax too. I'd already
met William Bell, remember, who'd played his own part in
establishing the label with "You Don't Miss Your Water" back
in 1961. And I'd also met Carla Thomas. This would have
been in 1963. The Falcons were playing a club called the New
Era on Charlotte Avenue in Nashville. Etta James recorded
her live album *Rocks The House* there right round the same
time. The house group was Johnny Jones's the Imperials, and
they had another guitarist that night, a crazy cat who played
his guitar with his teeth, I remember that well. He would
reappear a few years later using the name Jimi Hendrix. But,
as far as I was concerned, Carla was the big star in the house
that night—even though she wasn't singing.

"I was in college then," recalls Carla. "That was a club we
were not supposed to go to. But it was a matinee, and a young
lady that had been in this group the Teen Town Singers with
me back in Memphis, she said, 'Do you want to go down to the
New Era to see the Falcons?' I said, 'The Falcons! Do you know

what that means?' I first heard 'You're so Fine' when I was a little bitty girl. I *loved* the Falcons."

Someone introduced me to Carla that night. There was no big conversation; I didn't realize what a future we'd have together. It just meant a lot that someone whose music I loved loved the music that I made too.

All of which brings us back to Al Bell. It was at the start of the '60s, just as Stax picked up distribution through Atlantic, that Al got his radio gig in Memphis. Like any R&B fan in that city at that time, he picked up most of his new records from Ms. Axton's Satellite shop out front of Stax. In turn, Estelle and Jim hipped Al to their own releases, especially a singer out of Macon, Georgia, they had signed by the name of Otis Redding. Otis took what my friend William Bell was doing and ramped all of it—the emotion, the tempo, the feel, the velocity—up by a factor of about five. While William was off doing his two-year service in the military, Otis hit the charts in late 1963 with the searing ballad "These Arms of Mine." That song was a game-changer.

Al Bell championed Stax's music on the local airwaves, and when he moved up to WUST in D.C., he figured to just bring his taste in music with him. He had to battle his station managers over the matter—they called the Southern soul "'Bama music" after my home state, and not as a compliment—but once he won that fight, he became a major figure on the city's music scene. He brought Otis Redding up to play the Howard, and recalls that Ladybird Johnson—the US president's wife—would call his show in person to request a song!

Successful as he was at radio, Al always had plans to *make* music. "I'd started a record label when I was in Little Rock and continued it in Memphis," he recalls. "It was just a small label, four or five releases, none of them hit and none of the acts went on to anything, and I closed it down before I came up to D.C. I was still just learning the business, learning the creative side. But after I'd won over D.C., I figured on starting another label, doing it right this time. That's when I got talking to Chester Simmons. He said, 'You need to meet Eddie Floyd. He's a great singer, a great writer, and a great person. You'll work well with Eddie. You'll like Eddie. And I'll work with you also.'"

And that's what we did. We set up our label and called it Safice: like Stax, it was made up of our last names' initials, though I'll leave you to figure out the order of them! A lot of people don't know much about Safice; it's one of those labels got lost in the shuffle of time, but we recorded a *lot* of music in just a year or so—from about the middle of '64 to the middle of '65. I guess Al Bell must have seen something in me.

"Eddie didn't know this," Al recalls. "But after a couple of meetings with Eddie, based on what Chester had said about the writing, I started listening and talking to him, and said, 'Holy . . . he *is* a writer.' I wasn't and am not a writer, but I knew how writers wrote. I even developed a formula, from just listening to and writing down the lyrics to the songs. And I listened to Eddie Floyd and said, 'Yeah, he's *it*.' As a matter of fact, Eddie Floyd was to me as a writer what Smokey Robinson was to Berry Gordy."

We kicked off the Safice label with a local D.C. group called the Mystics, and a doo-wop song I wrote for them with our pianist Al Haskins. Al and Chester got it sold to Ewart Abner, who'd just left Vee-Jay to start a label called Constellation. Al remembers that it was Abner who then told him—but politely— to look elsewhere next time. "You need to go to Atlantic and deal with Jerry Wexler," Abner told Bell, "because I can't market that music as effectively." Jerry Wexler, just like my uncle, knew the value of having a disc jockey like Al Bell on his team and agreed to distribute Safice straight away. That meant my first single on Safice, just like my last single on Lu Pine, had Atlantic behind it.

Both sides were solo compositions. "Never Get Enough of Your Love" was the first song of mine that tipped towards the sound of Otis and William Bell, that Southern soul ballad feel as opposed to the doo-wop I'd grown up with in Detroit. "Baby, Bye" the other side, was much more of an R&B thing, even had a bit of a Motown feel to it, so Detroit must have been sticking with me even as I traveled. Still, I opened it with a line about my new home—"You've been running around, all over D.C. town"—and it went on from there. A good song should tell a story, and a good story needs some detail. A location always helps.

What I liked about that single was not only that I wrote both sides on my own and that I was proud of them but that my voice came through loud and clear; the three of us were obviously working well together. And Al Bell was benefiting from his closer ties to Atlantic. Jim Medlin, the label's head of national promotion, introduced Al to Milt Gabler, who ran A&R at Decca. Milt was well known, a sophisticated jazz man, and he brought us the singer Grover Mitchell.

I loved Grover. He was from Georgia, had already bounced round a whole load of labels without a whole load of success. But the man had a voice that would give Wilson Pickett a run for his money, and you can hear it on the song I wrote for him called "Midnight Tears." (And in case you're wondering about the title, this is *before* Pickett came up with "In the Midnight Hour.") For the flip side of the next single we did for Grover, he sung a ballad that I wrote with Chester and Al, called "I Will Always Have Faith in You." Nobody really heard it at the time, but it's a song with a deep gospel feel to it that would come back for me many times over. Our songwriting was starting to take shape.

For Grover's third single on Decca, Milt Gabler came to Washington and got the Howard Theater Orchestra to play behind us on my composition "Take Your Time and Love Me," which would then get a very different, very Motown arrangement when re-recorded the next year on Josie. But then *I* got put in with the orchestra too. My first solo single on Safice having made a little bit of noise, Jerry Wexler suggested I put my next 45 out straight through Atlantic. Thing is, Atlantic was into big arrangements and productions; just when we're getting things together in our own musical field, in what's now being commonly called "soul" music, I'm back in that Don Costa world. I gave it my best, but on that single—"Hush Hush" and the ballad "Drive On"—my voice is buried by the orchestra. You can't win them all.

Still, by this point the three of us—Al, Chester, and me— figured that we just about knew what we were doing, which is why, when Al Bell told me that Carla Thomas was attending college at Howard University—right in the heart of the D.C. music scene, close to the theater and the night clubs and my apartment—I pushed for him to arrange a meeting. I knew that opportunities like this didn't come along often.

Fortunately, Carla felt the vibes, and they were good. "It must have been some kind of karma," she recalls. "By Eddie coming to Washington, by me being at Howard University. There was just something about me and Washington, and Eddie and Washington."

In short, when Al called her up, Carla expressed interest in working together. It might have been the very next day we came up with "Stop! Look What You're Doin'." And maybe even that same day, "Comfort Me." Both were ballads, in the 6/8 time signature, smooth rhythm & blues tailored especially for Carla's voice. I wrote both of them with Al; I was generally the one who came up with the melody, and Al saw his strength as being to help tell the story.

"It was, Cause in the first verse, the Effect in the second verse, then the bridge, and then the Solution," says Al. "So you create a Cause, the Effect of the cause, and then a Solution. I felt like that and I wrote like that. In writing with Eddie, once we set up the Cause, my mind went straight to Solution. So I would contribute what I had heard in other songs, how people approached Cause, Effect, and Solution, that influenced my thinking. And it flowed so well with the two of us . . ."

Now, here's how *I* go about writing a song. Most times it starts with a title. Get a title in. Then, whatever the title feels like dictates the speed of the song: slow, fast, a ballad. Certain things you see or say, for example, you just know it's meant to be a ballad. Then you try to come up with a concept of lyrics. And then that melody will come to you—if you're a songwriter, that is. *If* you know how to do that. If you just wrote some lyrics and didn't know how to sing nothing, it wouldn't mean nothing. But I know how to project, looking at those lyrics and how it becomes a melody, and I feel a melody in it, and make it be a melody just in the words that I see: So a simple phrase like "Come on and comfort me . . ." It's almost like I'm singing when I'm seeing the words. I'll sing it to you instead of talking to you.

Next, decide on what key you're going to sing something in. A lot people used to play all their songs in one key. I would sing a song in almost every key, and it might not even sound like me, because if you sing one register, your voice sounds one way, and if you sing another register, it's going to sound a little different. I could hear another artist sing, and they would sound the very same on every record that he sung; that's because they were singing in one key. I just didn't find that as being exciting.

With our songs in the bag, Carla said she'd come down to Al's radio studio after her classes. At seven o'clock we're at the studio in D.C. with our guitarist Al McCleod, we teach the song to Carla, and she sings it. She was—and is—a natural, and a good soul singer doesn't need more than a couple of takes. So now we got a demo of the songs. All we have to do is convince Stax to record one of them.

Carla might have been able to call that one on her own, but it certainly didn't harm to have Al on the team. "Jim Stewart would call me in D.C., ask me about the new Stax music, and ask me what I thought of it," he recalls. "He wouldn't ask me to play it on the radio because he was too diplomatic! But, of course, I was playing it anyway. So I had an opportunity to talk to him about this demo for Carla Thomas, and we sent it down to him, and almost immediately, he calls me back and says that they'd like to record 'Stop! Look What You're Doin'' at Stax. I said, 'Well, she's not going to fully understand the songs unless Eddie explains and sings it to her, so he needs to be there too.'"

Down we all go to Memphis. It was the summer of '65, and although I can't remember exactly who was on that first session I witnessed, that's partly because *everyone* seemed to be there. Even those who weren't on a session would be in the building, likely in the studio as well, offering ideas, helping out where needed.

A few weeks later, "Stop! Look What You're Doin'" comes out on Stax, and immediately I'm hearing it on the radio everywhere. I've had hits before, of course, with the Falcons, but not on a song *I've* written, and not for someone I already consider to be a star. It makes it all the way to the Top 30.

For me, this is the moment it all comes together. Having Carla take a song of mine into the charts is like opening a door from one world into another, this one full of artistic activity at a higher level. Al gets talking with Jerry Wexler some more, and next I know, we're writing for the great Solomon Burke, which means soon we'll have another hit when he sings our "Someone Is Watching" in that comforting preacher style of his. Carla follows up by recording "Comfort Me," which is another great honor. I wasn't there for this session, though; I was out performing on my own, and it was only when Carla and I were on a radio interview together in 2017 that I heard who actually sang back-up: Gladys Knight & The Pips, the same group I'd been so impressed by in Chattanooga back in 1961! They're still not on Motown yet, but at least we're all moving forward together. Then Al gets talking with Jim Stewart again, and next I know, we're all headed back to Stax—this time to record our own singles on Safice. (Jim was letting a lot of outside artists use the building at that time, especially those that had a connection to Atlantic.) We've got this guy Roy Arlington who we figure to be our potential star solo singer, and we've written a ballad for him called "Everybody Makes a Mistake Sometimes." It's a classic guy-playing-the-field-and-losing-his-girl number, and it would become well known soon enough.

Down at Stax, we get to cut a single on me as well, a song called "Make Up Your Mind" that I wrote on my own. It was one hell of an experience, recording at Stax that first time. We brought Al McLeod with us—Steve Cropper stayed up in the booth as producer—but otherwise we were working with the Stax house band. In D.C. we would have different musicians that played with us, might not even know half of them. But at Stax, that was a family. It was the Mar-Keys! It was the M.G.'s! And they're already proven, because they're already recorded behind other people. So, when you get down there and hear that, how can you miss? You're with the real guys.

These guys were so committed. Every morning everyone would come to the studio, and if there were any songs to be played, they would all join in and play on the songs. Not necessarily working because it was a regular job, but just showing up because they could possibly make some music. And they had the time available to come in and play. It was just family, the attitude of everybody. You had no tension in any kind of way. It was all about the music.

I've been asked the question millions of times, "How was it back then, them being white and you being black?" Well, don't forget I put an integrated group together ten years earlier, when I formed the Falcons, so this is nothing new to me. But for another thing, there were maybe four white people in the studio, and all the rest were black. So it wasn't too much different from anything else, it really wasn't. It was Wayne Jackson, the trumpet player who always seemed happy to be in the studio. And then it was Donald "Duck" Dunn on bass and Steve Cropper on guitar. I sang, and it worked out just fine! Just go back to everything we did: it speaks for itself. I loved to hear Steve Cropper play, and I definitely loved to hear Duck play bass. Listen to him on "Make Up Your Mind." He's up and down that Fender Precision like a hound dog in a rabbit hole. Duck was a very genuine person. I loved him with all my heart. He was the kind of guy who laughed a lot and said funny things all the time. Never seen him frown. There was just always a smile; that's the way he was.

Everything at Stax was done live. Nobody stopped you just 'cause somebody coughed. We tried to be quiet when it was time to be quiet, and we sang when it was time to sing. We had the barriers and the separations and that, and a little corner where we used to sing. But it was a big room, and nobody had headphones. Cropper said he always measured his guitar playing to the beat, not by listening to Al Jackson but by looking at him: when Al's wrist would come down on that snare, *that's* when Steve would hit the guitar.

We came back up to D.C. with four solid tracks. Really good tracks. Did they hit? Well, both my single and Roy Arlington's made some noise, especially in D.C., but not quite enough. Maybe if people knew they'd been recorded at Stax it would have made the difference; if they'd been *on* Stax then I'm sure it would. As for Atlantic, we had their distribution, but we didn't have their promotion. What we had at Safice was Al Bell, and good at promotion that he was, he had a day job as a disc jockey. When all was said and done, ours was a tiny little label, and Al—well, he was always thinking big. And now, so were the people at Stax. They wanted to lure Al back to Memphis.

"I knew Al to be a good contributor of ideas," says Steve Cropper. "Also, a good songwriter and so forth. But the reason we really needed Al Bell was because he knew everybody in the business. We needed to be able to get into people's offices and say, 'Listen to this.' I knew that if I played people a Stax record they'd go, 'Man, I got to put that on the air!' because it was just the right music at the time. But there were so many doors that were closed, unless we had somebody like an Al Bell to call a friend and say, 'Hey, listen to this.' Without that, you don't have a chance."

Al recalls it playing out as follows. "Jim calls and says, 'Al, we're about to go under, we're $90,000 in the hole, and you know our music. Can you come down and take over the promotion?' So I called Jim Medlin at Atlantic. He said, 'Al, you know I know this business. I know you. Take that job and go do what you know how to do. That's the only company around here that has the kind of bottom sound that's in Stax Records.' I said, 'What do you mean, the bottom sound?' He said, 'I'm talking about the bass drum and the bass guitar, there's no other bottom sound like that in this industry, and it's going to be huge. And the way you know how to do things, you can go in and help turn this company around.' So I asked Jim how much he'd pay me. He said, 'I can give you $100 a week, and Jerry Wexler said he will give you $100 a week—and we can give it to you in cash.' I said, 'Do you know what I'm making in D.C.?' I was making mid–high five figures in D.C. at that time, and they're offering me $10,000 a year!"

But hey, I guess Al lowered his salary, because next I know, we're closing up Safice. Chester Simmons gets himself a job doing promotion for Chess in Chicago, and Al's telling me I'm going to be a permanent part of Stax. Memphis, here we come.

Chapter 7
634-5789

When I first came down to work at Stax, in 1965, I was the new guy, the unknown quantity, looking to fit in to what I knew was a tight-knit family. There were plenty people had been there a while already and had built the label up into something. Not just artists like Carla or William, who I respected enormously, or the members of the M.G.'s, who I'd already hit it off with when I came down for Carla's session. There were also people like David Porter, the first songwriter on staff there; David wrote alongside Isaac Hayes, who'd taken the place of Booker T. Jones at the keyboards when Booker went off to college.

But the thing about Stax being a family, even a tight-knit one, was that it still welcomed newcomers. "When I found out

Eddie had sung with groups that had name recognition, like
the Falcons, I was blown away," says David of my arrival. "And
Eddie was not one of those loud, in-your-face kind of guys. He
was laid back; by no means would I call him an extrovert. So he
wasn't bragging about what he had done. But I could tell he was
ambitious, we all were."

Then there was Deanie Parker, who'd been signed as an artist
in 1963 but quickly shifted over to become the label's publicist, its
first full-time female staff member. Deannie was Stax's arbiter of
taste, the kind of woman who commanded respect. It's interesting
to hear her take on my arrival, all these years later. "It's very clear
that Al Bell was Eddie's conduit to Stax," is how she puts it. "And
if he had been a joke, if he had been a no-talented individual,
a hanger-on, I don't think he would have been accepted or
welcomed into the Stax family without any hesitation. But when
Eddie came, he had in his arsenal of assets, much knowledge about
the music industry and how songs are structured and what stage
delivery is like, and I think he had his finger on the pulse of the
music industry. And Al Bell was that lifeline to the career that he
sought, which enabled him to develop many talents that he had."

Whether or not Al was my "lifeline," he was going to be too
busy running the promotional department at Stax to carry on
writing many songs with me. I was assigned Steve Cropper as my
writing partner. Steve had already helped flesh out "Comfort Me"
for Carla and got his name on the writing credits for it, so we've
got something of a rapport. But he's also got his name on hits like
"Green Onions," "These Arms of Mine," "Mr. Pitiful," and a
song called "In the Midnight Hour." What does he need *me* for?

Well, the short answer is that if it wasn't me, it was going to be
someone else. Cropper is the first to admit that he hates writing
by himself. "I have nothing to spin off of," he says. "What am
I going to do? Sing to a wall, say 'tell me what you think?'

Nothing's going to come back! If I cowrite, they're going to say, 'Hey that's good,' 'Do it again,' 'What did you say?' That kind of thing. It's all about inspiring somebody to do a little better."

Cropper and I hit it off immediately. We would just find a room and write. "He knew what I was thinking, and I knew what he was thinking," Steve says now. "And we didn't say, 'Man that sucks'—you'd pat each other on the back and you'd get along. Somebody might write something you don't really like, but you don't really hate it, so you don't smile as big, but if somebody hits it, you jump up and go, 'Man, that's it, that's the one we've been looking for.' So that excitement right there alone, it's a hit before you ever take it to the studio—Eddie and I knew that feeling."

Steve Cropper and I would write a *lot* of hits together in the years to come. But what many people don't realize is that we wrote one of our biggest hits almost as soon as we got together. Stax put me up at the Lorraine Motel, on Mulberry Street. The Lorraine was like the Stax social club, or its rec room, a place where black and white musicians could hang out together without anyone coming down on them for it. The musicians often went over there for lunch, dinner, or just to relax by the pool. The owner, Mr. Bailey (he named it the Lorraine after his daughter), he took a liking to me, and the place felt like home. On this first writing trip, I've barely checked in before they sent Steve over to join me. And it seems like we've barely sat down together in a room, than Al Bell tells me Wilson Pickett is coming in to record at Stax. Can we come up with songs for him?

Pickett? I'm going to write songs for Pickett? Last I checked he didn't need any help from *me*. After splitting from the Falcons, he'd split from Detroit too, heading to New York and teaming up with Lloyd Price at the singer's new Double L label. There he had a couple of big hits with "If You Need Me" and "It's Too Late," but then the pair of them fell out, and Pickett went over to Jerry Wexler at Atlantic. Jerry put him in with Brill Building songwriters and surrounded him with those big arrangements they liked to do up in New York. But it wasn't soul.

Pickett always said it was hearing Otis's "These Arms of Mine" that convinced him he should go record at Stax, and maybe that was true. Whatever, once he got with Steve Cropper and they fleshed out some songs together, the change worked wonders for him. That spring of '65, they wrote and recorded "In the Midnight Hour" together and, all of a sudden, Pickett's world changed. You could say, so did the whole world of soul music. But fine, we can write for Wilson Pickett. It's not like I don't know the guy, after all.

Now, it just happened to be right around that time that they changed the prefix on the telephones to all numbers. Used to be you'd call the operator and say, "Beechwood 4–5789," to use the example of that song by the Marvelettes on Motown in 1962. I thought it would be really funny to write a number that was *all numbers*. Far as I knew, nobody had done that. But when someone did write a song with numbers, it was usually a hit.

So Steve and I go to a room and, just that quick, I start singing a melody, Steve starts playing, and we put it in a structure. Okay, he's got a lead-in, I got the 634–5789; we know that's going to be in the background each time we do it. So now, the opening line:

"If you need a little loving, call on me."

Well think about this. Wilson Pickett's first big solo song was:

"If you need me, call me."

I won't say that's what I was thinking of, but it could have been! It's a combination of different melodies. In my mind—and I might not even tell this to the person I'm writing with, that being Cropper—I just sung it in the feel of "The Hucklebuck." That was the big hit by Paul Williams out of Detroit, who I told you about earlier. And that's the way the horns go if you listen to that song; it's got that same swing to it.

There were no cassette players to put any copies down. We had to remember everything. I would remember what I remembered, and Cropper would remember what he remembered, and we'd hope we'd remember the same song the next morning! I gave him the benefit of the doubt—there's a possibility I forgot half of it and sung something else and it became a hit! But once you start doing on tape, that's what it is.

So, anyway, now we have the song, and we figure we have something good, and the next day Pickett comes down to the studio. He and I haven't seen each other for a long time, pretty much since he walked out on the Falcons.

Cropper loves telling the story of how we met Pickett at the airport, brought him to the studio, and played him the demo of "634–5789" that we'd done the night before. "Pickett's listening to it," recalls Cropper, "reading the lyrics, and then he just takes the lyrics and wads it up and throws it across the room, like trash. And about that time, I see Eddie Floyd flying in front of me, and he just blind tackles Wilson and there they are wrestling on the studio floor. I thought, 'The session's going to get canceled, I'm going to get fired, this is the end of the end . . . ' And Eddie said later, 'Oh we would do that all the time, we would wrestle around in the dressing room,' like two brothers. And I found out after that how much Wilson respected Eddie and so forth."

I remember things a little differently. It might well have been that Pickett thought he was writing his own songs with Cropper and did not like the idea of me taking his place in that partnership; after all, they'd already come up with "In the Midnight Hour" and "Don't Fight It." And yeah, it's possible he figured that "634–5789" wasn't his kind of song. When I write a song like that, I'm thinking about Sam Cooke, because of his pronunciation. And maybe that wasn't what Pickett thought he was about at the time. All I know is the minute we said two words between us, Steve was gone, up to the office. He wouldn't even have had time to see if we wrestled or not! And he came back down quickly enough and told Wilson he was needed upstairs. I never went up there, never saw what happened. But Wilson came back and said, "Okay, play the song again." I don't think he just talked to Jim Stewart upstairs. I think they got him on the phone with Jerry in New York, and he was told to go along with it all. Or else. And so, he went along with it. He came back down to the studio and said, "Play the song."

We played it, Wilson learned it, and we recorded it that day—and we had one helluva band to do so. You got Steve on guitar, Duck on bass, Al Jackson Jr. on drums, and Isaac Hayes on piano. Add to that the brass: Wayne Jackson on trumpet, Andrew Love on tenor sax, and Floyd Newman on baritone sax. All of it done live to tape; the backing vocals got added later down the line, in New York. It was Patti LaBelle and the Bluebelles as far as I understand, so you can add Nona Hendryx, Sarah Dash, Cindy Birdsong, and of course Patti herself to the list of fine people on that cut.

We recorded a couple more songs at that session, one of which Pickett, Cropper, and I wrote together right before we went in to record. "Ninety-Nine and a Half (Won't Do)." This one is Pickett's idea, 'cause it's a gospel thing. I'd heard that phrase with a gospel group way before Pickett tells me the words. It's an old Holiness Church standard, "Lord I'm Running, Trying to Make 100, Because 99 and a Half Won't Do." There was a lot of that going on at the time, taking a gospel song and turning the lyrics from sacred to secular. Pickett had already done it with "I Found a Love." It wasn't theft, it was just what you did—passing the baton, if you like, same way I thought back to "The Hucklebuck" and "If You Need Me" for "634–5789." That was a great song, "Ninety-Nine and a Half." Cropper did some real interesting things with the guitar that were unique, but listening to the bass line that Duck came up with . . . I don't believe it would have happened if it weren't for that bass line.

"Ninety-Nine and a Half" would become a hit a few months down the line, but first we had the fun of watching "634–5789" take off. It was released at the start of 1966, on Atlantic, and when I saw a copy, somebody had added the words "(Soulsville, U.S.A.)" to the title.

Turns out it was Al Bell: "Motown was 'Hitsville U.S.A.' and I thought that was magic," he explains, "because that's what Motown was. I recognized that Berry had figured out how to record black music and mix and master it in such a manner that it was more acceptable to pop radio, which would not play very much black music at that time. You'd get played on the black stations, and by the time you got on forty or fifty of those across the country, some pop act would have covered your song and that would be the end of it. You'd have to go back and do something else . . . And I said, 'Well, where we are coming from is not Hitsville, U.S.A.; we are African Americans in this African-American community, and I'm not worried about hits, I'm worried about authenticity. I loved Motown but that to me was the distinct difference between Motown and Stax, from a producer's standpoint. With Berry, you'd hear an artist sing 'Owwww' but Berry would take and mix it back to where you could feel it, but you wouldn't hear it. But with Jim Stewart and what we were doing, it would be right up front in your face, it was authentic. This is *Soulsville* U.S.A. We are soul music, we are soul in a soul community. That's what gave birth to that, and I started pushing it and pushing it."

So there you are. I guess that means I wrote the song that established Stax as Soulsville. Funny thing is, some people liken "634–5789" to a Motown song anyway. And of course, the single didn't come out on Stax; Pickett was on Atlantic. Still, it was written at Stax and recorded there, and as Al Bell says, "I didn't waste any time letting every disk jockey I'd ever known know where it was recorded and produced. So that they know we're not just putting out those "Bama records.' Black stations that were saying that, I could say to them, 'Well, listen to *this* song.'"

Or as Deanie Parker puts it, "When it hit the market, there was no question about where it was from. Everybody knew that we had a relationship with Atlantic and that Atlantic wasn't producing anything, they weren't creating a damn thing."

One thing Atlantic definitely did have was promotional muscle. Although I'd been involved in a few hits before, I'd never seen a record take off like this. "634–5789" spent seven straight weeks on top of the R&B charts in the spring of 1966. That, to us, was *the* chart. That was the chart we went after.

But then "634–5789" almost made the pop Top 10 too. I mean, this was a big, *big* hit. And people actually had that phone number. Buffalo, New York, I remember had it. Miami had it. And Atlantic was getting calls from these folks saying, "Please can you stop people from calling my house?" Well, it was a little too late for that; the phone number was blaring out from the radio all over the country. I was told that "634–5789" was the first and last song to use a real phone number: after that, if a song ended up being all numbers, it's got to be some crazy number you can't dial.

I was still based up in D.C. at the time, coming and going from Memphis, and after the song went to number one, I heard Wilson Pickett was going to be playing at the Coliseum in Baltimore. So I went over and saw him. He brought me up on stage and introduced me as the person who wrote the song. That was real nice of him. But you know what? I never saw Pickett really sing that song much after that. He might have thought it was a little light. Technically, after that, "634–5789" became my song. I mean, it's been covered by everyone from James Brown and Willie Mitchell to Tina Turner and Bruce Springsteen, but somehow it's become one of my theme songs. Everywhere I go, they want me to sing it.

Why do they know me for the song when Pickett was the star and I was just the writer? Because once I'd written a hit that big at Stax—and pretty much at the first attempt—it was obvious they'd need to let me record under my own name too. Eddie Floyd's solo career was truly about to begin.

Chapter 8
KNOCK ON WOOD

In early 1966, on another of my visits to Memphis, Steve Cropper and I wrote a song together called "Things Get Better." We took the title from the "Things Go Better with Coke" slogan, which had been the company's tag line for the last couple of years. Except, of course, I sang about love: "Things get better, baby, when I'm with you." It was an upbeat title and an upbeat song. The way I remember it playing out is that we recorded a demo, with me singing it, to have on hand for any other Stax singer coming through looking for a song. Jim Stewart must have liked it, because he said, "Well, you can come back and record it for yourself." And that was it: I had my first single on Stax.

Obviously, I hoped for the best from it. Al Bell fell in love with the title message, what he called the "social science point of view," and worked it as hard as he could. But nothing happened. The disc jockeys reported back to Al that it didn't fit what they were playing at the time.

Funny how that stuff goes. Over a year later, "Things Get Better" was a big hit in the UK. Still gets played to this day. And the flip side, a ballad called "Good Love Bad Love"—a song I wrote with Al back in D.C.—was picked up a solid four *decades* later for a Quentin Tarantino movie. A song is never dead just because it doesn't come alive the moment it's released.

Fortunately, I was having a lot of success as a writer. At least every month, someone else was going into the studio at Stax to record one of my songs, often from a demo that had my own voice on it. Among them was Sam & Dave, the barn-stormin' duo I'd first met down in Miami when I was touring "I'll Be Home." Sam Moore and Dave Prater could put on a hell of a live show, and they came to represent the hard-hitting side of Stax soul—but they were never best of buddies. Around the time I hit Stax, I got a side on the follow-up to their first big hit, "You Don't Know Like I Know." My side was the ballad "I Got Everything I Need," and they did it justice. Same with Carla Thomas on a song I'd written with Al up in D.C., "Another Night without My Man." It became the title track of an LP she put out. The Mad Lads—a well-named group of young singers straight out the Memphis scene—cut another song I'd written with Al, "Sugar Sugar," as a single. And then my friend William Bell comes back from doing service—he'd been stationed in Hawaii for a year and a half, where he mainly heard surf music—and I've got a song ready for him too.

"Everyone was writing songs for me and giving songs to me," he recalls. "'Marching Off to War'" was one of those songs, and I could identify with it. That's the unique thing about Eddie, that he's able to look at another artist and get their personality and their experience and write about it so that the other artist could identify with the song. So, sure, when I heard the lyrics, it was just a song I could identify with."

There was never a problem, as far as the music process went at Stax. Things were happening, and if you stayed busy . . . "Anybody got some songs?" "Yeah! I got songs." So boom! Here we go. You got a hit this time, but that's as far as it went. Didn't mean you'd get the next one. Whatever was the best song available at any moment in time, that's the one that got recorded.

That makes it all the more interesting about how my most famous song came about—or how it almost did not. Steve and I were writing at the Lorraine one night; nothing unusual about that. And as always, we want to start with a title, a subject for the story that will become the song. But in this case, we're having a hard time coming up with the *right* title.

We knew we wanted to write a song about superstitions, but we couldn't find the right one. "We went through the gamut of everything known to man," recalls Cropper. "Rabbit feet, going under ladders, black cats, throwing salt over your shoulder, breaking a champagne glass, all of that. I said, 'That ain't it,' and Eddie said, '*That* ain't it.' And finally, I said, 'Eddie, what do people do for good luck?' He knocks on the wooden table three times, and I said, 'There's our hit right there!' The whole attitude changed, about, I'm going to knock on wood for good luck that I keep this wonderful woman that I have, that I don't lose this great love. *I don't want to lose this good thing . . .*"

We weren't the first to use the title "Knock on Wood." You can take it back to the 1940s and the scene in *Casablanca* where Dooley Wilson is at the piano when entrepreneur Humphrey

Bogart first meets the black-market nightclub owner Peter
Lorre; he plays a song of that name, and the whole audience
sings along. Or you can cut to the movie *Knock on Wood* from
the 1950s, an Irish romp starring Danny Kaye, also with a song
of that name. But Steve and I, when we came up with that,
well, we had our own angle. There was a big storm going on
that night, with thunder and lightning. Memphis is set on the
Mississippi, and the winds come over the river from the bluff
in West Memphis on the Arkansas side and gain power as they
rise up to the higher bluff on the Tennessee side. You get used
to some bad weather here: Memphis gets more rain than the
national average and a fair number of tornadoes too. Same thing
back home in Alabama. Just because it's hot down there doesn't
mean it don't get storms; if anything, it means it gets more of
them. When we were little kids, and those storms would come
sweeping in to Montgomery, like I told you earlier, my little
brother Joe and I would hide under the bed—we got so scared.
I was telling Steve all this, how we'd be frightened and take
refuge. And all of a sudden, I've got a rhyme: *It's like thunder,
lightning, the way you love me is frightening.*

So, now we got this great song that we'd been writing and
writing, and we were so sure of it and enthused about it that
Cropper called Wayne Jackson on his gig over in West Memphis.
Cropper said, 'Wayne, when you get off your gig get over here
because we got a hit.' And he did just that. He sat there at two
o'clock in the morning and worked on the horn lines.

"But then," recalls Cropper, "we couldn't come up with an
intro. And I was kind of known as the musician who could put
an intro on things. I think I said, in desperation, 'Well, I wonder
what "In the Midnight Hour" sounds like backwards, and it was
just, "Follow the dots" on the guitar.' 'In the Midnight Hour'
runs from a D major on the 10th fret all the way down to an

open E major. And for 'Knock on Wood,' I just ran my fingers up the other way!"

I thought that was pretty clever of Steve. If you can turn a riff around and get away with it, that's OK. They don't sound alike, "In the Midnight Hour" and "Knock on Wood," but they got that feel of both being from the same time. But I didn't realize at the time that he'd turned it around. I'm hearing all of that mentioned *after* we made the record. It's like on "634–5789," he's not hearing "The Hucklebuck." I am.

I still say about "Knock on Wood," though, that I can't see it being a hit record just with Steve Cropper and I writing it in the hotel. The song wasn't complete yet. That only happened once we got to the studio to record the demo, and there are *other people*. The main one is Al Jackson. He hears us play through the song a couple of times, along with the other M.G.'s, and then he says to me, "Come here, George." Al used to call everyone George!

"Yeah, what's happening?"

"Can you sing up in the high register on 'Knock on Wood'? *High* register."

"Oh, OK." I came all the way up, a full octave from where I'd been when writing it with Steve, and that's what you hear to this day. And then, right in the middle, Al Jackson—again!—stops it and says, "Let's make a break," and when I sang "I gotta knock . . ." he went *boom-boom-boom*. You know what I heard in my head when he said that? I heard this old comedian all the way back in the day, Dusty Fletcher, with the phrase, "Open the door, Richard . . . Richard, why don't you open the door?" It was an old vaudeville routine—Pigmeat Markham used to do it at the Apollo—that got turned into a hit record, and if you listen to Fletcher's recording from 1947, there's a triple "knock" of the snare at the end of the first verse. Was Al Jackson thinking the same thing that day at Stax? I never asked him!

Nowadays, I can't even imagine it not having that break. The melody would have been the same, but it wouldn't have had the dynamic feel that it had. And that was totally Al's idea.

But we're not done. Next, in walks Isaac Hayes and says, "I got an idea; let me play *this*." He sits down with the piano, where Booker is, and basically creates the middle eight, that keyboard-and-brass line, before it goes right back into the verse. And everybody laughed and said, "Wow, that sounds like a soap opera." Just think about it. You know it wouldn't have been a record without it. The brass section picked straight up on it: Wayne Jackson on trumpet, Floyd Newman on baritone sax, and . . . I'm not quite sure who was on tenor sax. There were so many great brass players who would show up for Stax sessions, you couldn't keep track of them all!

By this point, we're thinking that "Knock on Wood" could work well for Otis next time he comes through. "When you listen to the horns on 'Knock on Wood,'" says David Porter, "you can understand what Isaac was thinking, about something musically that would be a complement to Otis Redding, in terms of intricacies, of colors for horn like that."

David would know, because he's in the studio as well, so we recruit him for backing vocals. And William Bell and a guy by the name of Quincy Phillips too. But it's David who comes up with the idea of a high note—better "knock!"—just before the second and third chorus. And if all of this make it sound like this was a team effort, well, it was.

In fact, says David Porter, "'Knock on Wood' embodies that family vibe at Stax more than any other song. Because that was the stage where we were open to things. We were trying to find all the right goodies for it. Steve was trying to find the right complements. Eddie was always open for suggestions. We were all pulling for it. 'Knock on Wood' was to me the only song that everybody came together with an energy that complemented and stayed true to the credibility of what Eddie and Steve had initially created. And I think that's why everybody felt good about it. It was not compromised."

Everybody played their part on that song. I've got to give respect to Cropper for his guitar playing, Booker for the piano—and then especially Donald "Duck" Dunn for that bass line. We didn't hear the bass line when we're writing it; we're hearing only the guitar, not hearing the drums or nothing like that. We're just hearing the song moving, but then it really comes alive when you get it off in the studio that morning. If Duck didn't play it like that, there wouldn't be no song. It's hard to be that simple and that effective. People have been marveling at the bass line on "Knock on Wood" ever since. And then of course there's the *way* that he plays it, too; no one could play like Duck. He had this beautiful 1959 Fender Precision bass he used on just about every session. Eventually he wore down the wood above the pick guard just from keeping his thumb there while he hammered the strings with his first two fingers!

Believe it or not, everything I just described took place in about three hours. And that was a long time at Stax! "Knock on Wood" popped up and came out, like perfect, and everybody knew the song had a possibility. Except Jim Stewart. He didn't like it!

"Eddie knew it, I knew it, Estelle Axton knew it, and Al Bell knew it was a hit," recalls Steve Cropper. "But Jim Stewart would not put it out. He thought it sounded too much like 'In the Midnight Hour.' I said, 'Jim, this song is a hit. And you know why it's a hit? Because everybody wants to knock on wood for good luck.'"

"I just knew 'Knock on Wood' would get people's attentions," says Al Bell. "Disc jockeys first, that they'd say, 'Hmmm, 'Knock on Wood,' what's that about?' and then, when you listen to it . . .

Here was what was considered a demo, but it wasn't a demo, it was a work of art. I didn't know no damn thing about no damn demo. I heard a masterpiece when I heard 'Knock on Wood.'"

The way Cropper remembers it—and he was the one closest to Jim Stewart at the time—it stayed in the can for a while, and eventually, after Mrs. Axton put pressure on Jim and so did Al Bell, he said, "OK, you can put it out." But let's give Jim the benefit of the doubt. He's a fiddle player, country and western, and then all of a sudden, he's seeing all of these crazies doing songs like "Walking the Dog," "Jelly Bread," and "Can Your Monkey Do the Dog." He might have been like, "I *hope* they're right." Because nobody knew who was right, you just knew how it felt. And I figure that's what he was going by. A lot of times he may have been a little reluctant on stuff until it was proven. So what if he didn't jump at the song like we did? Well, maybe he doesn't want to spend his money unless it's something he's sure of. And that's all right by me. Because all through this, I never heard him down anybody. Jim was—and remains—a gentleman.

You also have to look at what else was going on with Stax at that time. The label couldn't stop releasing hit records in 1966. The A-side to that ballad I wrote for Sam & Dave I told you about ("I Got Everything I Need") was an Isaac Hayes and David Porter composition, "Hold On, I'm Comin'." I figure you know that one: it went to number one, the label's first and only since "Green Onions" and considered one of *the* Stax classics to this day. And Carla Thomas had a smash with "B-A-B-Y," and Mable John had a Top 10 of her own with "Your Good Thing (Is About to End)." Johnny Taylor, the Mad Lads, the Mar-Keys, the M.G.'s, the blues guitarist Albert King . . . Everyone was having hits. As for Otis, the label's flagship artist—even though his records were on the Stax subsidiary, Volt—he came off the back of the ground-breaking "Respect" with the equally foot-stomping "I Can't Turn You Loose," and then had a crossover smash with the Rolling Stones' "Satisfaction." And when he did finally pick up on one of my songs, it was "Don't Mess with Cupid," which I'd written with Steve and Deanie Parker—who was an artist, remember, before she ever took the office job. That song was the flip side to "My Lover's Prayer," yet another Top 10 for him and the label. So if Otis decided not to cut "Knock on Wood" for now, and we'd figured it was meant for Otis all along, then Jim might have been asking why he needed to risk cutting it on Eddie Floyd.

As I remember, it was months before Al Bell convinced Jim to release it. And when they did, my recollection is that "Knock on Wood" happened real slow, maybe because I waited so long just for this "demo" to get released. Al Bell recalls different.

"It wasn't too much of a struggle," he says now. "I went to Washington, D.C. to spend two weeks in every retail outlet, every store, the radio stations and all of that, and got 'Knock on Wood' played in D.C. I knew that market, I knew Eddie's popularity in that market and how well he was known, generally speaking, in that market. And by the time I finished in D.C., it was breaking and selling there, and there was no question in my mind that that was a hit record—and I took the time to let everybody that I talk to know that there's no question that this is a hit record because of what's happened in D.C. Well, back in those days, those of us in the industry knew that if you get D.C., then it's Philadelphia, it's Boston, then Hartford, then New York City. If you got D.C., you got it: you're in the south, but you move out of the south, in every direction."

The way it worked between Stax and Atlantic was that Atlantic only picked up records for distribution that they thought they could take all the way. They didn't jump on "Knock on Wood" until after it had gotten all that action that Al Bell's talking about. But when they did, then—as David Porter puts it—the single "flat out exploded." "Knock on Wood" hit the charts in August and kept climbing. And climbing. Eventually, in November—the other end of '66 from when we recorded it—the song hits number one. It's only the third time Stax has put a single on top of the R&B charts, but it's the label's second within a few months, coming fast on the back of Sam & Dave. It's my second number one of '66 as well, because I had "634–5789" with Pickett at the start of the year on Atlantic. For that matter, given that I had the B-side to "Hold On, I'm Comin','" it might even have been my third.

But really, we weren't thinking of it that way at the time. You might have a hit, but it wasn't like someone told you about it at a given time of day. We were too busy to stop and celebrate. After all, "Knock on Wood" could have been one of those songs that hit big at the time and then faded away. But in this case, it went the opposite way. First, "Knock on Wood" goes Top 30 in the Hot 100, which is quite rare for a Stax single, and by the time we're done, we've sold almost 750,000 copies! And by then, the cover versions have started rolling in. My man Wilson Pickett records it almost straight away—while it's still climbing the R&B charts—over at FAME in Muscle Shoals, and the whole team there did it proud. The Capitols and James & Bobby Purify also got on it real quick. Maybe that was to be expected. In the soul field, it was commonplace for us to pick up on someone else's song while it was still fresh; it was like we were helping promote something we believed in.

But I knew we really had something with "Knock on Wood" when it quickly spread to other styles of music. Willie Bobo, the great Latin percussionist, put out a fierce instrumental on it. Prince Buster, the bluebeat kingpin in Jamaica, he cut it to a storming rhythm track that you just know filled the dance floor down there. The Buena Vistas, a side project from some of the past and present Motown session musicians, they record a burnin' instrumental. Next, the white garage bands get on it, and not just American ones but groups out of Canada and New Zealand too. But what really took my interest was when I heard that we had a hit with the song in the UK—and that it had inspired Georgie Fame, who was like the Booker T. Jones of the UK, to do a version that was filling the clubs in London and beyond, with some gorgeous organ work that Booker himself would have been proud of.

It continued this way for a couple more years, long after I'd moved on to other songs and other sounds too. It was a nonstop barrage of cover versions, until one day, I heard it on Ella Fitzgerald, and . . . well, that was the pinnacle of making it. Ella Fitzgerald! The First Lady of Song herself. The woman I had so admired as a child, when my mother took me to those concerts in Detroit. Back then, however much I knew I wanted to write songs, I could never have imagined Ella would one day be singing one of mine. And she did it just beautiful, too, closing out an album of contemporary songs, simply titled *Ella*, with a big brass section that sounded about ten times the size of the one we had at Stax.

Somewhere in the middle of all these cover versions, Otis finally records "Knock on Wood" like he was meant to all along, using pretty much the same musicians as recorded our "demo" of a year earlier. But he does so alongside Carla Thomas, as part of their *King and Queen* album that also included that funny and furious duet, "Tramp." I knew Otis would have his own concept on feel and groove, that he wouldn't do it exactly the way I did it, and he was the only one I heard who was singing all the way up. Plus, he sung it much faster than I did. And for all those changes, he and Carla still had a big enough hit with it, too, the second time it made the Top 10 within a year.

You have to think about it. If Otis had shown up when he was meant to, I might never have gotten heard. Otis would have had another hit record, I'm sure, but maybe not as big a hit as I did. My little demo would probably still be on the shelf, and the world might never have heard of Mr. Eddie Floyd.

You can call it a lucky accident. But the way I look at it: you got to do something, to create something to have an accident. You got to form the accident too. I totally believe what's meant to be will be. My good luck with "Knock on Wood" is my proof.

Chapter 9
HIT THE ROAD, STAX

I'd had a routine going for a while now. Every time I came down to Memphis from D.C., first thing I'd do after dropping off my bag would be to check out the Tiki Club, which was William Bell's nightspot. He'd gotten it together after coming out of the military, helping redecorate an existing club with a silent partner, and naming it for the environment he'd experienced in Hawaii. The Tiki was the place to be, where I could expect to see all my musician friends from Stax if they weren't working that night. And some of them even if they were!

The house band at the Tiki was the Bar-Kays, the group of fifteen- and sixteen-year-olds from Memphis who were knocking on the doors of Stax. Of course they couldn't travel or work that much at that age, but William got permission from their parents for them to play at the Tiki on Friday and Saturday nights. There they made some noise, in more ways than one. It was evident a new generation was coming up at Stax, inspired by the one before it.

The Tiki Club was right off of McLemore, on Highway 51, which is Elvis Presley Boulevard now. It was a block south of McLemore, very close to Stax. "A lot of the artists, when they were in town, that was the hangout for them," says William. "We had it laid out with the VIP area, so they could come in and have a good time after a concert or something and wouldn't be bothered at all. The Tiki was the spot! If you didn't get there before 8:30 or so, there was a line down the block. Unless you were Eddie Floyd or someone, of course."

And I *was* Eddie Floyd, so I got that VIP treatment! Soon, I was enjoying Memphis so much that I moved down there permanently with my second wife, Sonja, who I'd met in D.C. We got ourselves a place on Kerr Avenue, near Stax, put in a bamboo bar, and got the carpets and walls done in leopard skin! Elvis himself would have been jealous. Only problem was, I didn't really have enough time to enjoy it. Things were suddenly getting *very* busy.

You may know about the way it goes in the music industry. Or at least the way it was back then: you have yourself an unexpected hit single, suddenly you need an album out. Like, *now*. So, as "Knock on Wood" made its way to the top of the charts, and at the end of a year where I'd had to push to get a single out on me in the first place, all of a sudden Stax wants an LP's worth of material.

I recorded it with Booker T. & The M.G.'s at the end of 1966, in the break between Christmas and New Year. Really, though, there was no break: we were just working and working! Now,

having written so many songs for other people that year, I didn't
have a ton of them left. So we recorded a lot of other people's
songs, which was always part of the soul music process anyways.
Some of them had been big hits that year: "Warm and Tender
Love" for Percy Sledge, who'd also had the very first Hot 100
number-one soul single in '66 with "When A Man Loves A
Woman"; "Something You Got," which had hit for both Alvin
Robinson and Ramsey Lewis; "Hi-Heel Sneakers," which had
topped the charts for Tommy Tucker; and J. J. Jackson's wonderful
"But It's All right," the original of which he had recorded earlier
that year in England with a top jazz act. Going back further, I
also cut Chuck Jackson's breakthrough hit "I Don't Want to Cry."
There's one other "cover" as well: My version of "634–5789,"
which, although it was never released as a single, soon became the
recording everyone turns to when they think of that song.

We were also given the green light to record a couple of my
cowrites with Cropper for my next single. The A-side was "Raise
Your Hand." It started with a fanfare—one of those classic Cropper
introductions—and went onwards and upwards from there.

Cropper sometimes does himself down as a guitarist. "I'm
the most uneducated guitar player probably on the planet," he'll
tell you. "I never did learn how to play the guitar. I didn't have
time. I was too busy making records!"

And what records they were. Like with "Raise Your Hand,"
the production wasn't necessarily amazing. It's mostly just two
chords going back and forth, with a great call-and-response
courtesy of anybody who was available that day in the studio,
and a real emphasis on the off-beat—the "jerk"—that Cropper
and Al Jackson were so damn good at. It's representative of
how things were at Stax at that time, the mood of the place,
the sound of it, the feel, the *soul*! Jim Stewart obviously thought
as much, because he had Stax put it out about two weeks after

we'd recorded it, and it quickly got me another Top 20 single. So already, I was never going to be a one-hit wonder.

The *Knock on Wood* LP came out around much the same time. When I showed up for the photo session, we went over to the local park, and I was handed an axe by the photographer. Now that would have made sense if the album was called *Chop on Wood*. But it's *Knock on Wood*. I always assumed it was Deanie Parker's idea but she says it was Atlantic's.

"I told them at the time, 'That does not make sense! What does Eddie taking an axe to cut down a tree have to do with "Knock on Wood?" Where is your imagination? Where is your closer understanding of this? Give me a break!'" Nowadays, a copy of the *Knock on Wood* LP is worth quite a lot of money. Deanie jokes that it's because "People are still trying to figure out that riddle."

I mentioned already about "Knock on Wood" becoming a hit in the UK. Well, a lot of the Stax artists were getting attention in Europe. In '66, Otis went over for a tour, got a rapturous reception, and put in a stunning live TV special for *Ready Steady Go!* as well, which brought him an even bigger audience. I was thrilled that he'd recently recorded another of my compositions, "Everybody Makes a Mistake"—the song we originally cut with Roy Arlington for Safice—along with "634–5789," for his next LP, which would be called *The Soul Album*. On his version of Pickett's number-one hit, you can hear Al Jackson slam that snare the way he was famous for, but I'm more taken with the emotion Otis poured into the ballad. After all, "634–5789" was already well known; "Everybody Makes a Mistake" had slipped by unnoticed the first time we cut it. A year or two later, it was cut as an A-side by Mitty Collier, on Chess. She imbued it with the real gospel feeling I'd always felt in the song—which may explain how or why she eventually became a pastor up in Chicago. That line between the sacred and secular is always real thin.

It was in large part thanks to the success of Otis's European tour that, early in '67, just as I've got the *Knock on Wood* LP coming out and "Raise Your Hand" is heading on up the charts, that people at Stax—along with Otis's manager Phil Walden, and Phil's brother Alan, who runs a booking agency that many of us are using—start talking about taking a revue of the main artists on the label on a tour of Europe. That's Otis Redding, Sam & Dave, Carla Thomas—and Mr. Eddie Floyd. All of a sudden, I'm considered one of the label's stars?

But the stage is where I know I come good. I've been performing for well over a decade already, ever since I moved up to Detroit as a teenager. I've sweated with various versions of the Falcons, and, for the last few years, under my own name too. All through this period at Stax I've been continuing to perform, picking up club dates, playing the chitlin' circuit, doing the beach clubs, occasionally getting on the bill at the great black theaters. Still, I've never been outside of the United States before. None of us performers have, except Otis, and him only the year before for that tour of Britain. This is going to be something new. What makes it all the more special is that, unlike my regular dates, where I'd be playing with a local house band, we're taking our *own* house band: Booker T. & The M.G.'s, along with the Mar-Keys horns: Wayne Jackson, Andrew Love, and Joe Arnold. They've played on just about everybody's hit records who was going on that tour.

The one exception was Arthur Conley, who Otis Redding had recently picked up for his own label, Jotis. Conley had just released the sensational "Sweet Soul Music," which Redding had produced on him at FAME in Muscle Shoals, and, for whatever reason, it was decided that Conley would replace Percy Sledge, the original choice for a non-Stax guest slot. (Sledge's name ended up in the programs for the tour, so I guess that switch was made late in the day.) "Sweet Soul Music" was largely a rewrite of Sam Cooke's "Yeah Man," and its new lyrics celebrated our music by name-checking some of its biggest stars: Otis (of course!), Sam & Dave, "the Wicked" Wilson Pickett, Lou Rawls, and "the King of them all y'all," James Brown. When "Sweet Soul Music" exploded early in 1967 (it went all the way to number two on the Hot 100), it took soul music a significant step further into the international consciousness while demonstrating that we were all in this together, to the point of singing and chanting each other's names.

Still, no question but that I felt fortunate to be invited on that Stax/Volt tour. Rufus Thomas didn't go. William Bell didn't go. And Carla had to come home after three or four shows because she had another commitment in the States—a benefit that Al Bell had signed her up for, about which she was not thrilled. This meant she missed out on the one concert that was filmed, which we'll come to in a minute.

Right before the tour set off, Otis went to record a new single—a song I had written especially for him with Booker T. Jones, a searing ballad called "I Love You More Than Words Can Say." Otis gave the song everything he had, and it was further elevated by the use of strings—a violin section being heard for what I think was the first time on a Stax single. Otis was already a proven master of the ballad, but people heard "I Love You More Than Words Can Say" as something different on him, perhaps a sign of a new direction. We would see.

It's interesting to hear what Al Bell has to say about how Otis and I worked. "There was something that they brought in: they didn't just come in and go to the studio and start writing, they'd be all over the place—they knew everybody. They interacted. Not that others didn't have something similar, but there was something special about Eddie Floyd and Otis Redding. I could see it, I could feel it. I don't know whether Eddie even realized it."

I'm not sure that I did. I was just glad to be doing what I was doing in a place where I enjoyed doing it. And now that would mean doing it in Europe too. The tour there has been remembered as simply the Stax/Volt Revue, though we had our own name for it: Hit the Road, Stax. And that's what we did. We all flew over from Memphis to Dulles in D.C., catching an Eastern Airlines plane from Dulles to London. In the years since, I've been on maybe thousands of plane rides, but I still remember the details of that particular journey. Everyone was so darn excited.

A lot has been said about how we were received in Europe. And a lot of it is true. What we found was that there was an appreciation for the music from America—going all the way back to the 1920s and early jazz. They were used to the music, to *our* music. And for that, I have to say thank you for keeping our music alive. Thank you very much.

"There is no way to express in a digestible way the impact that it had on all of us going to that part of the world," says David Porter of the experience. "Seeing that, not only did the people know who we were, they know where we came from, our mothers and fathers, our sisters and brothers. Even though Isaac and I were writers, they knew who Hayes & Porter were, which was amazing. So I saw, first hand, a level of appreciation for all of us, that was unlike anything we'd seen in America. Even though we had hit records in the States, it was amazing for us to have that experience of people getting beyond the bullshit. They were open."

I read something somewhere that when we checked in to the Cumberland Hotel in London, the black musicians went around the back to the service entrance out of habit. That's some bullshit! We had enough respect for ourselves we would never stoop to that in America, let alone in England. Besides, we'd been welcomed like stars: the Beatles sent their limousines to pick us up at the airport.

Paul McCartney showed up for the first gig too, a private affair at this swanky little nightclub in the center of London's Soho called the Bag O'Nails, where the M.G.'s and Carla performed and the rest of us watched. McCartney was just Paul McCartney, and as far as I was concerned, the Beatles were just a group starting out. I know what you might say to that, and maybe it just means I had my own worldview and that up until then Beatlemania had passed me by. It was the same with Elvis. When we were up in Detroit in the 1950s, Elvis didn't mean nothing to us. We barely knew his name. Not like we knew Hank Ballard or Frankie Lymon: *those* were our idols.

Still, the Beatles loved what we were doing at Stax, so much so that they had been hoping to record at East McLemore in 1966, but word had gotten out, the local paper wrote about it, and they canceled. They went back to Abbey Road in London, but when you listen to the songs on their 1966 LP, *Revolver*, you can only imagine what "Got to Get You into My Life" and "Good Day Sunshine" might have sounded like had they been mixed with some of that Memphis stew.

I guess Carla must have known more about the Beatles than I did, because she followed Paul McCartney all round that club that night. She had decided to include Paul's recent Beatles composition "Yesterday" in her live set, even learning some of it in French for when we played in Paris, so it was a real honor for her that Paul came to hear her sing it that night. It was such a shame when Carla had to go home early: not only was she the only woman on the bill, but she was, even at her young age, the longest-serving Stax artist. The Revue was lesser without her.

The promoters set us up in London, doing interviews left, right, and center. Seemed like everyone in Europe wanted to talk to us. I was looking back recently at an interview I did with the English weekly the *New Musical Express,* and I said this:

"When am I gonna get a chance to get another record in the charts? 'Knock on Wood's bin selling for close on a year now. When's it gonna lay down and die? A man has to progress sometime, man! But this record keeps comin' back at me over and over again!"

I shouldn't have complained! "Knock on Wood" had gone back into the UK charts just before we went over—right at the same time that "Raise Your Hand," along with the latest singles by Otis and Sam & Dave, was released as part of a new Stax distribution deal in the UK with the label Polydor. So now I got *two* record companies pushing *two* different singles on me, and both are getting played at the same time. Matter of fact, and I remember this like it was yesterday, at one of the first shows we did, they brought along this American radio DJ, "Emperor" Rosko from the pirate station Radio Caroline, and I guess they must have been playing my songs out there at sea, because he introduced me by saying, "Eddie Floyd has not only the number-*one* song on the charts but also the number *two* . . ."

Those European shows were truly amazing. Every single one of them. For the M.G.'s and the Mar-Keys, who rarely got outside of Memphis to perform, it was an eye-opener: they had no idea just how much impact they had around the world. Booker and Co. responded by upping the tempo, increasing the volume, and quickly raising the roof, starting off each night with a set of instrumentals— and when they hit "Green Onions," the venues went crazy. It was almost impossible to understand how big that cut had been around Europe until we saw the audiences dancing to it and clapping along to it and cheering every solo. And it was a mixed crowd— black kids as well as white. That's important to note.

The Mar-Keys would then join the M.G.'s for their own hits, "Last Night" and "Philly Dog," after which it was Arthur

Conley and Carla's turns. Arthur was good—he was a solid down-to-earth soul man, and he covered the main soul hits of the time, like "In the Midnight Hour" and "Land of 1000 Dances." By the end of the tour, "Sweet Soul Music" was considered one of them. As for Carla, she excelled, always. "Yesterday" was a highlight of the short time she was with us.

I had the honor of opening the second set. I did so, initially, with "If I Had a Hammer." It had been the first track on Sam Cooke's live *At the Copa* LP from 1964: it's not like I was covering a folk song, as some people know it for, but that I was paying tribute to the King of Soul. Otis did the same thing in his set, with Sam's "Shake." I rehearsed up a number of the cover songs from the *Knock on Wood* LP, and among those we definitely performed were "I Don't Wanna Cry," "But It's Alright," and "Something You Got." All these went down well, but when I got to my own songs, I noticed that the audience would sing along to every word of "Knock on Wood"—and when I implored them to "Raise Your Hand," well, they didn't take much convincing. These songs were also fresh enough for the M.G.'s that none of us barely had to look at each other to understand where to go at any given moment, whether to raise the groove high or take that rhythm down low.

Then, when I was done with the audience, on came Sam & Dave, Double Dynamite. Stepping, sliding, spinning, sweating, swapping places at each other's microphones almost every other line, they had these perfectly rehearsed introductions, moves, and fake endings that looked like they were all being made up on the spot. They could crack you up—Duck could barely keep a straight face behind them—but they never let it affect their singing or their dancing, which was always on the money. People in Europe already knew them for "Hold On, I'm Comin'" and "You Don't Know Like I Know," though I doubt they'd ever *seen* anything like it. When they left the stage, even the walls were dripping sweat.

Weren't many people who could follow an act like that, but Otis Redding wasn't most people, and the one of him could hold his own against the two of Sam & Dave. After all, Otis was a superstar in Europe already, and most of the songs in his set—"Satisfaction," "Respect," "Fa-Fa-Fa-Fa-Fa (Sad Song)," "Try a Little Tenderness"—had already been hits there. Plus, people had already had a chance to see him the previous year; they knew he could deliver. Chances are you already know what kind of a performer Otis Redding was on any given night, and even if your only proof is from television and concert footage, you won't be surprised to hear that he brought the show home, without fail.

A lot of people have said about that first Stax tour, the way that they saw that it got stronger and stronger and stronger as the night went on, "Well you guys were obviously in competition with each other." I've always said no! We considered ourselves soul singers—and that's all it was. Nobody was going to try and go up there and *not* do it right. It would just continue to escalate, and that's the way it should be. None of the artists were ever in competition with one another.

We automatically knew that each one of us onstage was giving 100 percent. He's giving all of him, and I'm looking forward to seeing him do it. There's no malice, because I'm singing my thing, and he's singing something different. And we didn't have no conflict with the band either, because the band's supporting everybody. I know what I did, and I did everything I was supposed to be doing. If someone did a little less, it wasn't me!

Tom Dowd, the producer from Atlantic Records, joined us for those opening shows. He recorded the concerts at the London Astoria on March 17—we performed two shows a night—and again, four days later in Paris. Stax/Atlantic got two live LPs out of it, with myself featured on both of them. You can hear the energy on those records; everything seems to be peaking, like the needle is in the red, but Tom's mix keeps it all just under control—which is testament to him, because he was mixing it right there, in the concert hall that night; he didn't have the multiple tracks that would be available nowadays.

I guess we knocked them dead that first night in London. The man from the *Melody Maker* wrote that "the Stax Show must be one of the raviest, grooviest, slickest tour packages that Britain has ever seen," which definitely dates the review to 1967! But he also credited us on our "sheer professionalism—a professionalism that hasn't yet come to Britain's pop music ranks." We didn't know anything about that; we were just doing what we did all the time!

After Paris, we bounced back to England, playing an old train shed in North London called the Roundhouse, then going up to Manchester, Leeds, Leicester, and more—all cities in England I'd get to know well over the years. Then we took off for Scandinavia for one show each in Denmark, Sweden, and Norway. We were all total tourists at this point, fascinated by all the architecture, the language, the clothes, the vehicles. Some of the guys had brought home movie cameras with them, and you can see footage of us on the Stax documentary *Respect Yourself*. We struggled some with the food—wasn't much Southern barbeque in Manchester!—but that was all right; wasn't half as much of a struggle as getting some sleep. Nobody wanted to miss out on anything, so it felt like no one went to bed for a month.

We traveled on a bus—not one of those tour buses like you get nowadays, with the tables and the bunk beds and the televisions and all of that. Just a regular bus with forward-facing seats. Even so, we used the time to write and work on songs. I recently heard Emperor Rosko, who came on the bus with us in Britain, say as much on a radio documentary about the tour. We were motivated to keep writing, because the reception was really like nothing we'd imagined. It took me back to the days of touring with the Falcons when we had a couple of Top 10 hits, and the girls would scream at us and try and grab our legs onstage. But in Europe, it was the boys doing it as well. In Glasgow, they dragged Otis offstage to mob him. In Paris, at the Olympia, Wayne Jackson remembers the owner coming to stop the show because the balcony was swaying so much he thought it would collapse! Kids would be running after our tour bus. We were so popular in England, in particular, that at the end of the tour we came back to London and played yet another two nights, this time at the Hammersmith Odeon—and they both sold out!

The longer the tour went on, the more I started focusing on my own hit singles rather than the cover versions I'd started the tour with. And by the time we got to Oslo, in Norway, where the show was televised—the only one of the entire tour—I had a better idea of my strengths as a performer. Like I said at the beginning of this book, my attitude is, no matter what gig I got, take no prisoners. The film of me extending "Raise Your Hand" to a full seven minutes in Oslo is evidence of that, I'd like to think.

Now, it's important to understand that a soul concert is meant to be like a church service—the call-and-response is a vital part of the singer's role on stage any night, just like it is for the preacher at his pulpit every Sunday morning. So when I encourage the crowd to "clap your hands a little bit louder" and they oblige, then I know that I'm doing my job. And when I shout, "Let me hear you say 'YEAH!'" and they come back with a "YEAH!" so loud that the sound recording distorts, then I *really* know that I'm doing my job.

And you can see it in that crowd in Oslo the same as you can hear it on the recordings from London and Paris: they're young, they're beautiful, they're excited to be there, and they're up on their feet. When the security tries to get them to sit down again, well then I walk down into the audience myself and immediately, they're back up on their feet, and there ain't much anyone can do about it—not even the army.

That was the strange thing about that Norway concert: they had the army working as security, on a TV show! Guess there weren't any wars for them to fight! There's a point where I reach out to them—"I wonder if I can get all the soldiers here on the front line here to just turn around and clap your hands here one time"—but you know, they had their orders! If you've seen that clip, you'll know that I'm having myself a grand old time down there in the front rows, but eventually Al Jackson hits his cymbal a couple of times loudly and goes into a lengthy snare role, and I realize he's saying to me, "It's time to go." But then, when I get back on stage finally, for some reason the band goes into another breakdown like they must be loving this as well. I take advantage to start talking the crowd up again, and the song goes a little bit longer. Sure I'm milking it, but it was like, how many songs they got you singing? You ain't got many, you might as well milk the one you got! Might have been the only song I got to play that night, I ran so over time.

Talking of my performances on those European shows, Wayne Jackson wrote in his autobiography, *In My Wildest Dreams*, that I'm a "master crowd manipulator." I think he meant it as a compliment! I'll certainly take it as one.

You can definitely say that that Stax/Volt tour helped make me who I am in Europe, but it's not what I was thinking at the time. For me, I'm singing just like I did my whole life, and whenever I achieved something, well, that's a plus. But I'm not thinking, If I just go do *this*, I can get *that*. 'Cause if you think like that, you won't get anything. No, just stay straight. Just work at it. That's all you do. I love the music, I write the music, and when I realize the people love the music that I write . . . I'm good to go.

And as far as that Stax/Volt tour of Europe went, it was perfect. Just perfect.

Chapter 10
GET ON UP, BIG BIRD

All things was happening then, buddy; 1967 was one busy year. My family was growing as Sonja and I had a daughter, Nicholle, that year. I'd end up with seven children in all, and my relationships with the three mothers has been close all the way down the line, just like it has been with the children themselves. I'd been going back up to Detroit to see the kids from my first marriage, but now with "Knock on Wood" such a big hit in the States, I get up there to sing under my own name as well, and I play the Greystone, one of the greatest rooms anywhere for a singer. All the original Falcons come to the show and everyone's genuinely happy for me. When it's over, I take Mack Rice aside. Mack has carried on releasing some singles of his own, but the main thing he's got going for himself is that Wilson Pickett just covered his recent single "Mustang Sally." Mack wrote it, in true Motor City style, about a girl and her new Ford Mustang, and Pickett's version—recorded at FAME Studios in Muscle Shoals after Al Bell and Jim Stewart decided to keep Stax exclusively for Stax artists from now on—is everywhere. It's like "Knock on Wood": it's crossed over from R&B to pop and rock, and it's exploding overseas as well. This is Mack's moment.

"You want to go down to Memphis with me," I tell him. "It's really happening down there. Stax is the right place for you, man."

I knew Mack was the only one from the Falcons who would want to travel. Willie was long off the road, and Joe Stubbs was locked in at Motown. At first Joe was with the Contours—they had a big hit round this same time with "Just a Little Misunderstanding"—and then he was put on lead with the Originals, on a cover of Lead Belly's "Goodnight Irene." The Originals did a lot of backing vocals at Motown too. Joe cut a couple of songs under his own name for the label, but nothing came of it. Joe may have felt he was standing in the shadows of his brother Levi because the Four Tops were turning out number-one singles at the time like nobody's business. But I think it was mainly that Joe wasn't really trying to reach anymore, he was just happy doing the shows that came his way and not thinking any other way. Most people are like that.

But not Mack Rice. I felt that I had enough respect at Stax now that I could invite him down to Memphis and know that they'd take a meeting with him. I mean, you gotta figure they'd want to meet the man who wrote "Mustang Sally." So I told him, "I'll get you a ticket, and it will be at the airport tomorrow. Come on man, go for it."

I thought he wasn't going to come because he didn't like to fly. Nobody liked it back then—and for good reason, as we're about to confirm. Anyway, I'm at the airport the next afternoon, and the flight is getting ready to board. There's no sign of him, and I figure he's not going to take up my offer. And then, right as we start boarding, I see Mack running through the waiting area. In Memphis, I introduce him to the people at Stax, and he instantly starts writing songs. His first single for the label comes out shortly after we get back from Europe; it's called "Mini-Skirt Minnie" and although it isn't a hit on him, it certainly is once—yeah, you guessed it—Wilson Pickett gets his hands on it down in Muscle Shoals later on in the year. Mack would commute back and forth a lot from Detroit to Memphis— he still had his own family up there to take care of, just like me—but now there are three of us Falcons doing some serious business under our own names, and all of us connected one way or another to Memphis and Muscle Shoals, as well as Detroit. Plus, I got one of my best friends in at the Stax family.

Mack and I didn't write together at this point; it would be a few years before that would happen. Officially, Cropper was still my writing partner, and we were on a roll.

"Writing with Eddie was fun," recalls Steve. "If we got something out of a writing session, great. If we didn't, we had a good time doing it—as far as I remember. We used to drink a little rum, have a good time. It was just a chance for us to let our hair down, have fun. Writing late at night most of the time was like a way to get out of the house! So some nights we'd write our butts off. Other times we'd find something else to do."

We quickly followed up "Raise Your Hand" with "Love Is a Doggone Good Thing," a solid groover, which Cropper says is "musically, probably the only song I co-wrote I tried to put a Motown feel to it." I guess he doesn't count "634–5789"! Then, within a couple of months, we followed it with another hit, "On a Saturday Night." As I told *Hit Parader* back at the time,

"I wanted it to be in the old style with a spiritual flavor. I got the spiritual group the Dixie Nightingales to do the harmony part. I got the bass line from one of those old 'doo-wop' groups. Then I got the guitar idea from Hank Ballard and the Midnighters. I think it was 'There's A Thrill Up on The Hill.' You know, that old tinny guitar. Then I put in the shuffle beat."

Some people like to pretend that they pull songs straight out of thin air. I've always been honest about the various influences that go into a hit record. Either way, the result was one of my most popular and enduring songs in the States. It's a staple on the beach circuit, and we play it in the Blues Brothers Band to this very day—"we" meaning me and Cropper, who gave it one of his classic guitar introductions in the studio.

Steve told me his favorite line is this: "If we're going to have a good time, then it might as well be a good time . . . me and my baby and a glass of wine, on a Saturday night." It still don't get much better than that!

"On A Saturday Night" has a real party feel to it, with some fantastic piano and brass along with the great backing vocals. Stax was starting to finally upgrade its equipment, and it was getting a little easier to overdub down there—but we still did the core backing track in one take, live to tape. For the flip side, I recorded a Hayes-Porter song, "Under My Nose." Even though I was close friends with Isaac and David, that was the only time I ever did one of their songs: they had their own artists they were writing for, and I was pretty comfortable writing for myself. Like David Porter says, "We didn't have to jump on board and ride that train."

In the States, "On a Saturday Night" was my fourth single of 1967 already—and my third Top 30 R&B hit. I had three proper hits in the UK as well that year, though with different songs. I've already mentioned "Knock on Wood" and "Raise Your Hand" competing against each other in the charts when we hit London for the Stax-Volt Revue tour back in March. "Knock on Wood" won, if that's how you want to look at it, spending four whole months in the British pop charts. When it finally eased off in the summer, Stax rereleased my debut, "Things Get Better," and that one charted as well. A single we couldn't give away in the States eighteen months earlier was now a hit 4,000 miles away, and I got invited back over for a headlining tour. This was when I really cemented my connection with the British audience. On the Stax/Volt Revue, wonderful as it was, I had just a very short time to make my connection with the crowd. As a headliner, though, I was able to work my way through a whole set and really show what I was capable of.

Everything seemed to be going just perfect. Not just for me, but for everyone at Stax. The European tour had done wonders for all of our profiles, helping turn Sam & Dave into international stars and further confirming Otis Redding as probably the greatest crossover soul singer of them all. In June, the Big O had played at the Monterey Pop Festival and won over what he called the "Love Crowd" with his performance, helped along in no small part by having the M.G.'s and Mar-Keys behind him. Fair to say most of the young hippies in the crowd that day had never been taken to church like that before—though those of us who grew up in a gospel environment and sung our souls out every day and night maybe took it more for granted. But I was happy for Otis. He was my friend, and what was good for him was good for all of us. Fact, he took two of my songs into the charts that summer: as well as his duet with Carla on "Knock on Wood," there was also "I Love You More Than Words Can Say," the ballad I wrote with Booker. Round this time Carla also recorded "I Will Always Have Faith in You," which had slipped by unnoticed when Grover Mitchell cut it on our D.C. label, Safice; Carla's recording added strings, which was something still new for Stax in general. It was beautiful. The single was massive on R&B and crossed over to pop as well. I remain so proud of that one.

For all that the hippie rock thing was starting to happen, soul was very much the sound of America at this point, proving the wisdom of Al Bell claiming "Soulsville" for Stax in response to Motown's "Hitsville" back at the start of '66. The word showed up in our label's two biggest singles of '67. Sam & Dave had a number one in the summer with Hayes & Porter's enduring "Soul Man." But before that, the Bar-Kays, those kids who weren't even old enough to drink at the nightspots they played, had scored almost every bit as big with the instrumental "Soul Finger." Both are stone Stax classics, but "Soul Finger" is perhaps truer to the real Stax spirit: David Porter says it's the only session that had a sense of total collaboration in the studio similar to that of "Knock on Wood." The Bar-Kays, who'd named themselves partly after the Mar-Keys, were emerging now as the next generation's M.G.'s. Perhaps because the original M.G.'s were always needed in the studio, Otis took on the younger band as his own. He brought them up to New York with him for a residency at the Apollo, alongside James Brown, and after they graduated high school that summer, he took them all over the country too. The Bar-Kays—James Alexander, Jimmy King, Carl Cunningham, Ben Cauley, Ronnie Caldwell, and Phalon Jones—were like our kid brothers. We loved them.

Otis had some throat problems that fall, and he had to come off the road, have an operation, and wait several weeks for the results; he wasn't allowed to sing in the meantime. But the operation was deemed a success, and at the start of December he returned to the Stax studio, where he recorded a real soft song called "(Sittin' On) the Dock of the Bay" that was unlike anything he'd done before. He wrote it with Cropper, who played acoustic guitar on it, which was almost unheard of at Stax. Otis cut almost a full album's worth of material at the same time, including "Hard to Handle." He was back on a roll. Then, the weekend of December 8–10, he took the Bar-Kays with him for dates in Nashville, Cleveland, and Madison, Wisconsin.

Otis was a real star, traveled in a private plane, and that summer he had upgraded to an eight-seater, in part so he could fit the Bar-Kays in alongside him. Well, there was more than eight of them in the whole touring setup, so a couple of guys would take turns to drive the others in rental cars to the airport and then take a commercial flight. That's how it went that particular weekend. On Saturday December 9, prior to his concert that night, Otis appeared live on the Cleveland TV show *Upbeat*, closing it out by singing "Knock on Wood" as a duet alongside Mitch Ryder from the Detroit Wheels, the Bar-Kays holding down the fort behind him. The next day, a Sunday, it was the turn of bassist James Alexander, along with the roadie, Carl Sims, to drive; the others got in the Beechcraft 8-seater to fly on up to Madison. But there was bad weather outside of Madison, and the plane was apparently low on battery, which might have affected the engines or the instrument panel because, as you probably know, Otis's plane never made it to Madison: it crashed in the icy waters of Lake Monona just a couple of miles short of its destination. Everyone but Ben Cauley was killed, either on impact or from drowning. Ben was seconds from giving into hypothermia and going under himself when the emergency crews got there, just seventeen minutes after the crash, and pulled him out of the water. The average age of the four deceased Bar-Kays and their valet Matthew Kelly was just eighteen. Otis Redding, like his pilot Richard Fraser, was all of twenty-six.

I was in England when we got the news, in London at the Cumberland Hotel. I was woken up to it at 6 a.m. in the morning, by the BBC asking me for a statement. I was shell-shocked. Nothing like this had happened to any of us before. Maybe we'd had a death in the family back home, but not seven of them all at once, not that of a close friend who's also one of the world's great singers and performers, one of the world's true nice guys. We'd certainly never experienced the deaths of four talented, fun, hard-working teenagers you're expecting to see grow into their adulthood right around you.

That Monday, as we digested the news, I wasn't sure what I was meant to do. It was still the middle of the night back at Stax, and besides, turned out everyone there had flown up to Madison, where the search for bodies went on for the next week. Eventually, word came through that Otis's funeral would take place on Monday the eighteenth and that I should see out my tour. I was told there wasn't much I could do back home that others weren't taking care of, and if we could avoid canceling any shows, we should.

So that's what we did. But it meant that my first real European headlining tour was not the high point I might have expected it to be. Those last few dates were something of a blur.

Come the day for me to fly home, the plan is to catch a plane to New York, then another to Atlanta, and from there drive down to Macon, where the service for Otis is being held in his hometown. We board our plane, and soon enough we're taxiing down the runway. Suddenly we hear a noise, the plane swerves, and then stops, and they tell us the plane has to return to the gate. When it does, we get sent back into the lobby of the airport and we sit there for hours. At first we figure they're going to find us a different aircraft, but instead they decide to fix our plane. I'd never seen that before. We're sat in the lobby of the airport, wondering, *Do they know what they're doing?*

Well, it takes about five hours, and when we finally get back on board, it's obvious I'm going to miss my connecting flight, which means I'm going to miss the funeral. And after what's just happened I can't help but worry, *Is my plane heading for disaster too?* By the time we're finally taxiing back down the runway again, everyone on board is clearly nervous after what happened first time around, several hours ago, and I find myself willing the plane into the air for a safe journey across the Atlantic.

"Get on up, big bird, 'cause I got to make it."

Then it hits me: I've got a song title!

Well, as you must have figured, our plane made it to New York in one piece and, as I'd already figured out too, I missed Otis's funeral. Every other person from Stax was there. So was James Brown, Wilson Pickett, Solomon Burke, Joe Tex, Percy Sledge, Arthur Conley, Joe Simon, Gene Chandler . . . And of course there was Otis's family: his wife Zelma, and the three little kids left behind, Karla, Dexter, and Otis Redding III. It broke my heart to miss the funeral, but over the years I've become very close friends with Otis III, and every year, when it's Otis Redding Day in Macon, Georgia, I go down there to sing or whatever else they want from me. Macon has become like a second home for me. The day before Otis's service, a joint funeral for three of the Bar-Kays had been held in Memphis, where almost as many people showed up as did in Macon. In the middle of the service, it was announced they'd finally found the body of the fourth. No words I write in this book can begin to address the scale of the tragedy.

But at the same time, there is no choice but to get on with our lives. This is what we do at Stax: we write songs, we record them, we release them, and hopefully people get something from them. None of us can bring Otis back, or the Bar-Kays, but we *can* carry on making music. So while Stax releases "(Sittin' On) The Dock of the Bay" and it goes all the way to number one on both the pop and R&B charts the way posthumous singles have a habit of doing, I get together with Booker to flesh out this "Big Bird" song idea.

Why Booker? Why not Steve? There's a lot of stories about some things that happened on the European tour, about some kind of show-down, the result of which saw Al Bell promoted to head of A&R and Steve Cropper demoted from that position, and there are people who will tell you things weren't the same at Stax after we all got back, that egos started acting out and getting in the way. But that's not what I saw through 1967. I saw a label going from strength to strength. I saw the Mar-Keys finally get put on wages—too late for Joe Arnold, who quit, but just in time for Wayne Jackson and Andrew Love to commit themselves to the company—and with the four M.G.'s plus Hayes and Porter all getting an equal split of the action, there were enough reasons for everyone to remain fully committed to the company. You couldn't dispute that, since he'd joined, Al Bell had turned Stax from a regional record label, with the occasional breakout single, to a national record company that was delivering major commercial hits on a regular, worldwide basis, while retaining total credibility with its core audience. The tragedy that was Otis Redding's death did not alter that.

So it wasn't that I called on Booker to write with me, or that he called on me. Remember, we'd just recently had a hit together for Otis, so this was not something brand new. Maybe Steve was doing something with another artist that day. And that's fine. But Booker and I, well we'd always been looking for a reason to write further together, and here's our opportunity.

Now, I've never said that the song "Big Bird" was *for* Otis— Booker wrote a song with William Bell called "Tribute to a King," which took care of that. But if somebody asked the question, I'm saying it's sort of *about* Otis because he's on my mind while I'm flying. "Get on up, big bird . . ." You wouldn't know the reason I said that unless you know that I've just lost someone, and that has never happened personally before.

I told Booker about the flight, the whole bit, and I guess he just started playing guitar—because Booker, like I told you way back, could play just about anything—and he put in a little intro, and I heard it right away, melody-wise.

"Open up the skies, 'cause I'm coming up to you."

And now we got a verse going. Then, all of a sudden, Booker makes the change-up, and I'm singing:

"You know I'm standing at the station, ready to go
Oh, big 'ol aeroplane, I'm trusting you so."

The song is rising at this point, and it keeps rising, but then it levels off with the chorus, like the plane is finally in the air. And that's the feel too, to this day, when we're onstage playing it.

By the time we finished writing it, I knew I had a great lyric. The chorus is saying, "Get on up, big bird, to my baby's love" and so you can think of it as a love song. But that other part of the chorus, the first part that I came up with, well, that's obviously me willing a plane to just get up in the air and not kill us all! And then the second verse, well, once you know when and how I wrote it, you can understand why some people might say it is about Otis:

"With me down here
And you up there
Now all I know is
It ain't fair."

Well, we're at Booker's house, and he's got the song in his mind all right, and I got it in mine, so we go straight to the studio the next morning on that one. And we introduce it to Al Jackson, but he's the only other one of the M.G.'s who's there. We don't mind. As long as we got the drummer, we're good to go. Remember, Stax is multi-track now. Plus, we got the brass section, and the brass is central to the song; it really signifies that plane taking off.

In the studio that day, Booker ends up playing guitar, bass, *and* piano. It always blows peoples' minds when they find out that's Booker on the guitar, because "Big Bird" is my rock song, my psychedelic rock song. And people figure Steve Cropper to be a rock guitarist, and as for Booker, even if they know he plays instruments other than the organ, they figure he can't possibly be a rocker as well. To be fair, it was amazing to me, too, that he could play all those instruments on that song—and feel it so well. It's like "Knock on Wood": who knows what would have happened had Otis jumped on the song when it was available to him? And who knows what would have happened to "Big Bird" if Steve and Duck had played on it? It might actually have been better! But this was Booker's sound. And I loved it.

On "Big Bird" you can hear me sing differently than my previous singles. I'm reaching more. I'm stronger. Louder. Maybe it's all the performances in Europe. Maybe it's the exposure to the rock scene over there. And the backing vocals follow suit—it's more like they're being shouted than sung. This is one loud record. I was so enthused about it all that I never corrected the one line that didn't make sense: why am I standing at the *station* waiting for an aeroplane? I should be standing at the airport! But nobody ever mentions it: at a certain point, a song becomes familiar just the way it is. And it's all part of what makes "Big Bird" unique, because it's one of those songs that can be about whatever you want it to be about: an airplane journey, death, your love, all of those things.

These days, "Big Bird" is considered one of my greatest songs. I've seen it described as "one of the most thrilling singles ever made." I've had people tell me it's their favorite song in the world. But I guess it was a little unusual for Stax at the time to have a rock-sounding record like that, because when they released it at the start of 1968 . . . man, it died a death! Although I was *never* the kind of person to watch the charts, I've been informed it was the only one of my singles from 1966, when "Knock on Wood" came out, all the way through until 1971, that did not make either the American pop *or* R&B charts. Other than that, I had a run of about thirteen or fourteen hits in a row. "Big Bird"? I guess people just didn't get it at the time.

The American singer Rosetta Hightower, who had been in the Philadelphia girl group the Orlons earlier in the 1960s, she recorded an amazing version of "Big Bird" in London later that same year. Her voice brought it just a little further back into soul territory, but the band she had over there, and the producer she used, together they ensured it also appealed to the rock crowd. That version wasn't a hit either, but given that copies now go for about $200, you have to figure she did something right with it! Meantime, for the next twenty years, I would hear a voice in the crowd every night, somewhere, calling for it. Then, in the early 1980s, about fifteen years after it first came out, I heard that a group called The Jam had put out a live version in Britain. People told me they were the biggest band in the UK, that they were so popular their singles would go *into* the charts at number one. So that was an honor. Fast forward yet another ten years, to the early 1990s, I was in New York City, and this guy told me, "Do you know there's a club here has been playing 'Big Bird' for years and it's still number one?" I said, Let's go! Someone took me down to the Village, to the Empire State Soul Club on a Thursday night. Here's the *New York Times* writing about the place in 1992, when it had already been up and running for several years:

At midnight, the Soul Club hits its peak. That's when it's time for Eddie Floyd's "Big Bird," the Soul Club anthem. As the horns trumpet

their message, the beat pounds higher and higher and Mr. Floyd's voice
reaches a fever pitch.

That night I went to the Empire State Soul Club, a melting
pot of people of all descriptions you want to name, and they
were waiting when I walked through the door. I guess they
knew I was coming! They started playing it, and I just walked
straight up on stage and started singing "Big Bird." Didn't do a
full show but they didn't ask me to. They just honored me, and I
honored them in return.

So, songs like that, might be that nobody calls them a hit, but
they still get famous. I call them underground. Fact is, here we
are talking about it fifty years later. Got to be doing something
right!

That's what I keep telling young people: if you don't do
nothing you won't *be* nothing. So just keep doing it. Some
people, they just get halfway, and just don't quite understand
where to go or how to go. I say, keep doing what you doing. Is
it a little better than the last thing you did? Okay, that's it, that's
all you're going to get out of this one. Now do another one, and
see what happens.

Chapter 11
I'VE NEVER FOUND A GIRL

Early in 1968, word came down from New York that Ahmet
Ertegun and Jerry Wexler were selling Atlantic Records to
Warner Bros. for a cool $17.5 million. That inspired some
animated conversations in Memphis. Why? Well, as Al Bell puts
it, "Atlantic would be getting their money based on revenue
projections going forward, which was itself based on history—
and a great deal of that history came from Stax." Atlantic had
plenty artists of its own—Aretha Franklin was selling up a storm,
Pickett was holding his own, and Solomon Burke, Ben E. King,
Percy Sledge, and others were coming up with occasional hits—
but Stax was its real R&B hit factory. "(Sittin' on) The Dock of
the Bay" had gone to number-one pop, of course, and whether

that was because of, or despite Otis Redding's death was hard to say; maybe that kind of hit was coming his way regardless by then. After all, Sam & Dave hit the pop Top 10 with "I Thank You" round the same time, just like they'd done the previous year with "Soul Man," and they were still very much with us.

Otis was selling albums too, and many other acts on Stax were delivering hits of varying degrees, myself included. So, you can understand why Warner Bros. wanted to be sure that Stax stayed on board as part of the deal, and why Jerry Wexler would have schmoozed Al Bell to ensure as much, bringing Al up to his home in suburban New York, hosting parties for him, trying to make sure it was personally worth his while. "I was doing for Stax through Atlantic what Atlantic was supposed to be doing for Stax," Al says, looking back on it all. "I was doing the promotion, talking to all of the independent distributors, about twenty-five of them across the country. I knew all their sales people, all the promo people, and I would call the guy who was overseeing single sales at Atlantic and say, 'This market is ready, and this is what you should try to sell them,'—and why. When Jim Stewart brought me in, he thought it was for the relationship with the jocks. Well, I had that relationship and knew what to send to them, but I understood distribution too, and I studied it."

The reason that Jerry had to engage in all this schmoozing was that the contract Jim had signed between Stax and Atlantic, in May 1965 just before I came down to join the label with Al Bell, contained what was called a "key man" clause. Basically, Jim had so much respect for Jerry Wexler that he couldn't imagine an Atlantic Records without him, so he'd had a clause put in to say that if ever Jerry ceased being an owner of the label, Stax could end the deal. The way the sale of Atlantic to Warner Bros. was being constructed, Jerry *would* still be a part of Atlantic Records—he and Ahmet were staying on as high-salaried employees—but they'd no longer be shareholders. As that deal neared completion, Jim and Al grew increasingly frustrated by what they thought were low-ball offers for their share of the money from Warner Bros., and in the end, they decided to enact that "key man" clause. They figured, and not without good reason, that they could secure a better distribution deal for Stax elsewhere. After all, the catalog ran pretty damn deep by this point.

That's when they found out what else was in that contract from 1965. Turned out there *was* no catalog: Atlantic owned every single master recording of Stax that it had distributed, going all the way back to Carla's "Gee Whiz" in 1961—and this despite the fact that Stax had paid for all the sessions, recorded in their own building down in Memphis! Jim Stewart, it turned out, had not read the small print back in '65; he was a Southern gentleman who believed in handshake agreements. Jerry was a man he respected and trusted; that's why he'd insisted on the "key man" clause in the first place.

Al Bell was no less astonished; the Stax deal with Atlantic was worse than the one he'd struck with Jerry to distribute our tiny Safice label in D.C. We didn't have any hits—but at least we still owned our masters.

Jerry Wexler would go to his grave insisting he knew nothing about the small print in that Stax deal, blaming it on the Atlantic lawyers who put it together. That was cold comfort to a Stax label that, while still grieving over the death of its most popular artist, Otis Redding, now discovered that it did not actually own the rights to his hits in the first place—nor those of its *other* artists these last seven years. That included myself, and my major records "Knock on Wood" and "Raise Your Hand." Going forward, those songs would become part of the Atlantic catalog, just as the Falcons hits also found their way into that vast vault of R&B classics. To make matters worse, it was also clarified that Sam & Dave were never actually signed to Stax. They were merely "on loan" from Atlantic which, now that Stax decided to look elsewhere for distribution, took the duo back—ironically, on my song "You Don't Know What It Means to Me."

"At the end of the day there's no question, Atlantic took advantage," says Al Bell. "But Jim was a mortgage banker—he didn't know anything about the music business."

A series of crushing body blows like these would have felled a lesser company. But Stax was a family, and the best and strongest families stick together in a crisis. And so, with complete confidence in our abilities, we pushed on. Stax still had a roster that included Rufus Thomas, Carla Thomas, William Bell, Albert King, Johnnie Taylor, Mable John, and more, hit-makers every one of them. It had as its house band none other than Booker T. & The M.G.'s, who were proven hit-makers in their own right. It had the songwriting partnership of Isaac Hayes & David Porter. And it had me, a songwriter, singer, and ongoing hit-maker. None of us asked to leave; in fact, Sam & Dave were *devastated* to find they'd be off the label in the near future. So while Jim and Al went off to look for new financial backing and distribution, we all stayed busy doing what we did best, which was what came naturally to us—writing songs and then getting into the studio to record them.

As the weeks went by, we heard that Gulf & Western was looking to buy Stax. They weren't exactly the kind of music people you had over at Atlantic, but they had recently bought Paramount Records, which had an R&B catalog of its own, and they had a lot more money at hand than Atlantic ever did. A deal was worked out that had Stax reporting to Paramount, and then Al Bell, with Jim Stewart's blessing, got to work on creating a bigger and better Stax than the rest of the music world could ever have imagined. He signed the Staple Singers, the family led

by "Pops" Staples, who were living legends to many of us for
their perfect union of gospel, R&B, and protest music. And he
brought in a new producer, Don Davis, from Detroit. I knew
Don from all the way back with the Falcons; he played guitar
with us a couple of times back in the old days. He played on
some of the early Motown hits too, before taking a backroom
role in that company. So bringing him down to Memphis was an
ambitious effort on Al's part to give our Southern soul some of
that Motor City flavor. Soulsville, U.S.A., meet Hitsville U.S.A.

Meantime, other stuff was going on in Memphis that was going
to affect not just Stax, but the whole country. In the years since
Dr. Martin Luther King Jr. had first become known for leading the
Montgomery Bus Boycott, right on the block where I grew up, the
Civil Rights movement had grown beyond what we might once
have ever dared imagine. The struggles had not been easy, and
they didn't come without bloodshed, but we'd seen the results with
the Civil Rights Act in 1964 and the Voting Rights Act in 1965.
Dr. King had now shifted some of his focus to economic issues, to
the racism endemic within the workforce. He came to Memphis in
the spring of 1968 to bring attention to, and show solidarity with,
the city's sanitation workers, all of them black, who had gone on
strike to protest their appalling conditions. These workers walked
a picket line in the city every day during their strike, standing up
for their dignity with signs and sandwich boards that read "I Am
a Man." But late in March, the police disbanded them violently,
and the tensions between the city authorities and the workers grew
increasingly hostile. Meantime, Dr. King was also speaking out
against the war in Vietnam, and championing an upcoming "Poor
People's March" to D.C. in May. For a lot of folk, he was now in
the news for the wrong reasons.

Al Bell knew Dr. King from working with him back in the
1950s, of course, and I guess he had concerns about the march.

"It looked like it was going to be more white people going into Washington than black people. I said to myself, 'It's all right if he goes into D.C. with a million black people, this black man, but going in with all these white people, that's a problem. When you get to that state they call it incipient insurrection, the overthrow of government. They can't let that black man come in with all those white people, that's dangerous.' I really wanted him to take a sabbatical. And that's because of many conversations in the past between Dr. King and me. And I felt he needed to back up at that point in time."

To get the point across, Al came up with the idea for a song, about a "winding, winding road" which would "send peace and harmony home." But he needed help with it. So he came to Booker and me. Neither of us had really worked on a lyric like this before, in terms of addressing what was going on in our nation, and we didn't want to be too direct about it either. But we sat down with Al and fleshed it out until we had something we were all happy with. We found a tempo somewhere between ballad and upbeat, and Al marked "Send Peace and Harmony Home" for a singer by the name of Shirley Walton, who he had just launched on a new Stax subsidiary called Enterprise.

The recording session took place on April 4, 1968. Al was the producer on the cut. "Shirley sang it," he remembers. "But she couldn't get it. I'd done about eight or ten takes, and she still couldn't get it. And then Homer Banks [who was one of the new writers at Stax] opened the door to the studio just as we were about to do another take and said, 'Dr. Martin Luther King just got shot and killed at the Lorraine Motel.' Shirley started singing at that moment, 'cause the tape was rolling, and we let it keep rolling. She cried as she sang the song."

Dr. King. Assassinated. And at the very hotel where all of us from Stax hung out together. It's like Booker later remembered:

"It wasn't just that it happened in Memphis, he was shot at the Lorraine Motel, and the Lorraine Motel was where we had our meetings on Monday morning. We used their dining room for our meeting hall, and the Lorraine Motel was the place where Steve Cropper and Eddie Floyd wrote 'Knock on Wood.' We ate there on a regular basis. It was an institution for us. And so it couldn't have been any closer had he been shot at 926 McLemore."

But here's how I feel about all of this: King's death was nothing to do with what we did. *Everybody* came to the Lorraine if they wanted to. But they could have gone to the Holiday Inn; back during that time there wasn't much difference. The way I look at it, that part of history with Dr. King speaks for itself, and we'll speak for Memphis music. We're at the same place, and at the same time, and I know that, and I don't need anyone to tell me what a great man Dr. King was, not when my grandma was out there bringing water to the crowds on Holt Street at the start of the Montgomery bus boycott. But I just don't want the story of our music—which is a positive story—tied in to the story of Dr. King's death, which is not.

As for the way Al Bell tells it about Shirley Walton, well, there was another single that got cut around much the same time, "Long Walk to D.C.," by the Staple Singers. That song was *definitely* written about the March on D.C., and given that it was Homer Banks who wrote it, let's just say it's hard to remember what went on exactly fifty years ago. I thought for sure I was in the studio that day—and there was only two studios at Stax— because my memory is that the moment we heard Dr. King got shot, we all figured to close up and get home as soon as we could. We knew all hell was going to break loose on the streets. I didn't even go to Kerr Street, where I was staying round by the Tiki—that would have been farther to go, and things were happening in the street already. I went to Booker's instead.

As regards "Send Peace and Harmony Home," Al Jackson and I produced the flip side, a Hayes-Porter song, and then Al Bell put the single out on Enterprise, sending the lyrics out to the media in advance, the day after Dr. King's assassination. It didn't sell. I'm not sure the soul audience was really feeling peace and harmony at that moment.

People are always asking, "How did everything change at Stax after Dr. King was shot?" Well, in one sense, nothing really changed. I went right back to the studio and recorded another song. It wasn't like we couldn't record no more songs because *that* took place; it wasn't like that. What happened is, Dr. King got shot in Memphis and the whole *era* changed.

It's like my friend William Bell says. "Dr. King was everything. Not just to the black community but to the world in general. And once he was killed, the whole mood—not only in Memphis but all around the country—changed. And music changed to a degree as well."

Damn right. The mood changed at Stax, but it changed at the grocery store right next door too. Everything changed, period.

I've read the stories about the M.G.'s getting shaken down outside the studio by local hoodlums after King's death. Years later, Duck went on camera saying that Al Bell gave him money to go across the Arkansas border to West Memphis to purchase half a dozen pistols for self-defense, telling him, "If anyone threatens you, pull the trigger." So let me just say this: I was there every day, but I don't remember no pistols. No half a dozen pistols for what? Ain't nobody afraid of nobody on that block. Well, Eddie wasn't. I never saw any threats on the block. I don't know anything about it; I never heard that! And I don't believe any of those guys in the M.G.'s was brave enough to shoot anybody! Now, if they was some badasses, I'd be the first one to say. As for me, I ain't trying to be a badass, but I'm just saying

I never had no encounters with nobody to know. I never saw nothing outside of Stax like that, and I knew all the local people too. They were still just local people on the block. And we were still just trying to get along and make music like we always had.

Here's your case in point. In the middle of all this turmoil, right in the wake of Dr. King's murder and all the unrest that went on around the nation, we got to write and record my favorite song of them all. "We" meant myself, Booker T. Jones, and that old songwriting partner of mine from D.C., that very same Alvertis Isbell. It was Al who came up with the opening lyrics, about a "burning fire, shut up in my bones." He got it from a gospel song by Cleophus Robinson, released way back to the early 1960s, and Robinson had gotten it from the Book of Jeremiah to begin with. The original reference was sacred. But Al figured it was a perfect description of the love he felt for his wife, so now it's a secular thing. A love thing.

Booker and I took it from there. I heard him play a little rhythm, and I'm singing a little melody, and we got Al Bell's opening verse. Well, we know we got something good going already, and soon enough we got the concept, and the chorus, and the title that comes from that chorus: "I've Never Found a Girl (To Love Me Like You Do)." It's three o'clock in the morning when we're done, but we know we can always wake up the drummer. Sure enough, within half an hour of us calling him, Al Jackson meets us at East McLemore: he didn't live far from Stax anyways. He hears what Booker's playing and starts right on in. Booker might have recorded that bass line first—I'm almost sure he did. Then he would have added the piano part—those eighth notes that really helps make the song what it is. And our lyrics were there by this point: "You're every poor boy's dream, and every rich man's prayer, but I don't need money, honey, because you're always there." When I finally got into the studio to sing it, I added something to the song title that closed out each chorus: "And that's the truth." It gave the declaration of love that little extra validation.

Now that we had more tracks to work with at Stax—eight of them!—Booker was able to overdub a couple of his parts without trouble, and then we focused on the coloring. As far as I remember, the brass was mainly driven by a flugelhorn, and I think Booker played that too! Then he brought in a string section from Memphis State University, and that was the icing on the cake. I like "I've Never Found a Girl" song more than any song I ever did. No contest. I always say that that was my "uptown" song.

"I've Never Found a Girl (To Love Me Like You Do)" came out in June 1968, catalog number Stax 0002, the second release as part of the label's new deal with Gulf & Western. (Stax 0001 was Booker T. and the M.G.'s "Soul Limbo," which went Top 10 on the pop charts. Booker had it going on at that point, man!) Immediately it was all over the radio. It became *the* summer jam. And you know, it's important to note that, for all people might be talking about how things had changed in America after King's assassination—that people were angry (and they were!) and that the streets were on fire and race relations sank to a new low—well, those same people still be falling in love. And they still needed songs to express that for them. "I've Never Found a Girl (To Love Me Like You Do)" went to number two on the R&B charts, spent a couple of weeks there in fact, and it got me back into the pop charts as well. Sold over half a million copies in the process. And it may say something for me—and Booker, my co-writer at the time—that my previous single had been a psychedelic rocker, "Big Bird," and now here I am with this beautiful soul ballad with strings, and that, depending who you ask, where they come from in life and what they listen to, different people might say *either* one is their favorite song of mine.

And some people might go beyond that. Many years down the line, Daryl Hall of Hall & Oates, what we would have called a "blue-eyed soul" duo in the old days, had Booker come in and play the Hammond on his TV show *Daryl's House*. They performed a lovely version of "I've Never Found a Girl," and Daryl, who sung lead on it, spoke over the introduction.

"This is my favorite song in the world," he said, and then, quoting straight from the song itself, he added, "and that's the truth."

Chapter 12
CALIFORNIA GIRL

I've heard it said that 80 percent of success is "showing up." Well, in the summer of 1968, I was in at Stax, and Isaac Hayes was rehearsing up an arrangement of the Sam Cooke ballad "Bring It on Home to Me" for a different Sam—Sam Moore and his singing partner Dave Prater. To ease some of the bad blood over the fact that Atlantic had only ever loaned Sam & Dave to Stax, it had been agreed that the duo would record their next few singles exclusively for "us" before being taken back.

But Sam & Dave didn't show that day, and I did. So I said to Isaac, "Well, do it on me!" Isaac's arrangement was quite a bit faster than Sam Cooke's, and of course once it fell into the hands of the M.G.'s it quickly took on a very Memphis sound, also different from Sam's original. Compare the backing tracks and you'll hear exactly what I mean. And if you do so, you can't say I sung it like Sam Cooke either; I sung it different because Isaac was playing it different, and my voice just went along with the melody. We put brass on it, got the backing vocalists in—Ollie and the Nightingales were the regulars for that work at that time—and put it on the market. Coming hot on the heels of "I've Never Found a Girl (To Love Me Like You Do)," I guess the public—and radio—was ready to embrace me some more, and "Bring It on Home to Me" went Top 5 R&B and Top 20 pop.

Quite a few other artists took on that same song in 1968, including Aretha and Wilson. It's one of those things with soul music, how a certain song will become popular for a period of time and the public wants to hear their favorite singer(s) put a personal spin on it. For whatever reason, mine scored biggest. Sadly, I don't sing it live too often; the house musicians would only know Sam Cooke's arrangement, and I'd be saying, "Well, now you have to learn mine." Often it was easier to leave it alone. It's not like I don't have other songs in my bag!

If my last couple of singles had cemented my standing with a certain kind of soul audience, my earlier ones on Stax were beginning to show their far-reaching appeal. In December of '68, a young woman by the name of Janis Joplin came to town to play at what we had called the "Stax/Volt Yuletide Thing." As with "Hit the Road Stax," when Arthur Conley came on board, it seemed a good idea to include a special guest from outside of Stax. Janis had appeared at Monterey the previous year, fronting Big Brother & the Holding Company, and her love of rhythm & blues was apparent from her inclusion of Big Mama Thornton's "Ball and Chain." Now she had broken up that group and put together a new one, the Kozmic Blues Band which, we were told, she intended to sound very much in the vein of what she

The only photograph I have of my father, Prince Edward Floyd, a welterweight who trained at the same gym in Detroit as Joe Louis.

My mother, Florence Marie West, in the mid-1970s. I recorded the single "Mother Dear Mother" for her. Any words of wisdom you hear from Eddie Floyd come from her.

The earliest photo I have of myself, taken in a booth in
Montgomery, Alabama, when I was around thirteen years old.

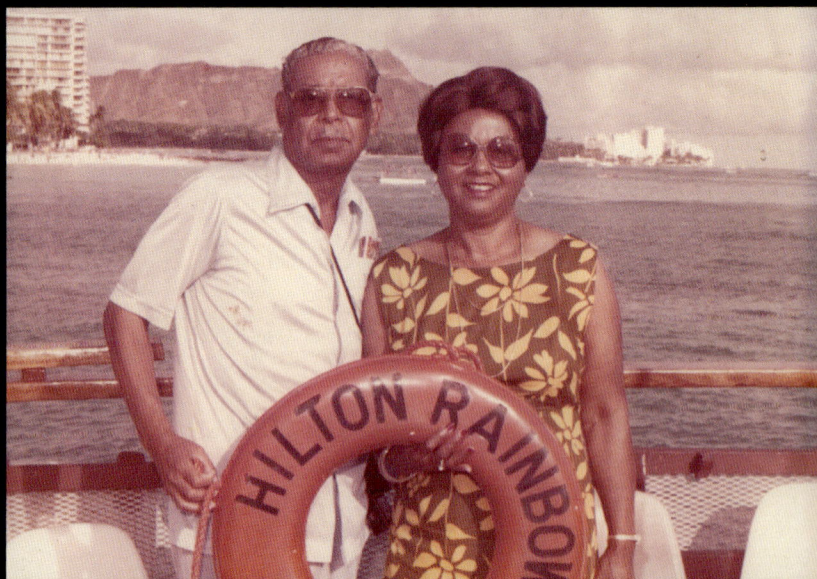

My uncle and aunt, Robert and Catherine West, later in their lives. Robert managed the Falcons
and ran several great record labels in Detroit, where I lived with him and Catherine in the 1950s.

My Life In Soul

The only photo of the original 1956 lineup of the Falcons, performing live at a radio hop (L-R): me, Tom Shetler, Bob Manardo, Willie Schofield, and Arnett Robinson.

The Falcons lineup in 1957, after we left Mercury (L-R): Willie Schofield, Arnett Robinson, Joe Stubbs, Eddie Floyd. My preference was always for Joe Stubbs as lead singer.

P3

A promo shot from soon after I signed to Stax in the mid-1960s.

Givin' all I got onstage in the mid-1960s.

With Steve Cropper at Stax. Almost as soon as we got together we wrote "634-5789," "Knock on Wood," and several more big hits.

Stax on tour in Europe, 1967 (L-R): Duck Dunn, Arthur Conley, Wayne Jackson, Otis Redding, Sam Moore, Steve Cropper, and me.

At the Mayfair Hotel in London, 1967.

My Life In Soul

Looking dapper in the 1960s.

Isaac Hayes and me outside Stax in 1968. As the 1960s progressed, the look and image changed for many of us. Photo by Don Paulsen.

Me and Al Bell in the parking lot behind the Stax studio, 1969.

My Life In Soul

Signing Lynyrd Skynyrd to Hustlers, Inc., the management company I ran with Alan Walden (seen wearing a tie standing behind my chair), 1970. Photo by W. Robert Johnson.

Backstage with Bruce Springsteen, the night he invited me onstage at the Ellis Auditorium in Memphis, April, 1976.

In Amsterdam in 1987. Photo by Frans Schellekens.

Onstage—just about—in Norway in the 1990s. I always like to get close to the audience.

The Blues Brothers Band onstage (L-R): Steve Cropper, Donald "Duck" Dunn, me, Matt "Guitar" Murphy, and Dan Aykroyd.

With Wilson Pickett on the set of *Blues Brothers 2000* in Toronto, 1998. We had history together dating back to "634-5789" and the Falcons before that.

A photo I took of two of my greatest soul brothers, Percy Sledge and Wilson Pickett. Sadly, both have now passed.

The Champ! Muhammad Ali and me at my birthday party in Vandalia, Michigan on June 25, 2006.

I joined Bill Wyman's group, the Rhythm Kings, in 2004 and continued singing with them for the next five years.

With my British band—"The Boys" as I call them—who stuck with me from the mid-1980s onwards.

My Life In Soul

Still goin' strong!

P14

With William Bell, who I first met on tour with the Falcons in 1962. We've been best friends ever since. In the late 1980s, I recorded for his label.

I wrote most of my big hits with either Steve Cropper (far right) or Booker T. Jones (seated); we're seen here with James Morrison and Jools Holland at the Royal Albert Hall, September 2017.

With Tom Jones at the Royal Albert Hall, 2017. Ain't no doubt about it, Tom's got soul.

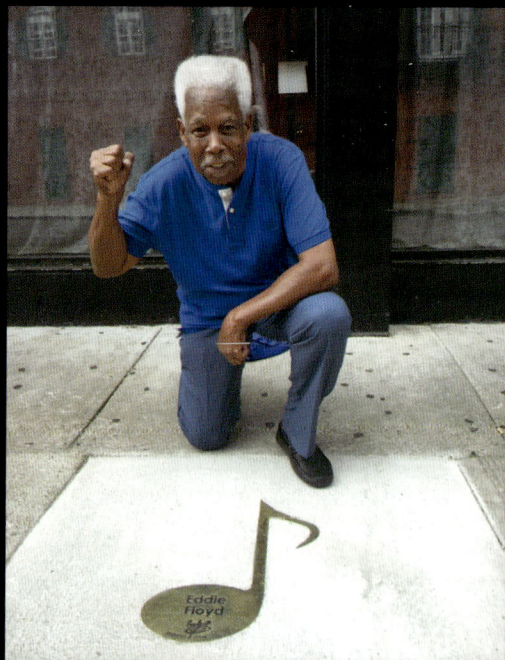

In 2016, I was celebrated in Memphis with a Beale Street Brass Note.

heard coming out of East McLemore. Any which way, she and her new musicians showed up the day before the December 21 concert at the Mid-South Coliseum to rehearse in our studio, and that's when I learned that they were including "Raise Your Hand" in their set. Her new keyboard player Bill King had performed it in his old garage band, and he had recommended it to the singer. I'd heard some cover versions on it by now and, as with "Knock on Wood," I knew that the song had crossed over to more of a rock audience, but this was the first time the evidence was being brought on home to me.

The next night, at the Mid-South Coliseum, Janis was placed high on the bill, just beneath Johnnie Taylor, who had the number-one R&B single, and a Top 5 pop hit at the time, with "Who's Making Love." It had been written by an in-house trio of Homer Banks, Raymond Jackson, and Bettye Crutcher; lots more songwriters were coming on board as the roster of artists kept growing. "Who's Making Love" was produced by Don Davis, my old friend from Detroit who quickly made his mark in Memphis—and beyond—with *that* one! The rest of the bill for the Stax Yuletide Thing included the M.G.'s, Rufus Thomas, Carla Thomas, William Bell, the Staple Singers, the Mad Lads, Albert King, myself—and, we were all happy to see, the Bar-Kays, who had built back up almost from nothing by its two surviving members, James Alexander and Ben Cauley.

Janis Joplin's performance that night has often been criticized, including by her own band. As Bill King later wrote, the odds were kind of against them from the start. "Even with the best soul intention, a bunch of white pretenders in psychedelic gear were no competition for the clean manicured presence of Johnnie Taylor and Eddie Floyd."

That's as may be, but my feeling was that she turned "Raise Your Hand" inside out, and I recall my immediate response being, it really comes out better with a female singing it. Whatever the response—or lack of it—from our Memphis soul audience, she came to join us at the party afterwards, which Jim Stewart hosted at the mansion he'd bought with some of the proceeds from the deal with Gulf & Western. (Like Jerry Wexler, who frequently hosted music industry barbeques at his Long Island home, Jim enjoyed having people on the property.) Janis was memorable company that night; she had a wild streak, but she was sincere and fun at the same time, a combination you can only pull off if your heart is in the right place.

Regardless of how she went down in Memphis, big things were happening for Janis. In March of 1969, she went on the Ed Sullivan Show and opened with "Raise Your Hand." She did the same that summer when she played the Woodstock Festival in upstate New York, though her version was so wild, it would be hard put to know it was my song unless I told you so! The performance I'd *really* encourage you to check out is the one she did, also in 1969, as a live duet with Tom Jones on his television show. I love Tom—we got ourselves a good long history together—and ain't no doubt about it, he's got soul. But so did Janis, especially on that occasion. Man, she pushes him so hard. There's a light in both their sets of eyes because they're clearly having such a good time with it, and Janis gets some dirty dancing in with Tom in the process; you can see her try and grind and Tom gently back off so that he doesn't get in trouble with the television company! It's one of my favorite clips of anyone performing a song of mine and really *reaching* with it. Sadly, it was only a year later that Janis was gone, at age twenty-seven. Some people just ain't built to make old bones.

The male-female duet thing was one of the many ideas on Al Bell's mind at the time too. After the death of Otis, the loss of the masters, and the departure of Sam & Dave, he figured that the best way to announce that Stax was back in business was not to just keep releasing hit singles—something we were clearly very good at—but to release albums, which were now overtaking singles as the main music medium. And not just a few albums. *Lots* of them. A full catalog's worth, all at one go. Al's brainwave, if you can call it that, was to release an album by every single artist on Stax, along with a double album of duets that featured a whole number of us, plus a few compilations, and *all at the same time*. And being Al, he saw it through. The "Soul Explosion" would find Stax unveiling twenty-eight albums simultaneously during its sales conference in May of 1969.

I'd recently put my second album out on the back of—and named after—"I've Never Found a Girl." We'd been able to take our time with this one compared to *Knock on Wood*, and it showed. As well as my recent hit singles and what I thought were their excellent flip sides ("I'm Just the Kind of Fool" and "Sweet Things You Do," both written with Booker), there were some real solid songs I wrote with Cropper: "I Need You Woman," which probably could have been a single in its own right, "Hobo," and "Water." Another highlight was a ballad I had penned with Al, "Girl I Love You," which Cropper made his own with a delightful guitar arpeggio—though it's always hard to single out a member of the M.G.'s or Mar-Keys for their contributions down at Stax. Fact, when I look back on it, *I've Never Found a Girl* is a great example of team effort all around: it has probably the most even distribution of songwriting partners of anything I did on Stax, and perhaps the most consistent sound too.

Now, just a few months later, all focus was on the upcoming "Soul Explosion," and I seemed to have as big a share of it as anyone. You see, as well as putting us all in the studio to record new albums, Al Bell had the idea of a *Rare Stamps* series of compilations for those artists, like me and Johnnie Taylor, who'd released a lot of singles that had never shown up on LPs. In my case, this gave the public a chance to own "Things Get Better," "On a Saturday Night" and "Big Bird," among other, all on one LP—and not only was my *Rare Stamps* record a big success, but I liked the way it reflected how I'd happily swung left and right with my songwriting and singing during my first couple of years at Stax.

Then, when it came to a promotional compilation, a double album trailering the whole launch by the name of *Soul Explosion*, I not only got my two most recent hits on there, but also a recording that never showed up anywhere else, ever again, "It's Wrong to Be Loving You," and one for Carla likewise, "Book of Love." Both were cowrites with Cropper, and I forgot all about them for many years! There was just so much music going on at the time. For the compilation of duets, another double LP's worth entitled *Boy Meets Girl*, I was pulled in as songwriter *and* singer. My songs "Ain't That Good" and "Never Never Let You Go" saw me team up with Mavis Staples, which was of course an honor, and the second of those songs has followed me around over the years. We also had fun singing together on the Erma Franklin classic "Piece of My Heart." Plus, I got to duet with Carla at last, on a couple of songs written by Carl Smith. We didn't get to sing in the same room at the same time, unfortunately. Things were too busy to get all that together, and *Boy Meets Girl* ended up being cut partly at Stax, partly at Ardent in Memphis, and then some of it down at FAME in Muscle Shoals, where the house band of Jimmy Johnson, Spooner Oldham, Tommy Cogbill, and Roger Hawkins was about the only studio team within a thousand miles that could give Booker & The M.G.'s a real run for their money.

Also for *Boy Meets Girl*, Booker and I wrote "Love's Sweet Sensation" for William Bell and Mavis Staples. William and Carla then took on "I Need You Woman" from my last album,

while Johnnie Taylor and Carla went all the way back to the
"Raise Your Hand" B-side for "I've Just Been Feeling Bad."
And then *all of us* who were on that double LP participated in
the opening song, "Soul-a-lujah," written by the same team
as penned "Who's Making Love"—Homer Banks, Bettye
Crutcher, and Raymond Jackson. It can be hard to pull off a cut
like that when you've got a lot of people all at the microphone.
My belief is that it only becomes soul music when everyone
does what they're supposed to do and not jump on everyone
else. That's the way we knew to do it; maybe other people, in
later years, because they're new, they try to put themselves in,
and that's when things got strange. You've got to know when to
hold back, not claim it all for yourself.

By the time it was done, *Boy Meets Girl* was twenty-two cuts
in all—and Stax released about half a dozen as singles. Sadly,
none of them took off. Nor did my "new" solo album, released
on the same day as *Rare Stamps*, *Boy Meets Girl*, and the other
twenty-five long players! *That* record, *You've Got to Have Eddie*,
was almost entirely cover versions, and a lot of it of pop material.
Now, there's never anything wrong when a good singer decides
to pay tribute to someone else's songs. I was happy to take on
Creedence Clearwater Revival's "Proud Mary" and Tom Jones's
"It's Not Unusual," but truth is, you didn't hear an original Stax
composition until side two. On the plus side, of the two songs I
had a hand in writing with Booker for that LP, "Don't Tell Your
Mama" was one of the few major hits to come out of the whole
28 albums. And its B-side, "Consider Me," ended up with a
whole other life of its own. We'll get to that.

At the end of the day, Soul Explosion was a great concept,
and it made people sit up and pay attention to Stax, if they
hadn't already, and how we were upping our game. Still, how
could you expect radio to be playing twenty-five to thirty

different Stax songs at the same time? How many people had the money to go in and buy them all at once?

The only LP out of the whole Soul Explosion campaign that really "exploded" caught us all by surprise. Everyone knew Isaac Hayes as a songwriter—if they knew him at all outside Stax. But the man was also a master pianist and a natural arranger— as I knew from his contributions to some of my hits—and he would come down to the Tiki Club and perform as a singer at times too. Onstage at William Bell's club, he'd worked up an extended version of the Glen Campbell song "By the Time I Get to Phoenix," and it gave him the idea to do a similar thing with Burt Bacharach's "Walk on By." You see, there were few of us at Stax who felt we had to conform to an outside notion of rhythm & blues, or soul music as it was now being called where we came from. If we liked a song, we'd sing it—didn't matter if it was country, pop, jazz, you name it. Same thing with our songwriting if we were given half the chance. Al Bell did give Isaac Hayes that chance, and between some of the musicians we had in Memphis and the addition of Don Davis's connections in Detroit, Isaac ended up with an album that had just four long songs—four *very* long songs. And the public fell head over heels in love with those songs. Until *Hot Buttered Soul*, Isaac wasn't perceived as an artist, like us. But with that LP, he *became* one. On *Hot Buttered Soul*, you hear Isaac's natural voice, just exactly like he would sound when he talked. It's that deep bass. And those raps he had at the start of his arrangements, that's what he was doing when he was performing at the Tiki Club. He looked the part too, with that bald head and the permanent shades.

By the time Stax took a breath to stop counting, *Hot Buttered Soul* had cleared well over a million copies, dominating the jazz and easy-listening charts as well as R&B and pop sales. Along the way, the music industry had learned that black artists could sell albums as well as singles, and Isaac Hayes had become a superstar. It was a great thing all around. If Isaac was moving, everybody else was moving.

Sadly, some people moved on entirely. Miss Axton had given up the Satellite record shop because the label needed more space for recording studios and offices, but I guess with that she gave up her place in the whole company. She was a sweetheart, period, as far as I was concerned. Very friendly. She wasn't ever in the way. But maybe not everyone thought like that, because shortly after shutting up her shop, she sold out her 45 percent share of Stax, most of it to Al Bell. It wasn't the smoothest of deals either; one of the conditions was that she stay away from the recording industry for the next five years. Shortly after that five-year noncompete clause expired, she launched a new label and had one of the very first platinum singles in the music business—meaning a million sales—with Rick Dees's novelty smash "Disco Duck." Guess she always did know what record buyers were looking for!

Chapter 13
DOWN TO EARTH

Losing Miss Axton was a disappointment, but not something that necessarily affected me or my work personally. Losing Booker, though—that was a different story. We could see that things were changing in the administration part of the company; we weren't that naïve that we didn't know things weren't happening. What I see is that if Stax was a family, well at some point, people are going to grow up and leave home, simple as that. Booker had been with Stax since he was at high school, had given the label one of its biggest hits ever with "Green Onions"—and that was before he went off to college! He'd come back and recorded more hits, written more hits, and was known as a master session musician too. And yet, young as he was, he and the M.G.'s were already like the big brothers to the Bar-Kays, and maybe there was a feeling that the younger siblings were starting to encroach on their space at Stax as house band. Plus, when Booker went to the Monterey Festival in 1967, I think he fell in love with California itself. In the summer of 1969, when he couldn't work out whatever business differences he may have had with Jim and Al, he moved there permanently. Didn't leave Stax completely, didn't quit the M.G.'s—least not yet—but he's no longer coming to the studio every day and writing and recording songs with all of us either. Out in Los Angeles, he hung out his shingle and got himself more work, and probably at better pay, than he'd ever had before.

Steve Cropper and I were maybe more successful as a songwriting partnership, to a degree. "Knock on Wood" remains my signature song, after all. But I did way more songs with Booker, liked way more songs with him, would do anything, sing anything with him. With Booker, he can hear me, and I can change melodies and not feel restricted to do certain things. We're singing different types of songs with different arrangements. Booker was across the board. He could play anything. He was definitely my guy.

We had written a song, "People Get It Together," earlier in the summer of '69, when Stax did one of its last revue shows out at a college in El Paso, Texas. There'd been some racial unrest going on there before we arrived—sadly, that was the story across much of America at the time—and we took that into account. It's unusual for me to write directly about a subject like that, but it just reflected how we were thinking at the time: that people *weren't* getting it together. We wanted it to be uplifting rather than a criticism:

"You can be black or white, either way is out of sight, short or tall, fat or small, just gather round and have a ball."

What I was really liking about that song was the way that it was driving. It worked. And Booker really could make it happen too: the way that track sounds at the end, that's a lot different from Stax. In some ways, "People Get It Together" was comparable to "Big Bird," the way I was really letting my voice go for it, and the big punching brass. If the lyric was a reflection of changing times, so was the fact that we recorded it at Stax, but without Cropper and Duck. In their place were Bobby Manuel and Allen Jones. Everyone was so busy back then.

"People Get It Together" might have made for a really interesting A-side, but it ended up on the flip of another song I did with Booker round that time, "Why Is the Wine (Sweeter on the Other Side)." This one had a loose, sparse groove, a kind of upbeat ballad. The bass player on that cut is Roland Robinson, who'd made the move from Detroit to Memphis, where he hooked up with his cousin, guitarist Teenie Hodges, and played on a lot of sessions over at Hi. Roland was a key member of my band during those years and went to England with me when I went over on my own. And for that single, we put the strings on there again, and we got us a hit again.

I know by this point that I am definitely going to sound good with Booker putting it together. So what I do when Booker moves to California that same summer is, I go out there too. Not permanently, I'm not moving *my* life or anything. But if that's where I need to be to write with Booker, that's where I'll go. Booker picks me up at the airport, and he's got his wife from back then, Priscilla Coolidge, with him. And the first thing I notice is that the women out there are dressed totally different than elsewhere in the States. Priscilla's got on a halter top and some little short shorts, and that's about it. It's a California thing, she's a California girl. So we get to the hotel, and we got a little cassette player—things have moved on since the days Cropper and I had to hope we'd remember our songs after we wrote them!—and Booker's got an acoustic guitar. And we're sitting out on the balcony at this hotel looking out over Los Angeles, and I just totally ad lib:

"As I stand here this evening, looking out over the metropolis of Los Angeles, California, I can't help but think about the young lady that I met here. So I wrote a song tonight, and I called it my California Girl." In my mind, I want to sing it like a medium ballad. "California girl, you're living in a different world"—because it *was* different. LA to me was different.

As I'm singing, Booker is clever enough to make the change up that you hear on the final record. We carry those changes over to the next verse, and after the third verse, it changes up again, modulates. We put the song down on cassette and get into the studio out in LA to record it as soon as we can. Booker played all the band parts in the studio except the drums. I recorded the vocal in one take, two at most, and he got a couple of Raelettes and a couple of Ikettes in for backing vocals. Boom. We got it. "California Girl" was released in January 1970, and even though it maybe sounds like a summer jam, the fact that it's winter doesn't stop it becoming one of my bigger hits. At this point, as far as I'm concerned, with the run of success we've got between us—not just commercial success, but creative success, the feeling of doing good work together—I'll keep it going with Booker for as long as he wants to keep it going with me.

Early in 1970, Booker came back to Stax to do one more session with the M.G.'s—a reworking of the entire Beatles' *Abbey Road* album, which was called *McLemore Avenue* for reasons that should be obvious! I jumped on the opportunity to write and record three more tunes with Booker, including one in partnership with Deanie Parker, "Love Is You."

I was fully expecting to finish an album with Booker; we only needed one more session, and I would have been happy to go back out to Los Angeles to do it. But all of a sudden, Booker tells me he can't work on any more projects for *anyone*, even his close friends, if they are going to be released on Stax. His frustrations with the setup there—which aren't mine—have brought him to a decisive point in his life. I was disappointed but accepting: I guess Booker's desire to move on from Stax outweighed anything else on his mind at that point.

But we were all moving in one way or another. At my end, I was considering a partnership with Alan Walden, over in Macon, Georgia. Along with his older brother Phil, who had been Otis Redding's personal manager, Alan ran the Walden Artists and Promotions company, and had booked many of my gigs along the way (as the Waldens did for most of us soul singers living and working below the Mason-Dixon Line).

After the death of Otis, and especially after the assassination of Martin Luther King Jr. and how things changed around them, Alan and Phil started a rock label called Capricorn with funding from Jerry Wexler, who also brought them their first artist: Duane Allman. Duane came to prominence playing lead guitar on a version of "Hey Jude" that Wilson Pickett cut down at FAME in Muscle Shoals toward the end of 1968. Wexler bought out the session guitarist's contract from Rick Hall at FAME, reunited Duane with his organ-playing sibling Gregg, and the Allman Brothers Band was born. For Capricorn, there was no looking back. Over the next several years, based out of the Waldens'—and the Reddings'—home city of Macon, Capricorn would serve as headquarters for an international sound widely known as "southern rock."

Alan and I became good friends during this period. I used to go out to his log cabin in Bolingbrooke, which was next to Otis's ranch, and he and I hunted together. Otis had 276 acres of land at the time that was full of deer and turkey; it had a lot of game out there. "We enjoyed each other's company, hanging out," says Alan. "I'd go out to the black clubs he'd be performing at with him if they were within the two hundred mile range."

All was looking good in Alan's life. But he left Capricorn barely a year after the company got going, when Phil accused him of "riding his coattails." Given that Alan had run the Waldens' entire business while Phil was off in the service in the mid–1960s, you can understand why Alan had a problem with that, so he decided to prove he could cut it on his own. Still, he needed a headline act to launch with. Guess that's where I come in.

"Eddie and I hit it off so good that I asked him to be a partner in my company," recalls Alan. "And I enjoyed my relationship so much with Otis Redding, I thought, 'Well, I'll try and do the same thing with Eddie Floyd.' Plus, Eddie was a great writer. I've always been into the writing part of the business. It was really my favorite part of the whole business. We all thought songs all the time. Somebody would say something, and we'd say, 'Wait, that's a good song title!'"

But Alan had other motivations for bringing me in as well. "I'll openly admit that I was searching for another singer that I thought would be similar to Otis Redding. And I thought the idea of making Eddie a partner in the company would work similar to Otis with Redwall Music." That was the publishing company the Waldens founded with Otis, a source of considerable income. "I saw a business side to Eddie. I felt like he had the intelligence and the knowledge to actually manage other artists too."

But then, says Alan, "I was also looking at Eddie as a potential producer. I had counted on him helping me on promotion with all the black disc jockeys. Overall, he would be doing management and producing and being an artist himself. And songwriting too." In other words, I was to wear many hats—and wear every one of them well! That was quite a set of expectations!

As a good faith demonstration of his own capabilities, Alan assumed responsibility for the promotion of "California Girl." By the time we were done, "California Girl" peaked just one place outside both the R&B Top 10 *and* the pop Top 40.

And so, at the end of March 1970, I went in to the newly built Capricorn Studios in Macon for the first time and recorded alongside a rhythm section that included Jesse Carr on guitar; he'd been part of the Allman brothers' previous band the Hour Glass. They were still getting the premises together, there in Macon, and we were actually in a back room that was set to become Studio Two. Together, we completed what would become the *California Girl* album with a quartet of cover versions. These included the Delfonics' "Didn't I Blow Your Mind This Time" and Eddie Holman's "Hey There Lonely Girl," both of which were representative of the direction soul would take in the 1970s, with a higher vocal register, a slower tempo, a softer beat, and more by way of strings. For me, though, the standout was my take on Brook Benton's classic "Rainy Night in Georgia." We'd been working through the day and night and by now, it was about three in the morning, and I was feeling it. I figured now was the time to show I could sing just as low as Brook Benton. And I did! Never sung lower than that in my whole life, and most people don't even think it's me. The songs we recorded at Capricorn were sweetened by some gorgeous string arrangements, and—with "California Girl," the single, doing well in the charts—the *California Girl* album looked like it should have followed suit when it was released on Stax later in the spring of 1970. It sold well, for sure, but I always thought maybe it could have done better; there's a lot of good material on there beyond the couple of hit singles that would have driven people toward it in the first place.

A couple of days after we did that session in Macon, on April Fool's Day in fact, Alan and I officially incorporated our partnership under the name Hustler's Inc. Bear in mind there was no adult magazine of that name at the time: we were referring strictly to the fact that we were working so hard!

And work hard we did. Alan had an apartment at his office, and I'd often sleep there while in town. Our priority was to set about finding new artists to work with. Alan didn't feel it was right to raid the Capricorn stable—with the exception of the one major artist he'd brought to the company, Boz Scaggs. But Boz decided to stay put. We picked up a few guys whose names haven't really stood the test of time, though all of them made real good singles: Perk Badger, Bill Coday, Pep Brown. We were doing our recording mainly at Capricorn there in Macon, or at Muscle Shoals Sound, which had been set up by the old FAME house band known as the Swampers, also with a handout from Jerry Wexler. You'd normally find Jimmy Johnson at the board on those sessions, and chances were that David Hood, Roger Hawkins, and Spooner Oldham would be on the tracks as well. We shouldn't have been able to go wrong with that team!

We also partnered with another figure in Muscle Shoals: Quin Ivy, whose once tiny Norala Studios had been the location for Percy Sledge's legendary "When a Man Loves a Woman" session, back in 1966. Now Ivy had a larger studio called Quinvy, and we set up a production office with him there. A photograph in Billboard in December 1970 showed myself, Alan, and Quin clasping hands together and announcing as much.

All of this was within the soul music field, but Alan and I had every intention of expanding into rock as well. The way Alan tells it, he went on a talent search for that one perfect rock band, and out of the 187 that he claims to have auditioned, he kept the 'lucky' 13th through the doors: a hard-driving, hard-partying rock group from Jacksonville, Florida, barely out of their teens. Led by singer Ronnie Van Zant and guitarist Gary Rossington, they'd been together long enough to know exactly what they were doing, but not too long that they were getting jaded. They had recently renamed themselves Lynyrd Skynyrd, and we signed them to a management and production contract in 1970.

There's a wonderful photograph from that day: I'm sat at the desk at Hustler's Inc., the only black man in the picture, and behind me is this young band of seriously long-haired dudes—Leonard Skinner was the name of a high school teacher who liked to enforce the rules when it came to men's appearances!—along with Alan and a couple of our staff.

Lynyrd Skynyrd went on to become one of the great rock bands of the 1970s, as you may know. But they certainly didn't take off immediately. Alan and I brought the group down to Muscle Shoals, spent time recording an album's worth of demos, and every single record company rejected them, even though the demos included "Free Bird."

All our acts were costing us money to record and produce, and it wasn't helped by what Alan found to be the increasingly slow pace down in Muscle Shoals. ("Macon was like New York by comparison!") Soon we were a year or so into the company and short on deals, let alone hit records.

"We made all the mistakes of a new business," says Alan. "We overspent on doing the offices, and we expected my old connections to be right there, and they weren't. I'd apparently pissed a lot of people off when I was in the agency business, so some of the people I was counting on shut the door in my face. They were getting back at me for some of the things I'd done for making sure the artists got paid. I ran into situations where people shut the door when I didn't have any idea they would shut the door: I had thought we were tight!

"We found ourselves with very little money to run the company. And at that particular time, Eddie was not in great financial shape either, and he had some dealings, he got behind with the IRS." I was in a position right then where I needed to be putting money in the bank, not taking it out and lending it. As Alan recalls it, our main Hustler's Inc. employee, Gary Donahue, borrowed some cash from his father and bought out my shares. Alan was mad at me for a few years after that, and I guess I was frustrated too. That happens when you set after something you think will deliver you happiness, success, and make you money as well—and then it costs you in all those areas instead. I'm pleased to say that we made up down the line at an awards ceremony and became close friends again; I see Alan pretty much every year in Macon when I go there for the Otis Redding memorial event, and it's always good times.

The way I look back on our problems together with Hustler's Inc. is to say, well, that's the only time things ever went that way, and that's why I tend not to talk about it. It's not that I don't admit to things that don't work out; it's that I learn from them and move on. I can say it was a great thing to be there and to meet all those artists who later became very famous. And it worked out eventually for Alan. After we parted ways, he persisted with Lynyrd Skynyrd and was finally rewarded when the musician Al Kooper signed the group to a label he had just set up with MCA. All those songs that got rejected when we demo'd them? They became rock classics. Alan split from the band in 1974 but kept their early publishing, which proved to be a smart move. As you may know, three Lynyrd Skynyrd band members died in a plane crash in 1977, which put an end to the group's career at the peak of their fame, but long before he perished, Ronnie van Zant had recommended another Florida group, the Outlaws, to Alan, who managed them for a solid fifteen years of success. Alan Walden played a long game, and it paid off.

It was necessary for me to go through that experience with Alan. A lot of us soul brothers and sisters at the time were trying to show that we knew how to handle our own bottom lines, that we were more than just performers to be hired and fired. Still, I was known first and foremost as a singer, and I had no intent of letting that reputation slide. I had no intention of leaving Stax either, so with Booker no longer available as a partner there, I picked up right where I'd left off with Steve Cropper. Steve resumed his role as my producer, first with a cover of The Temptations' "My Girl" and then with a number Steve and I wrote together called "The Best Years of My Life," which had a full funky arrangement with strings, brass, lovely female backing vocals, and a twist at the end of the story.

And then, what do you know, but Cropper's gone from Stax, too! Watching the likes of Don Davis and other newcomers at Stax gain increased power in the production and A&R departments, knowing that Booker had already left, believing that Al Bell was no longer in his corner, Steve felt he had no choice but to move. But at least he had a choice about *how* to move on. He negotiated his way out of his various deals with Jim and Al, an agreement that kept him producing artists at Stax for the next couple of years. Then he drove his guitars and his amps five miles across town and carried on working just like he always had, only now he was based out of a new studio, Trans-Maximus Inc, which he co-owned along with one of the former Mar-Keys, Ronnie Stoots. As I was one of the artists Steve was contracted to keep producing for Stax, I followed right on over. If this is where we gotta be, then, hey, let's go!

The first single we put out from our time together at TMI turned out to be probably the most unusual of my career. And, at the time, one of my least successful! Steve had just opened up the studio; we were sitting round one night, and we got an idea. It's thunder and lightning—again! Steve opened up the back door, there was a big shower of rain coming down, so we put a microphone out there and recorded the rain and thunder. The studio had a metal awning, and you could really hear the sound of the rain coming down on that tin roof.

When Steve and Ronnie then played it on tape, I got to think of, *Oh how it rained*. Steve sat down with an acoustic guitar, he made a rhythm by tapping his feet, and we just formed the idea of a song. All of a sudden I'm with a woman, it's rainy and it's cloudy, and *I remember when you left me* . . . This, my friends, is the songwriting process. We just came out right with it, that night, straight on. I chose to sing it real low, which I have a tendency to want to do if it's three o'clock in the morning.

It was a moment that was happening that we wanted to capture, and it didn't call for us to write something like the songs that Stax had at the time, like the way we'd first worked together five years ago. It was just mellow, with the rain and the feel of that. Often Steve would have his electric guitar, but that night he had the acoustic, and when he started tapping his foot, you could hear the echo. We stuck a microphone just between him and me, and we did it. Whole different feel from anything we'd done before.

When we're finished with "Oh, How It Rained," we know it's not a "Knock on Wood," but we know it's a *song*. A good song at that. And a clever song too, so we give it to Stax, and they put it out. Wasn't like the old days when Jim Stewart would challenge everything you recorded, demand to know why you

thought it could be a hit. Now it was: "Hey, Eddie just gave
us a new song; let's release it." And with *that* song, wasn't even
probably a thought about it being a hit.

And guess what? It wasn't! Not of any kind. "Oh, How It
Rained" was my first solo single not to make *either* the pop or
R&B charts in two full years and ten releases, going all the way
back to "Big Bird." Just like "Big Bird," "Oh, How It Rained" got
lost in the shuffle at Stax because it didn't sound like Stax. The disc
jockeys didn't play it. Stax never even put it on an album!

But "Oh, How It Rained" stayed with me. We performed it
on a TV show in Houston, and the whole approach was different
from anything I'd done before. I'd normally be standing up at the
microphone doing all kinds of moving and stuff, but for this show
I was sitting on a stool. I felt like I needed that stool because it was
so quiet. We had an acoustic guitar with us too. Anyone thinks
I'm only about soul music, well, take a listen at this, brother. Just
a few years ago, Curtis Stigers recorded a lovely rendition of it for
an album, *Let's Go Out Tonight*. You'd be surprised how many
people dig "Oh, How It Rained." They just didn't at the time.

Cropper says how he wishes we'd had that song just a little
earlier, for the Staple Singers. He had worked on their first two
albums at Stax, but around the time he left to set up TMI, Al
Bell took over the family group's production for himself. Al
brought them down to Muscle Shoals to get himself away from
the telephone at the Stax office, but also from a studio where his
production capabilities might be second-guessed—and almost
immediately hit gold with the immortal "Respect Yourself."
That song was co-written by none other than my old friend
Mack Rice. "Respect Yourself" sounds just like Mack Rice
talking. *If you don't respect yourself, how can you respect anybody else?*
In fact, the song came out of a conversation Mack had been
having with Luther Ingram, a new artist at Stax, and, being

Mack, he gave Luther a cowrite as a result. Mack had been in and out of Stax for a few years now, and I was real happy for my old friend, that he finally got such a big hit with the label on such a meaningful and timeless song.

Mack *had* got some hits elsewhere though. It was no surprise that a writer like Mack, who came from the Motor City, would have continued to write for some of the artists up there. In 1968, he had given the song "Linda Sue Dixon" to the Detroit Wheels, and it was released on the Motown subsidiary Inferno. "Linda Sue Dixon" got a fair bit of attention but not too much radio play, which was no surprise when you look at the initials: like Mack wrote it and the Detroit Wheels sung it, "You're plain old LSD to me."

Well, now it's 1971, and once we get going with the album we're making at TMI, Mack comes on over to write with us, 'cause he was enthused by what we were doing, and Stax had no other outlet for that kind of sound that he was into. We wrote a couple of core songs together, the three of us: "My Mind Was Messed Around at The Time," which carries on with that theme of "Linda Sue Dixon," and "Salvation," which clocked in at a solid five and a half minutes. Even longer was my own composition, "When the Sun Goes Down," which was more like a southern blues-rock jam than anything you'd normally have expected from Mr. Eddie Floyd. These songs were totally different on purpose. We're not trying to portray Stax even. We're in a new sound, with new musicians, giving them a chance too. I especially remember Jay Spell, a real nice guy. Jay had been born in North Carolina and was legally blind—and if you were blind in North Carolina back in the fifties, you had no choice but to go to a special school, even if it meant boarding there. That's what happened to Jay and, like me at Mount Meigs, it turned out to be the best thing for him, because he got free piano and fiddle lessons after classes. And so, thanks to Jay, now I got fiddle on one of my records as well! Jay went on to play with Emmylou Harris, Tower of Power, all manner of people. Same with the drummer Richie Simpson, who went on to Roy Orbison, Jose Feliciano, and others. I think *Down To Earth*, as we titled the record, was the first album either was credited on. It was the nurturing of a new band. And for me, a new sound—although it still included Cropper of course, and we still brought in the Memphis Horns, which was the name Wayne Jackson and Andrew Love went by now that they too had gotten off the Stax payroll and put themselves out for hire instead.

Stax released *Down To Earth* in June 1971, but same as they didn't put "Oh, How It Rained" on there, they didn't release a single from the LP. They did send the opening track, a tough, bluesy, rocking version of Curtis Mayfield's "People Get Ready" out to radio, but that was about it. The rest of the album—all of our own songs plus "Linda Sue Dixon"—barely got heard.

You don't know that's going to be the case at the time, of course. *Billboard* gave *Down To Earth* a rave review, called it "an outstanding adventure in rock, rhythm & blues," compared it to Isaac Hayes's "modernization of soul" and called it my "brilliant return"—not that I had been away in hiding! We went on some radio stations that were receptive to this kind of music, but that was about it.

It's hard to know whether to point the finger at Stax, but maybe it wasn't coincidence that "Oh, How It Rained" was the first of my singles to list a new Stax address on the label: 98 North Avalon. The label had grown so big, it couldn't be sustained within the old cinema on East McLemore. And the new address brought changes galore, including the hiring of dozens of new people and Al moving out to oversee them. He wanted to keep the administrative people away from the creative people so we could all get on with our work, but he put himself in with the administration. All of a sudden he's blocks away; we're not seeing each other so much, not talking things through the way we used to.

David Porter has his own take on what was going on at the time, how things were changing now that people were moving away from East McLemore as their daily base. "The chemistry that gave lifeblood to what Eddie was doing, was *everybody* putting energy into what Eddie was doing. When that dissipated, that chemistry was lost. It would have been wonderful if Isaac and I stayed engaged in what Eddie and Steve were doing, not as writers but as complements to it, but we got so big that it fell away. And in my view, I believe that hurt Eddie to a certain extent. Because the creative juices that we were all bringing to the table as accompaniment to it, they were no longer there. So now you were looking at what all that Steve could do, or what Eddie could do alone, and a combination of the true complement to what Eddie needed was not necessarily there."

But here's something I have to say to that. Not once, not ever, have I thought about how much money I might make from a song, a recording, an album. Eventually you'll be with your accountant at royalty time and that's when you deal with it. You might be judging it by radio, and people talking about it when you go out to sing, how popular it is *when* you sing. That part of it, you can tell when something is maybe not as good, but even at that, hey, you recorded it, you still do it. With *Down To Earth*, that was life moving on, my brother. That was then, and this is now. So what's next?

Chapter 14
JAMAICA THIS MORNING

At the start of the 1970s, I got invited down to Jamaica for some shows. I didn't need to be asked twice, and not only because one of my aunts married a Jamaican. I was *always* happy to travel, go somewhere new, explore, find a new audience. And I was interested to learn more about the Jamaican music scene, about calypso, rocksteady, blue beat, and ska. Booker T. & the M.G.'s had embraced some of that West Indian steel band sound with "Soul Limbo." Al Bell was taking holidays to Jamaica, and of course he never missed a chance to promote Stax's music anywhere he went, so maybe it wasn't a total surprise to learn one of us was wanted down there.

The island did not disappoint. And in the capital of Kingston, which was a constant carnival of music with sound systems blasting the new reggae music all over the streets, I was thrilled by my reception. Seemed like people knew me. As often the case when I traveled, I went pretty much straight from the airport to the gig. There, for my first show, I played everything I figured they expected of me: "Knock on Wood," "Raise Your Hand," "I've Never Found a Girl," and more. As far as I was concerned, I delivered.

After the show, the promoter rushes back to the dressing room. I figure he wants to congratulate me.

"Oh God, mon," he says in that Kingston accent you'll recognize if you've ever heard it. "You don't do de song!"

"What are you talking about?" I say to him in return. "I did all my songs."

"No, mon. 'Consider Me.'"

"Who?"

"'Consider Me.' You don't play 'Consider Me'!"

He's talking about the B-side to "Don't Tell Your Mama," the single we put out in the middle of the Soul Explosion, in the spring of 1969. It was a beautiful song, for sure, a ballad I wrote with Booker that was all the more special for his organ countermelody that sounded almost *exactly* like a female voice. "Consider Me" had found its way onto *Rare Stamps*, one of the two LPs that Stax put out on me in the same week. But with all that Soul Explosion music hitting the stores at once, I was just happy that "Don't Tell Your Mama" got noticed; I had no idea that "Consider Me" had become a hit in the Islands.

It had, though. Big time, so much so that it had also traveled to Britain on the wave of musical migration that was taking place with the explosion of Jamaican reggae in the UK. It was in England that a guy by the name of Roy Gee came out with a full-blown reggae cover version. Roy Gee was to be a pseudonym for Dandy Livingston, a Jamaican immigrant to the UK you might know for his hit, "Suzanne, Beware of the Devil." That version had now traveled back to Jamaica and was a local hit—as was my original rendition.

That wasn't the only time the song got a reggae makeover—and Jamaica wasn't the only place "Consider Me" was a hit either. Just recently, I saw an article in an expat paper published in the States, a story that said how, "in the summer of 1969, 'Consider Me' absolutely ruled the jukebox in Belize City." Belize is tucked into a corner of the Caribbean coast, bordered by Mexico and Guatemala; most people couldn't find it even on a map of the region. Our music was *traveling*, man.

To get back to that particular trip to Kingston, though, I had to go out and get myself a copy of "Consider Me" to refresh myself—and the band—on the whole song! Fortunately, a copy wasn't hard to find in Kingston. Second night I'm performing down there, I make damn sure to sing it—and maybe more than once to make up for the first night!

That trip marked the start of a musical love affair with the Islands, Jamaica especially. In 1971, I joined Al Bell, Jim Stewart, Al Jackson, and Donald "Duck" Dunn to do some writing and recording there. We chose to set up at Byron Lee's studio in the heart of Kingston. Byron was one of the central figures in the Jamaican music scene. Born two years before me, he'd introduced the electric bass to the island, had taken his first band—the Dragonaires—professional around the same time the Falcons put out their debut single, produced the Maytals in the early 1960s, led package tours around the Island, headed up distribution in Jamaica for Atlantic Records, and even bought a recording studio from the future Prime Minister Edward Seaga! And it didn't harm his relations with Stax that he had recorded an authentic calypso cover of "Soul Limbo" right after Booker T. and the M.G.'s first released it.

That was a great time for us to have another country where we could do the music together. Some people thought Stax was starting to overreach by going there, but I say, "Really? They never been anywhere and now they going to Jamaica—where any tourist can easily go—and *that's* too much?" Why wouldn't you be reaching? That's part of life. Same as Stax setting up so many different labels. All the companies do that. You do something, it works, and then you reach for something else.

I had a song in my head right away, 'cause I loved the area, I loved the rhythm, I loved the music anyway. It was called "Baby, Lay Your Head Down," and I'm saying, "Well if we want the reggae feel, then we need to get the guys who play it," so the M.G.'s more or less watched Byron Lee's band record that one. I wrote another number in the hotel in Kingston that night too, an uplifting instrumental with Al Jackson and Duck called "Jamaica This Morning." That's one the M.G.'s did manage to record down there. When we took the tapes back to Memphis, we got Terry Manning, who had played the marimba on "Soul Limbo," to perform the same service. Jay Spellman added the organ, and because Booker wasn't a part of the group any more, the track was credited just to the M.G.'s. "Jamaica This Morning" was my first ever cowrite for the act that had played on all my early Stax records—and it turned out to be their last single. That, my friends, truly *was* the end of an era.

I'm not claiming to be the only soul singer going down to the islands and recording reggae. Johnny Nash, out of Texas, had been recording on and off in Jamaica since 1968, and when I'm hearing him, I'm thinking, "I want to do that!" In 1972 he took the concept of a soul-reggae crossover to the very top of the American Hot 100 with "I Can See Clearly Now," recorded in

London. We hadn't yet released "Baby, Lay Your Head Down," which was a shame, because by the time we did, it sounded like it was following a trend, when we really were quite ahead of it. Stax wasn't completely left behind, though. Earlier in '72, Al Bell had lifted the bass line from the 1969 reggae instrumental "The Liquidator," lock, stock, and two smoking barrels for the foundation of "I'll Take You There." It became a number one in its own right for the Staple Singers—and only the second Stax single ever to top the Hot 100. Al was credited as sole songwriter.

Back in Memphis, Steve Cropper, Mack Rice, and myself carried on writing together, recording at Muscle Shoals Sound Studio, where Barry Beckett, a masterful piano player, handled a lot of the arrangements. After the experiment that was *Down To Earth*, we decided to return to a groove that audiences expected of me, and it worked. I was straight back in the charts with the singles "Blood Is Thicker than Water" and "Yum Yum Yum." I returned to Britain again for my first tour in three years and found plenty of love waiting there for me. And in the middle of all this, Mack came down to Memphis from one of his trips home to Detroit, talking about a dance they were doing called "the Breakdown." So he and I worked up a song of that name, walked into Rufus Thomas's office at Stax—we all had offices at Stax by this point!—and presented it to him. Despite being well into his fifties, Rufus was on a roll at this point, hitting the pop charts and owning the R&B ones with dances like "Do the Funky Chicken" and "(Do The) Push and Pull Part 1." Rufus took one listen to "Do the Breakdown," added his own touches, and took it all the way to number two!

Steve, Mack, and I also worked together on the second of the two albums that Cropper produced for Stax at his new TMI studio (the first being *Down To Earth*), this one for a Canadian guy called Eric Mercury. My cowrite with Steve and Mack

174 KNOCK-KNOCK-KNOCK ON WOOD

was the opener, "I Can Smell That Funky Music," but if you think *that* was a good title, it was nothing compared to what Eric called his album: *Funky Sounds Nurtured in the Fertile Soil of Memphis That Sound Like Rock*. Come to think of it, that was a decent way of summing up *Down To Earth* too.

So, I was staying busy with my music. And the Stax people were staying busy trying to figure out a perfect business setup. In 1970, Jim Stewart and Al Bell had bought Stax back from Gulf & Western, using money fronted by Deutsche Grammophon, the records arm of Phillips, which took over international distribution and bought a minority share in Stax. Soon enough, Jim and Al decided they didn't like working for Phillips either, so in late 1971 they negotiated another buyout, partly with the cash that was flowing in from all the hit records and partly with a loan from their Memphis bank, Union Planters. The timing looked perfect for Jim and Al to finally own the company outright. Almost immediately, the Staple Singers hit number one on the Hot 100 with "I'll Take You There," and it looked good for Isaac Hayes, who had followed up *Hot Buttered Soul* with two more enormous hit albums. Now he got commissioned to write and record the soundtrack for a new black cop movie, *Shaft*. My old friend Charles "Skip" Pitts, from the D.C. group the Carltons, came to town and provided the theme song with a wah-wah guitar sound, which we all thought was amazing. Now Isaac Hayes has a number-one pop single too. But *Shaft* was about a lot more than just chart positions: the movie was a box office smash, one of the classics in that genre they called "blaxploitation." Isaac went on to win an Academy Award for the song—and three Grammys too. He'd become such a phenomenon that they called his next album *Black Moses*. To me, though, he was still just Isaac, ain't nothing changed.

Some things were changing around Stax regardless. Back in '68, after the assassination of Dr. Martin Luther King, when things in Memphis got real tense, Al Bell had hired two guys, Johnnie Baylor and Dino Woodward, to provide some security for the company. Johnnie, originally from Alabama, was a records man that Al had met in D.C.; he had his own label, Koko, which was how Luther Ingram got to Stax. Johnnie also liked to let you know he'd been in the Rangers, Special Ops division. You know, that he was a trained killer. He'd met Dino, a Memphis native, up in Harlem, where they'd both been around the boxing champion Sugar Ray Robinson.

If you've read much about Stax, or if you've seen the documentary movie, you'll have heard of these guys and their reputations, about how they got tight with Isaac and became closely involved in his business dealings and brought their guns to work every day. I know all the stories too, but I ain't got shit to do with that. I know it makes for good copy, but I'm here to talk about music, not thugs. What do I mean by that? I mean, if you portray like you're a thug, then you're a goddamn thug, that's all I can tell you. Just as long as you don't thug me. Ain't *nobody* going to approach me that way. So I heard all the stories, but I see that as gossip. When you speak of music, you got me. When you speak of people and the things that they do, you don't got me. I didn't deal with Johnnie and Dino, and I'm not threatened by somebody telling me this guy does this or he'll do that. Every time I saw Johnnie Baylor, the only thing we'd say was "Hello, homeboy," 'cause he's from Alabama too; that would have been *it*. I wasn't in their surroundings because we were each doing our own thing. And most of the things you hear about those guys would have been when they were on the road anyway. I wasn't seeing none of it at Stax. Not really. Isaac used to come in and record a lot at night. And when he was in there with his team, I never witnessed any of that stuff.

Meantime, come 1972, now that he was a co-owner of what he called a "full-service record company," Al Bell was expanding Stax like crazy and seemingly in every direction. Not all of it made sense—he pushed into musical theater, opened a West Coast office, signed a ten-year-old white female Scottish pop singer!—but one ambitious effort on his part paid dividends we would reap for the rest of our lives. In the summer of 1972, just about the entire company's roster went out to Los Angeles for the revue show to end all revue shows: Wattstax.

The last time Stax had done this in the States was way back in August 1965, shortly before I got to the label. That show had also taken place in Watts. Wilson Pickett was on top of the charts that week with "In the Midnight Hour," a single that had been recorded at Stax and helped along its way by the great disc jockey Magnificent Montague, who was now on air in LA and looking to make his name as a promoter too. The Stax show—with the label's major stars plus Pickett, headlining—took place at the 5/4 Ballroom in Watts, just three nights before the city went up in flames after an altercation between the police and a black driver they tried to arrest escalated out of control. There was a lot of pent-up aggression within the community out there, a lot of frustration over police racism, housing, education, all issues that affect black people every day, and I guess it just reached a boiling point with that one incident. The city burned for days, the National Guard was called in, and when the smoke cleared, there was a toll of thirty-four dead bodies, 300 destroyed buildings, and damage put at around $40,000,000.

Now, seven long years later, a period in which soul music had largely come to dominate black popular culture—and a good chunk of white popular culture too, and a lot of it thanks to

Stax—the label decided to revisit Watts and put the place back on the national map in the best way possible. Watts may have been viewed as a ghetto by many, but it was also home to the LA Coliseum, and on August 19, right after the LA Rams played an early season football game there, in rolled the sound trucks, up went a vast PA, and, the next day, the Coliseum opened its doors to the community. Over 100,000 people showed up, and just about all of them were of color. Stax provided its own security, in case the police got out of hand, and hired some dancers from Soul Train in case the crowd could not get in its own groove. There was no need for worries on either front. Whole families came out and spent the afternoon and evening soaking up the music, the vibes, and dancing to their heart's content. If there were arrests that glorious day, I never heard of none.

It was some lineup. We had Kim Weston singing what we called the black national anthem, "Lift Every Voice and Sing." Jesse Jackson led the crowd through his "I Am Somebody" call-and-response. The legendary Billy Eckstine—whose second album for Stax, *Senior Soul*, released that year, opened with his version of my ballad "I'll Always Have Faith in You"—joined Jackson, director Melvin Van Peebles, and William Bell, among others, as an MC. It was a day for Stax to celebrate and promote its ongoing success stories, be they old hands like the Staple Singers, the revamped and totally rejuvenated Bar-Kays, or new signings like the Emotions, Frederick Knight, Lee Sain, the Soul Children, and Mel & Tim. And it was an especially good day for those of us now seen as the "old guard." We were all told how important it was to do this, to film this, and that they wanted everyone to "do your thang," but keep it in order, don't try to excite nobody too much.

But it was also one long day. After showing up first thing in the morning, I went on stage about 4:30 in the afternoon, following William Bell as the last of a series of one-song solo performances. I was looking back at the movie recently, saw myself wearing African-design wide flares and waistcoat, a cross, and I got me a big old Afro as well—and I was one of the modest ones that day! I sung "Knock on Wood" with what they called the Wattstax Orchestra '72. Then I stayed on stage and we had a group session, of me, William, Frederick Knight, Eric Mercury, Lee Sain, and others who'd appeared on stage ahead of me: thirteen of us in all going back and forth on "Old Time Religion."

Later on in the day, Rufus Thomas came out in shorts, shirt, and cape—all in hot pink!—and called the crowd off the bleachers and on to the field to dance their asses off. Then, informed that the field was very much out of bounds and that the show was in danger of being stopped there and then, he somehow cajoled every single one of them back into the stands! Rufus was one of a kind, I tell you. His daughter Carla, my friends William Bell and David Porter—who'd launched a solo career of his own following his former songwriting partner's success—they all got to do their thing too. And then, at the end of the night, Isaac Hayes was driven right up to the stage to perform an hour-long set in resplendent chain mail top and bright red pants. He was at the peak of his popularity and his powers. It also happened to be the brother's thirtieth birthday. What a gift!

It was a great honor to do Wattstax, and see all those famous people, and now, all these many years later, to just look back at that and say, "Wow, I was part of that history." It's nice to be part of history. Naturally, Stax milked the concert for everything it was worth. There was the movie, *Wattstax*, which came out at the start of 1973. It had us Golden Thirteen, as we were called, doing "Old Time Religion" but no shots of me

on my own. That was all right. A lot of what was in the movie
was shot away from the Coliseum that day, in barber shops
and diners and on street corners round Watts, black people
discussing their lives. And then there's this one guy in that
movie we've never seen before, he's serious at parts, he's funny
at parts—and his name is Richard Pryor. He's just starting out.
History speaks for itself.

There was a double album that came out same time as the
movie, subtitled *The Living Word*, that had me singing "Knock
on Wood," but also included a new song of mine, "Lay Your
Loving on Me." That was Stax getting ahead of the game,
because "Lay Your Loving on Me" was my next single. Maybe
Stax figured they were doing me a favor by ensuring so many
people got to hear it (they did the same with the Staple Singers,
and a group Don Davis had brought down from Detroit, the
Dramatics). Trouble was, the album sold so well that few people
had a *need* to go out and buy my single.

"Lay Your Loving on Me" was mid-tempo, one of several
sweet songs I did with Dale Warren out in Los Angeles straight
after Wattstax. Dale was a Detroit guy, the nephew of Berry
Gordy's second wife, and had come up doing arrangements for the
Supremes at Motown and for my uncle's Lu Pine signing Bettye
LaVette. Like me, he made his way to Memphis via D.C., where
he'd worked for that city's key mid-'60s soul label, Shrine. Don
Davis brought him in to Stax, and Dale had earned his keep straight
away with the magnificent string arrangement for Isaac's "Walk on
By." He and I wrote a song together called "The Highway Man,"
and he produced a couple I wrote on my own, "Check Me Out"
and "What'cha Gonna Do with My Heart." They all reflected
the sound of '73, soul music with some good funky wah-wah
guitar, lots of strings, female backing singers, punchy brass. And of
course, at the heart of it all, me singing my heart out as always.

To finish off the new album, Al Bell and I finally get back in the studio together as coproducers, down at Muscle Shoals Sound. It was great working with Al again directly after all these years. We were both pleased with the results, and we had reasons to expect good sales from the album. We called it *Baby, Lay Your Head Down (Gently on My Bed)* for the song of that name, the one I'd recorded down in Kingston in 1971. I got on *Soul Train* for the first time performing a couple of songs from that album. The album held its own, but it didn't take off like we'd expected, or as much as Al had hoped for.

The way Al saw it, the success of Wattstax was a double-edged sword. "Stax became a threat to the American establishment and to the ruling class. When two or more of us got together we were a problem in general to white America, and certainly to the establishment. So to put 112,000 black people in there all day long . . ."

But if Al did think he'd become a threat to the establishment, it didn't stop him getting in bed with the establishment. At the end of 1972, he signed a distribution deal with Clive Davis at CBS Records, which brought Stax a massive advance—much of which went towards Al buying out Jim Stewart. Jim had had enough of all the wheeling and dealing, the ups and downs, the business triumphs, and then the disappointments. He saw what Al was doing with the company, especially within the black community, and he gave it his blessing, but still he wanted to cash in his chips. As these things often go, part of the agreement was that he didn't announce his departure; he kept the title of president even once he was gone.

The idea behind the new deal was that Stax would get access to more of the white record buyers through CBS's distribution, and CBS would get access to the black mom-and-pop stores through Stax. Al Bell was buying into Clive Davis's vision, and Clive was buying into Al's. Should have worked out for all concerned, and at first it looked just sweet: *Wattstax: The Living Word*, the one with both sides of my new single on it, went gold. (A second album, *The Living Word 2*, which featured our "Old Time Religion," also charted.) But the CBS connection didn't help *Baby, Lay Your Head Down* none. The title track, coupled with "Check Me Out" fared okay as a single; "Lay Your Loving on Me" and "I Wanna Do Things for You," not so well. Was it CBS? Was it Stax? Was it me? Or was it just the changing times?

Chapter 15
TALK TO THE MAN

In 1974, I made what turned out to be my last album for Stax, though, at the time, I never intended or expected that to be the case. We named it *Soul Street* for the intersection of Mississippi and Walker, the two streets just up above Stax, where there's a restaurant that's still there called the Four Way Grill. Best food in the world! Everybody who came from overseas, we'd take them to the Four Way. We had us a little party in studio A making the title track; I brought in about twenty bottles of liquor and got a whole vibe going that you can hear on the record. Had this new group Con Funk Shun in as my band. Got the Nightingales in there doing backing vocals, giving it a gospel feel. *What's that smell? Something's smelling good!*

Almost the entire album was recorded at East McLemore, and in some ways it was like a homecoming after doing my last few records in different places. At the same time, we got some new faces in the studio: not just Con Funk Shun, who went on to have a whole career of their own, but another house band, We Produce Rhythm. And the songs are coming from partners old and new. A couple of the finest, "I Don't Want to Be with Nobody but My Baby" and "I Am So Glad I Met You," I wrote with Joe Shamwell, who I knew from back in D.C., where we'd co-written "Got to Make a Comeback," the B-side of "Knock on Wood." And I wrote the finale, "Stick with Me Baby," with the great Luther Dixon, who'd been a partner in Scepter and Wand Records back in the early 1960s, writing hits for the Shirelles, Chuck Jackson, Jimmy Reed, and others. I happened to be with Luther down in Miami, and we just got to writing together. Don't matter where I am, who I'm with; if an idea for a song hits me, I'm ready to go to work!

The only song we didn't do at Stax was the first single from *Soul Street*, "Guess Who." For that, I went back up to Detroit, with Don Davis, to United Sound. That was one of the first studios I'd ever recorded at, back with the Falcons. During his time at Stax, Don made some big changes at the company, brought in some excellent people. Among them was Tim Whitsett to run the publishing companies. (I was signed to the main Stax songwriting arm, East Memphis, though there was another called Birdees.) But Don also upset a lot of people at Stax with his quick success and, after promoting him above some of the other people who'd been producing hits at Stax a lot longer than Don, Al Bell had to let him go. Don, though, was a savvy businessman and, back in Detroit, he purchased United Sound, modernized it, set up a publishing and production company called Groovesville, where he carried on making hit records.

Unfortunately, the song we did together, "Guess Who," wasn't one of them. It was real smooth—smoother than almost anything I'd done before—a good reflection of where Don was at, and a sound I was happy to get under my belt, though maybe not what people were expecting from me at the time. I didn't write the song either and wasn't too often I'd let that happen on a single unless, like "Bring It on Home to Me" or "My Girl," it was already well known and something I felt I could put my spin on.

But other than that, I think of *Soul Street* as my Memphis album, and partly because of the cover, probably the best album sleeve I got. The photographer came down to Main Street in Memphis and took a picture of me sitting on the steps of Sammy's, the finest tailors in the city at the time, with all other people going about their business on the street in front of me. Then they took that photograph and did a painting of it. All the people that you see on the cover—including the guy in the three-piece pink suit out front of Sammy's—were real people that were there that day. The picture captures the mood of that era, kind of a *Superfly* time. Sammy's has moved now—it's in midtown, in a mall—but at least it's still around.

That was more than was going to be said of Stax within a year. We knew it was falling apart because they weren't playing our records on the radio anymore. But at the same time, I wasn't in the administration part of it; I was a singer who doesn't walk into their office and ask them what bills they owe anybody. How would we know? You have to wait and hear what happens. You hope it's all going to work out.

But there were enough meetings and enough stories in the paper that we knew something had gone wrong. Or some *things*—very often, in a situation like this, it's not one problem that sends a company into a spiral but a series of them. For Stax, and this is really only from piecing it together from what

I learned down the line, you could say it started late in 1972 when Johnny Baylor was stopped at an airport on his way to Birmingham, Alabama, and found to be carrying $130,000 *cash* in his briefcase. Now, I'm not saying whose money it was or was not, what it was intended for or was not, but let's just say it was no surprise that the I.R.S. immediately announced an investigation into Stax's finances. Nor was it a shock that Stax promptly got pulled into an ongoing investigation into payola. Some people may have thought pay-to-play had gone out of fashion when the radio disc jockey Alan Freed, the guy they credited with popularizing the phrase rock 'n' roll, got scapegoated back in 1960, but we all knew damn well ain't no disc jockey going to play your record unless he gets some money.

In music, there's all kinds of off-the-books payments. Sometimes you get caught, sometimes you don't. And if you're a big company like CBS and you get caught, you just make sure to drop whoever was involved so you can claim you never knew nothing about it. That's what happened in May 1973, when CBS showed Clive Davis the door at Columbia Records (literally: they tossed him on to the street) when it became known that he'd used the company's money to pay for his lavish personal lifestyle. Clive, you may remember, was the man who did the massive deal with Al Bell to get Stax records into the high street stores and get Sony some access to the R&B distribution network in the process. Once he's gone, who at Columbia really cares about any of that? Sure, there were some money-making records getting sent up to New York—primarily from Isaac Hayes and the Staple Singers—but that's how companies like CBS/Columbia always work, by taking a big record and making it bigger. When it came to *breaking* new soul records, or just handling those artists in the middle of the marketplace, people like me, they weren't interested, or they didn't know how, which amounts to the same thing. In short, Columbia could get half a million copies of *Wattstax* into the high street record stores on the back of a hit movie that already had Isaac Hayes's picture plastered all over it, but they didn't grasp the importance of regional markets in black music, how a 45 might take months to break from one part of the country into another. At first, Stax keeps sending them product, figuring the more records CBS takes, the more money is in it for Stax. That's how it worked with the mom-and-pops, after all: they order it, they pay for it. But with CBS, it's different. CBS had the right to return unsold stock. So now Stax is running up bills with pressing plants for records it can't be sure it's going to get paid for. That's a fast route to a cash flow problem.

Al Bell soon concluded that CBS was ordering way more records than it could ever place in the stores, and he became convinced that it was deliberate, that they were trying to cause such a *big* cash flow problem that they could take Stax over. "This is capitalism, God bless America," is the way he looked at it. "The big fish is always meant to eat the little fish." Al refused to play the little fish and get eaten, so he brought a legal case against CBS, accusing them of manufacturing a hostile takeover. But a big fish like CBS? Not only do they have the lawyers to keep the little fish swimming in circles in his little goldfish bowl, but in this case, they're your distributors. You think you already have a problem getting your records into the stores? Now you *really* got a problem. Eighteen-wheelers start rolling up to the Stax warehouse, returning all the unsold product, my records among them. It's at least half of what they've ordered, maybe more. And CBS is now withholding the money for the records it has sold against *future* returns. So Stax's cash-flow problems have just doubled, even tripled—and on top of that, we *definitely* ain't getting our records into the stores right.

Next up: the bank. For years it's been easy street between Union Planters and Stax. The label—and the publishing–has been making so much money, the bank can't offer new loans quickly enough. But Union Planters is loaning money elsewhere in the local business world, and some of these loans are not doing so well. Fact, they're looking mighty dubious to begin with. The bank hones in on this guy, Joe Harwell, who's been making all these loans and, like CBS with Clive Davis, they drop him immediately and bring charges against him. But then what? The bank's got its own creditors to deal with. Banks can't be seen to collapse. And this bank has a parent bank in Atlanta with enough resources to send down the big guns. These heavyweight guys roll into Memphis, look around at the loans, see Isaac driving round in a gold Cadillac, all of us dressed to the nines, living large on our well-earned success, Al Bell with all his talk of black consciousness and economic empowerment, Jim Stewart with his mansion, and they figure, *This can't be right. That guy Joe Harwell that we just fired—Al Bell must have been in cahoots with him. Those loans can't have been honest. Let's call them in. Let's go after Stax!*

But, even as these problems are mounting, even as a recession is hitting, Al's vision for Stax shows no signs of slowing down. Stax is the fifth largest black business in America by 1974. Motown is number one. What does it take to catch up to Motown? The answer ought to be simple: more and bigger hit records. And it's true, Stax does put out *more* records than ever, but they're not *bigger*. Meantime, Stax purchases *another* building in Memphis for all the new staff Al keeps hiring, opens more offices around the world, makes plans to buy the local baseball team, and invests in more movies. Yet we can't find our own singles in the stores no more. The hits are drying up and with it, of course, the label's income.

The situation gets so bad that Jim Stewart comes out of retirement. Seeing the label that he started out of his garage struggling on the ropes, he puts his mansion and his future

Stax income on the line as collateral; he also puts $400,000 of his own cash money into the company to pay the bills. It's not enough, and when Stax can't meet its royalty payments to Isaac Hayes and Richard Pryor, they leave the company and go elsewhere. Of the other "staff" who used to get a one-sixth share of the income, Cropper and Booker have already departed, and now Donald "Duck" Dunn vacates his office too. Meantime, Al Jackson Jr., the last of the M.G.'s, is spending his time over at Hi with Willie Mitchell, cowriting massive hits for Al Green like "Let's Stay Together" and making records with Ann Peebles and Don Bryant and Otis Clay.

The only thing that's guaranteed to make money any more around Stax is the publishing. Now this was solid under Tim Whitsett. We all got our legitimate share, and no reason we shouldn't. At the end of the day, publishing is a real straightforward business: money comes into the publisher through airplay and record sales, and the publisher writes checks to the songwriters for their share of it. As long as a publisher has a good sense of what's happening with their catalog and don't overspend on overheads, no reason to ever go out of business.

But in November 1974, that's what happens. One morning, a Union Planters representative walks into Tim Whitsett's office and tells him *they* now own the company! You see, Stax no longer being in good shape, it had East Memphis and Birdees—the two publishing companies it owned—take out loans from the bank, and then Stax borrowed that money in-house. But as things went downhill on the records side, Stax couldn't repay its loans to its publishing arm, which means the publishing company couldn't repay the loans to the bank, and with all the problems they got going down all over the region, Union Planters looks at the publishing and says, *Now there's some collateral worth owning.* Overnight, the two companies are told to pack up and move into new offices right next door to the bank. All my writing contracts and copyrights for the last decade now belong to a bank! Tim keeps his job, but because he's now working for the bank and has to answer to them and not Al Bell, Stax makes *him* out to be the enemy. Meantime, people like me, songwriters at East Memphis who are also artists at Stax, we're caught in the middle. We're being asked to take sides, and that's not what we're here for. We're here to *make* sides.

"This was a rough time," recalls Deanie Parker. "I don't think any of us were feeling it. Some of us were supporting. But we were just trying to make sure that we had enough brake fluid there so that we could stop the car and not run into something cataclysmic. Things were changing all around us, not just at Stax but all around the industry. The recession is taking over in America at that time. Hell, things are so bad in Memphis that the damn Chamber went bankrupt. All of us were looking for a lifeline or revisiting the things we always said we would do if we ever experienced such turbulence."

That turbulence seeped into my songwriting. After a couple of the singles from *Soul Street* didn't do much—and there ain't nothing wrong with that album that some decent promotion and distribution couldn't have fixed—I wrote a new one with Joe Shamwell: "I Got a Reason to Smile ('Cause I Got You)." Sounds like another love song, and ultimately it is, but the first verse kicks right off talking about waking up in the morning to yesterday's problems, about having to get up and get on with the struggle. In my song, the resolution is that yeah, things may be hard, but I still got *you*. In Memphis, we were feeling that, yeah, things may be hard, but we still got *Stax*.

A similarly dark mood seeped into my very last new single for Stax, released in the spring of 1975. Just the title, "Talk to the Man," should give you a hint that it's not my usual fare, and sure enough, the end of each verse confirms as much: "We got to get on our knees every time we talk to the man." That was the state of the world at the time, and it was very much the state of things around Stax. In an attempt to stay positive—and also being unwilling to give up on a good song—we put "I Got a Reason to Smile" on the flip side this time.

If you know anything of me by now, you know that I work hard. I do what's necessary to assure myself of the best results possible. So I hear that there's a booking agency in Georgia, they're reporting on all these country stations playing "Talk to The Man," and that's a great thing for me: I have no musical boundaries. This booking agent, she's telling me she thinks the song can become a hit, certainly locally, but she can't get any help from Stax, that there's but nobody working there for her to talk to anymore. And now I'm getting action in Indiana as well, for "I Got a Reason to Smile," so I go up there to do a show. I get into town with my record and I actually go to the distributor, because that's what we would do in a lot of places; I'm trying to show good will, that I'm working my record, and that they should be getting it in the shops. And that's when they tell me they don't have the record because they can't *get* the record. Well, how come?

It was round that time that William Bell's contract expired, and he politely declined to renew. "It was tough going because Stax owed money to CBS," he recalls now, "and there were some other things going on with the systems changing, different personnel, so it was just a downward spiral for Stax. The originals like me and Eddie and Isaac who'd been there for a while, we could see the handwriting on the wall. For me I still had family, I had car notes and home payments that I've got to take care of, so I had to make the move." The Emotions got out of their deal round that time too. Then the Staple Singers demanded their freedom, and that ticked Al off to no end after all he felt he'd done for them. Another of the label's newer hit-makers, the Soul Children, left as well—for CBS, to be produced by Don Davis!

Me, I stayed right where I was. This is what I told the *Tri-State Defender*, the region's leading black newspaper, that June of 1975:

"I came to Stax with Al Bell. He brought me here and unless he puts me out, I'll be here 'till he takes me from here myself. I've had hard times before, but hard times they come and go. In the past, when they came, Stax stuck by me—so now I am sticking with Stax. I am sorry for the problems the company has had but I've never been sorry for a minute that I came here with Al."

And you know something, I've still never regretted that. Al and I had something deep, and it's obvious in what he said just recently, when we started working on this book. "What hurt me so badly, candidly, is that I couldn't do for and with Eddie what Berry Gordy was able to do with Smokey Robinson." I appreciate that he thought that much of me.

At the time though, it was tough. Later in the summer of 1975, like it was some kind of last-ditch effort, or maybe because they just needed to make sure they had some form of product in the marketplace, Stax released two more of my songs from *Soul Street:* "I'm So Glad I Met You" and "I Am So Grateful." It may have been the last single on the label.

The rest of the year was just one long slow death throe. In early September, a federal grand jury indicted Al Bell on fourteen charges of fraud, concerning the loans that had been secured from Union Planters bank. You can look at everything I've told you so far and draw whatever conclusions you want, but let me save you time: Al ended up fighting the charges and won, on every single count. Meantime, we took our distractions where we could get them and, on September 30, that was with a fight of a different kind, a heavyweight championship bout between Muhammad

Ali and Joe Frazier. I got some connections with both of these men, as you'll find out soon enough. They hyped up the match as the Thrilla in Manilla, and it lived up to the billing. One of the longest, toughest, most brutal fights you'd ever see; Ali only won it when Frazier's trainer refused to allow Joe to come out for the final, fifteenth round. Ali said afterwards that "it was like death."

My good friend Al Jackson, the M.G.'s drummer, watched the fight live at a downtown theater, after which he headed home. There, in his front room, he was shot to death, his body found lying on the floor in a pool of blood. His wife said they were victims of a home invasion. Others pointed out that the couple were in the middle of a difficult divorce that had already seen some violence; they noted that the house wasn't ransacked, that Al's wallet hadn't even been taken from him. But no one has ever been prosecuted for the crime. I went to a tribute event just a year back. Al's kid was there; so was Cropper and William Bell, and they said something about how the investigator was opening the case again. But this is forty-something years later: you really going to solve it now? Either way, you ain't bringing him back. Those of us in the Memphis community lost one of our best friends that night, the greatest of drummers, the finest of guys that we knew, one of the true ambassadors of our music.

On December 19 of that year, I had my own gun situation to deal with. I owned them, sure. That's the culture I come from. I have them to hunt, and I have them to protect myself. But that day, my daughter Nicholle got hold of my .32 Derringer and started playing round with it. She shot herself. I got her rushed to the hospital where they assured me everything would be okay—and it was, and she turned out just great—but of course they needed a whole boatload of insurance information from me. So I called Stax. I was told, "Sorry, we can't help you on that because the federal marshals are here right now and they're closing up the place."

"It was the bank that forced three creditors to close us," says Al Bell. "They'd already foreclosed on East Memphis Music illegally, bought it themselves, sold it to one of the bank directors and stockholders in the company for the same amount of money that was in the bank at the time. Once they'd done that, the guys that were handling it, they said, 'Okay we've taken that publishing company, we're going to come back and take that record company and put that nigga in jail.' So they got three customers—one who sold us our toilet paper, one who developed our film, and the other supplied some electronic parts—and they came in, on December 19th 1975 between 11:30 and 11:45 a.m., to 926 E McLemore. I get a call in my office: 'The federal marshal wants to see you up front.' At this point, CBS owes us a million dollars, and we're fighting on that. So Stax was limited on the cash flow side, but still not bankrupt. I said, 'How much is the amount?' The Marshal said, '$1800.' I said, 'Well I got that much in my pocket, let me give it to you now.' And one of the guys from the Bank said, 'Nigga, you got 15 minutes to get out of the building, now take us to the master tape vault.'"

They called it "involuntary bankruptcy," and that's as may be. But all that really mattered was the result: Stax was padlocked that day. It was, truly, the end of an era.

Chapter 16
RAISE YOUR HAND

That first part of 1976 is a difficult time for all of us who've stayed at Stax until the end. Got to be hard for those who left, as well, knowing that the buildings are all padlocked, that Al Bell's got court cases as far ahead as the eye can see, that Jim Stewart may have lost everything he ever earned, and that none of us know what's happening with the catalog, whether the label's going to be bought, sold, revived, or destroyed. Add to that, our songwriting catalog is being managed by the bank. It's extra hard because Stax was never a normal record company. Like David Porter says, "There was magic at Stax that only comes around in rare, *rare* occasions—and it happened with *us*." Doesn't feel too magical right this minute, but we're holding on to our memories of the good times and pushing onwards regardless.

What keeps me going is what's always kept me going: songwriting. I'm more fortunate that some—though you can say I've earned that fortune—because I've written hits. And these are the kind of hits that keep on coming. "Knock on Wood," in particular, just won't lay down. I thought Ella was going to be the tops—and in many ways, it was—but no sooner is she done with it than along comes Joe Frazier.

Yeah, you read that right. Joe Frazier, the boxer. There was a lot of crossover between boxing and R&B. No shortage of musicians had tried their hand in the ring, with some of them, like Jackie Wilson, getting pretty good at it for a while. But very few musicians could punch above their weight in the recording studio.

Frazier was that rare exception, and, though he wasn't the greatest singer in the world, Capitol signed him for a couple of singles in 1969, shortly before he became the greatest boxer in the world. The fight that got him that heavyweight title took place on February 16, 1970, when—with Muhammad Ali out of contention, having been stripped of his boxing license after refusing to be drafted for the Vietnam war—Frazier beat WBA champion Jimmy Ellis at Madison Square Garden. The night before that bout, Frazier appeared on the Ed Sullivan show, in the middle of a boxing ring, singing "Knock on Wood!"

When Alan Walden and I heard about this, we wasted no time getting him down to the offices in Macon for a photo opportunity, and sure enough, we got the shots printed all over. I'm the one who put up the dukes when they said, "Let's get a picture." I hit him on the arm, and man, it was like hitting a wall! It wasn't long after Joe became heavyweight champion that Ali got back in the ring—he'd appealed his conviction all the way to the Supreme Court—and the two men lined up for what they called the "Fight of the Century" in March 1971. I remember the night of the fight; I was in Memphis, and we were all listening to the radio. My friends were all for Muhammad. I was too, but I told them about the time I hit Joe Frazier with my hand and it was like hitting a brick wall. So I said, "You know he's probably going to knock Ali out." And, well, he didn't knock Ali out, but he won the fight, which went the full fifteen rounds. I think all the guys were mad at me, but I really wasn't against Muhammad. I'd met him back in Miami when he was still Cassius Clay, when we were all starting out. Ali loved our music too.

Many years later, on my sixty-ninth birthday, I met Muhammad Ali again. One of my brothers lives up in Vandalia, Michigan, and his wife, Yvette, taught Ali's youngest son. They'd always be inviting me to stop by and see him, but I never felt like I wanted to do that, because I knew he was not well in himself; he had Parkinson's disease. But in 2006, I came in straight from playing Europe. It was my birthday, and I was doing this show with my brother, with his little band, in this restaurant during the daytime. I was singing at the time when I saw this Winnebago pull up—that was Muhammad getting out. He only stayed for the one song, and we took the pictures, and we hugged, and we talked just briefly, and then they got him back in. You could see he wasn't doing great.

Back in the mid-seventies, though, he was the King. And in 1974, even though neither of them was the world champion at the time, people wanted to see a rematch between Ali and Joe Frazier. Joe was still releasing singles every few months, and ahead of this second confrontation with Ali he recorded "Knock on Wood" for a 45. It's a real solid version, very, very funky, doesn't even use Cropper's famous guitar riff but comes up with one of its own. You should check it out. Joe lost that fight by unanimous decision but still wasn't the last time the two would

face off against each other. And as you now know, the third
time they met was the night we lost Al Jackson Jr.

Joe Frazier wasn't the only one covering "Knock on Wood"
at that time. In the summer of 1974, I hear about this guy David
Bowie coming through town looking for me. He's fresh out of
England, supposedly the big thing there at the time, and he's got
to be doing something right because he's playing the Mid-South
Coliseum, putting 10,000 people in there. We're all invited to
his show, but I can't go; I'm playing over in Georgia that night.
A couple of my musicians who don't have to come with me that
night go see Bowie in my place, and when they go backstage,
Bowie says how he'd really wanted to meet me. A few months
later I find out why when he puts out a single from that tour,
recorded just a couple of weeks after the Memphis show, up in
Philadelphia, and it's—you guessed it—"Knock on Wood." His
version is a lot more faithful to our Stax original than Joe Frazier's,
and you've got to know I'm happy when it makes the UK Top 10.
Then the album comes out—*David Live*, a double LP—and I guess
David Bowie must really be the big thing at the time, because it
makes the Top 10 in Britain *and* America, and when I take a look
at the record, "Knock on Wood" is the only song on all four sides
he didn't write himself. Not that I ever doubted it, but it's evident
that my songs are built to last. And hey, it's always good to be in
the charts. Never did get to meet David Bowie though.

So when Stax gets padlocked, I continue writing songs,
and so does my old friend Mack Rice, and we continue to
show up at the publishing office to play them to people and to
plot our futures. And because it's being run by the bank, and
it's something of a cash cow, East Memphis carries on signing
writers. Early in '76, a thin young white guy arrives from New
York City by the name of Jon Tiven. Nice enough kid, seems
to love our Memphis music as much as he's pushing his own,

and I'm appointed as his creative mentor. Jon remembers the
situation he walked into:

"Things were really grim. It wasn't just that Stax had closed
down. The bank had taken it over, everyone knew that there
was a lot of funny business going on. Everyone was convinced
we'd never see anything from Stax ever again, and whatever was
left there, people were raiding because it was ultimately sold off
for far less than it was worth. All the writers were about to get
screwed while all the executives pulled off this coup. . . . There
was a fair amount of resentment toward what had gone on at
Stax. But I walked into the East Memphis music thing, and
Eddie and Mac were just real welcoming and real nice to me.
We didn't do anything creatively together except hang around at
a place called Fridays and drink, but that was fine by me; I was
in awe of these two guys! White kid from Orange, Connecticut,
way too green to be qualified to do soul music, but really
enjoyed Eddie and Mack 'cause they were just great guys."

One day right at the end of April, Jon Tiven comes in to the
office and says, "There's this guy performing in town tonight,
Bruce Springsteen. I just got a call from his record company.
They say he's a big fan of yours and wants to see if you'll come
down to the soundcheck and maybe join him on stage for one of
your songs."

I said, "Bruce *who?*"

I'll let Bruce Springsteen explain the history for himself. "In
New Jersey in the 1960s, when I had my first band called the
Castiles," he recalls now, "soul music was very popular. If you
were a playing band it was essential to have some soul under
your belt, because crowds were somewhat integrated. And if
you played soldiers' clubs like Fort Myers, you played to an
integrated crowd and so you had to have some soul music going
down. And we played some soul revues where if we didn't know

a good amount of soul we were sunk. So you had to have a
healthy repertoire of soul under your belt as well as the rock 'n'
roll. And this seemed to be the case along the Jersey Shore. A)
people just loved it, even the frat boys, and B) it was common
ground for everybody. You couldn't go wrong with it."

Well, by 1976 Bruce Springsteen is a name, and he's on the road,
and he's playing the Ellis Auditorium on Main Street, just down the
road from Sammy's, the tailors. Place holds a few thousand, which
sounds impressive, but it's not the Mid-South Coliseum, like David
Bowie was playing when he asked to meet me. What Bruce *does*
have in common with this guy Bowie is that he covers my songs.

"The first thing for me of Eddie Floyd's that I learned was
'Knock on Wood,' because it was a bar band staple," he recalls.
"We learned that even before knowing who sang it or wrote
it, and we played that regularly at all the clubs. Then when I
got together with the E. Street Band, my manager Jon Landau
was a huge soul music fan and he just turned me on to various
different things. So Jon played me 'Raise Your Hand' and
then 'Love Is a Doggone Good Thing.' And 'Big Bird.' And
these songs really came into our repertoire. But on that 1976
American tour for *Born to Run*, it was 'Raise Your Hand' that
we played regularly—as a show closer."

I had nothing to do that day in Memphis, so I got in the
car and drove down to meet Bruce. I didn't really want to go
by myself so this guy Carl Wise, who was employed at East
Memphis, he was a big fan of Bruce, and he came along with
me. At soundcheck, I met the E. Street Band—Steve Van Zandt,
Roy Bittan, Clarence Clemons—and it was obvious, they were
a good band. And I meet Bruce and he seems real excited about
it and he says he does five of my songs, and I'm thinking, he
does *five* of my songs? Is this man for real? But he told me the
titles, and then he actually played them for me, and one by one

I'm saying, "No I don't do that one anymore," and as this keeps happening, I'm laughing; this guy knows my songs better than me! The only two that I did myself as far as me out performing, was "Knock on Wood" and "Raise Your Hand." So we agreed we'd perform them together that night.

"This was a big deal," says Bruce, looking back on it. "I've never had anyone famous come join me on stage before now. But we're going to Memphis and somebody suggested, 'What about Eddie Floyd?' We ended up getting together and he came on stage, and it was a huge thrill and he sounded phenomenal. He was completely at his peak."

You might think this was a big deal for me as well, but the Ellis wasn't sold out. It was a good show, but it was still on the low key. Bruce was riding the bus just like everybody else. I think Jon Tiven told me he'd originally been booked into the Mid-South Coliseum but they moved the show because it hadn't sold well. I'm thinking, well, that's no surprise, nobody knows this guy and then, when I was getting ready to go out on stage, Bruce is playing this song; it's real long, called "Rosalita" I think. And I hear him saying something to the crowd about "I ain't no freak, 'cause I got my picture on the cover of *Time* and *Newsweek*." And that part of it was for real! It turns out he was on the brink of becoming a superstar—but down South, he was still something of an unknown quantity.

"He wasn't getting a lot of radio play," says Jon Tiven. "There wasn't a tremendous sense of cultural awareness of who Bruce Springsteen was in Memphis at that time. The *Born to Run* explosion was happening in certain territories in a big way, and in certain territories not at all, and Memphis was one of the 'not-at-alls.'"

Well, that's as may be. I certainly had fun that night, 'cause when they're finally done with this song "Rosalita," Bruce gives me this really nice introduction, went like this:

"I'm honored enough to have in the audience tonight a man I have admired and listened to his music for many years. Without his music I wouldn't be here because he's the guy turned me on to the whole Stax sound, the whole R&B sound, he's written so many great songs I can't even mention them. He's going to come out and do a few numbers with us. Please give a warm welcome for Mr. Eddie Floyd."

The guitarist, "Little" Stevie, plays the opening fanfare of "Raise Your Hands" just like Cropper, and then it's my turn. *Come on everybody clap your hands!* This is what I do. And in this environment, it's taking me back to Europe 1967.

"He was a classic full-on performer," recalls Bruce of my contribution. "He just came out and knocked the place out. It was our audience, which was a very young audience. So they may not have known who *he* was! All they knew was that he was a guest of ours, but then he came on stage and he was a storm, you know. He just went down incredible."

We do "Raise Your Hand" and "Knock on Wood" and at the end of "Knock on Wood" we vamp for a while on "Yum Yum Yum." Then as I'm leaving the stage, Bruce gives me an amazing compliment, calls me "the man that wrote the book."

"I was aware of the songs that he was singing," says Bruce. "I wasn't aware that he wrote '634–5789' and a variety of other things. That's some incredible writing. We still play 'Raise Your Hand' semi-regularly to this day. And we play '634' also. If I'm in a club, I play that."

Bruce asked, would I go down to Birmingham the next night, but I had a show of my own, and I couldn't go. We all got on with our lives. I'm not sure when I became aware that Bruce Springsteen had become one of the biggest names in American rock 'n' roll, *ever*. But the great thing about it was that he carried on playing my songs! When he released the record

Live/1975–85—five LPs worth!—he included "Raise Your Hand" from a 1978 show in LA that had gone out on the radio at the time. It's a real fired-up version. Bruce is saying to the crowd, "You want to play, you got to *pay!*" and telling people to turn up their radios, open their windows, and. . . . "Raise Your Hand." I understand that in England they camped out all night to buy the album. I was told that by Steve Cropper. I heard the record in Montgomery at home that night, a station I would probably never have turned to. Steve called me and, within minutes of my finding the station, they were playing the new Bruce, *75–85*. Recently I saw footage of him in 2012, singing "634-5789" at the Harlem Apollo—my old haunt!— and he's climbing up into the balcony while he does so! This is a performer after my own heart!

"Eddie's songs are all show stoppers," says Bruce today. "They're just great call-and-response songs. Y'know, the audience sings back tremendously on those. They all swing in a certain way and that's unique to them. It's like this. . . . It's the end of the night: 'Raise Your Hand!' You don't need anything else but that! That's what you're telling the crowd at the end of the night and it's just a perfect song to close the night with."

Amen.

Chapter 17
MOTHER, DEAR MOTHER

Just because Stax had gone out of business didn't mean that our music was on the skids. Far from it. The Staple Singers had a number-one single at the end of 1975 with "Let's Do It Again," their first release for Curtis Mayfield's Curtom label. And at the start of 1976, barely skipping a beat, Johnnie Taylor showed up on Columbia, the same label that had treated Stax so badly, with our old friend Don Davis producing, and got himself the first *ever* official platinum disc, for 1,000,000 sales. By the time "Disco Lady" had finished its run on top of both pop and R&B charts, it had doubled that! I guess Don and Johnnie knew which way the musical wind was blowing: the word *soul* had long given way to *funk* and was now being taken over by *disco.* Looking back on it all you can talk about the "era" of this or that but, at the time, the music itself just felt like a steady progression; wasn't too much that was different about Taylor's "Disco Lady" on Columbia than some of the later cuts on Stax that were still being called out as "soul."

My own focus shifted three hours south, to Jackson, state capital of Mississippi, and the home of Malaco Records. Malaco had grown out of a talent agency started in the early 1960s by Mitchell Malouf and Tommy Couch; by the end of the decade, they'd set up a recording studio, launched a small label, Chimneyville, and were looking to license out their recordings as often as they could. Like a lot of the independents of that era, they were just about holding on.

Then, in 1970, this guy around forty years old already, by the name of Wardell Quezerque, who had a history down the road in New Orleans extending back to Fats Domino and Professor Longhair, came to Malaco with a suggestion: give him the studio time and the session musicians so he could record some vocalists he had in mind on some songs he had in his bag, and Malaco could have first shot at the results. When Malaco went along with this, Wardell hired a damn school bus and brought five different artists up from New Orleans to record on the same day! Jean Knight and King Floyd were among them. King Floyd was no relation of mine, by the way—though you could say he had something royal in common with my father, Prince Floyd!

Anyway, Wardell recorded the songs he had in mind, and then Malaco shopped them, sending them up to Stax and other labels. They had a connection up there in Memphis in our publisher Tim Whitsett. Tim was from Jackson, had a band in the sixties called the Royal Imperials—he told me they played "Knock on Wood" up and down America—and for a while there that band had included a Jackson singer by the name of Dorothy Moore, whose father was one of the Five Blind Boys of Mississippi and who'd also had her own girl group, the Poppies. Tim liked what he heard, especially the Jean Knight record, "Mr. Big Stuff," but he couldn't get a commitment from Al Bell or Jim Stewart on either artist. So Malaco went ahead and put out King Floyd's "Groove Me" on their own little Chimneyville label, and when it got action, which was no surprise given how well it swung, Atlantic snapped it up for distribution. The single promptly spent a month on top of the R&B charts, hitting the pop Top 10 along the way. Back in Memphis, Tim went back to Al and Jim and said: "Are you *sure* you don't want to take a chance on 'Mr. Big Stuff'?"

Funny what someone else's hit record can do to your ears. Tim gets the green light, Stax signs Jean Knight, and six months after "Groove Me," "Mr. Big Stuff" also goes number one R&B, rises to number *two* pop—and sells two million damn copies. Malaco has its name on the map, Stax has more money in the bank—those were the good times!—and Wardell Quezerque has two new number ones under his belt, both recorded on the same day. And the best news of all is, he sticks around at Malaco to oversee and arrange a lot of the sessions.

After that, a lot of musicians came from Stax—and elsewhere—to Malaco to record. I was one of them. And some of the musicians came up from Jackson to Memphis. Tim Whitsett's brother Carson was one of *them*. There was talk of him taking Booker T. Jones's role in a reformed M.G.'s, because Carson plays organ, and he definitely was capable, that's for sure. But it didn't happen. Al Jackson's murder more than put the lid on that idea. When it was obvious that Stax was going under, Tim Whitsett suggested to some of us that we should talk to Mitchell and Tommy. So I go down to Malaco with a bag of songs in late 1975. When I get there, I find Dorothy Moore and this other girl, Jewel Bass, doing demos. They played me

Dorothy's take on the old country classic "Misty Blue," and I was just waiting for everyone to say the same thing: "That's a hit!"

Turned out "Misty Blue" had been cut two years earlier and rejected by every company Malaco sent it to. Some things just don't change! And during that time, King Floyd and Jean Knight had each dropped off the charts and lost their licensing deals. Strapped for money—again!—Couch and Malouf had taken another listen to "Misty Blue" and figured, "What do we have to lose?" They brought Dorothy back to add an introduction vocal, Jimmy Johnson popped down from Muscle Shoals to update a guitar track he'd laid down two years earlier, and Henry Stone in Miami agreed to distribute the track through his T.K. company, which was seriously happening at the time. The rest, as they say, is history. I was back down in Jackson a few weeks later when the song went 85 in *Billboard*—with a bullet. But it didn't stop there. "Misty Blue" ended up at number one R&B, number three pop, and was a Top 10 hit all around the world. Talk about perfect timing! The very month that Stax folds, the South has a new soul label to spread the musical gospel. And when I say gospel, I mean that for real, because right around that same time, Malaco signed up many of the vocal groups that had been on the old gospel highway, starting with the Jackson Southernaires and going on to include the Soul Stirrers, the Sensational Nightingales, and many more.

Well now, "Misty Blue" was such an international phenomenon that Dorothy Moore needed to cut an album, and soon. Me and Dorothy hit it off right away; she's a beautiful woman, wonderful voice, pure soul sister. We've been friends now for almost fifty years. For her *Misty Blue* album, she recorded "I Don't Want Nobody but You," which I'd put out on *Soul Street*, and proved my faith in the song as she took it all the way to church. Then she closed out the album with two new songs: "Too Much Love," a dirty funky track I wrote with

Carson, and "It's So Good," not so dirty musically but one of the more erotic lyrics I ever put down on paper. *Misty Blue* spent months in the album charts all over the world.

So Eddie Floyd, songwriter, is doing just fine, with old songs *and* new. As for Eddie Floyd the singer, he ain't down at Malaco with Dorothy but five minutes before he's invited to cut his own tracks too. Over the next couple of years, I released five singles on Malaco. One of them, "We Should Really Be in Love," was a duet with Dorothy that reworked my old B-side from "Blood Is Thicker than Water" and gave it some real passion. We backed it up with another duet, a song I'd written with Booker that had yet to see the light of day, "I'll Never Be Loved." Sweet single. If you've never heard it, do yourself the favor. Like my other releases for Malaco, it didn't chart, but the charts were changing anyway. Main thing was, we were having good times. My singles swung all over the place: "Chi Town Hustler" was me digging deep into disco a little ahead of the times, while "Somebody Touch Me" was more of a classic old-school soul stomper. A few of the tracks got released as singles in the UK on Contempo, a new label set up by John Abbey, the editor of *Blues and Soul*, and that gave me ongoing attention in Britain, which would serve me well down the line.

But one single from my time at Malaco stands out from the others. It was released at the end of 1976, my first holiday single since the Falcons put out "Can This Be Christmas" in 1957! The flip side, "Special Christmas Day," was clear on the subject. The A-side also mentioned Christmas, but only at the very beginning and end of the song. Other than that, "Mother, Dear Mother" was a song purely for my mom. I didn't care whoever else heard it. I mean, hopefully everyone who would hear the song would like the song, but it was for *her*. And when she heard the song and heard what I said, and, well, she didn't have to ask for no more explanation. It was a spiritual record about my unconditional love for my mother. In arrangement, melody, and delivery, it was the closest I'd ever got to gospel. "I know you taught me right from wrong/you said that God would protect me from all harm."

I say it was for my mom, but really it was for her *and* my grandma, just me and those two. After we got it pressed, I went over to Montgomery with it, got a little record player, and played it for them. And then I had to run left and right because both of them were breaking up! I had to come back and just embrace them both. That was a plus. After that, I started writing a lot of gospel songs. And they're all about my mother and my grandmother, every one of them. None of them has ever been released. They're for me—and for them.

This is going to sound funny, but my mother never saw me in a show. I know you say, how is that possible? But it's like, when I started singing, she wasn't around me, up in Detroit. And once I got big with the Falcons, my mom is beginning to age and she doesn't want to go to places so much, especially not the nightclubs.

So it was only once in Detroit that she came to see me. This is way back with the Falcons; we played a theater, and I had my driver take her and said, "Make sure my mom is down in the front seat so she can see the show up close," not really thinking. I come out and sing with the Falcons, don't see her. Can't wait to get off stage. What happened to her? The driver says he had to take her back to the hotel. Turned out the band started up in the theater, and it was so loud, and she's getting older, and she said it shook her up. She hadn't been in a theater since I was a kid; she wasn't used to that! It was just too loud for her. It was a matinee, and I thought if maybe she went to that where there weren't many people, it would be okay. But it wasn't. So that was a big mistake.

Still, everything that I've done, all the way through my whole career, for as long as she was with me on earth, I made sure she had it. Europe, America, any TV show I did, any record I made, I said I'm going to make sure you've got all the tapes. And if you went to the house, she'd make sure you heard it and saw it!

When Florence West Floyd did finally pass, in 1993, I sung "Mother, Dear Mother" at her funeral. Because, you know, the song did kind of anticipate that moment. "When He calls you to come home, I know He'll save a place for you by His throne." I've since heard from other people that they took comfort in that song when they lost their own mothers. That's a bonus.

The sessions at Malaco were generally real positive. It was a Mississippi thing, a different vibe from Memphis and just as good in its own way. When it came time to record an album there, I had Carson on keyboards, James Stroud on drums, Dino Zimmerman on guitar, and Don Barrett on bass. We brought the horn section down from Muscle Shoals—led by Harrison Callaway, who was also a songwriter. Wardell Quezerque arranged the strings, which was a home-grown group of Jackson players. And for background vocals I was truly blessed. Who wouldn't be if they could get the likes of King Floyd, Jewel Bass, Tommy Tate, and my old songwriting and recording friends Joe Shamwell and Mack Rice in the room with them?

Mack coproduced the album and wrote a couple of songs for me. We're twenty years on from the Falcons now and still tight as ever. With one exception, all the other songs were purely my own. *Experience* came out in 1977, the same year as that fine duet with Dorothy, but it was a strange time in music. Sounds started changing, ideas changing. Disco was the new thing. It wasn't like we didn't have the connections at Malaco, because Henry Stone and his T.K. company had KC & The Sunshine Band, George McRae and his sister Gwen, and his Miami studio hosted the Bee Gees for the sessions that made *Saturday Night*

Fever the biggest thing since sliced bread. So maybe Henry was focused on things other than Malaco. You only had to look at that movie to see that the music was being geared to a new, younger and—should I say it?—white audience. What we were doing down in Malaco was authentic, from the heart. Those who were listening to it dug it all right. But I was forty years old now and maybe, at this moment, at least when it came down to me, what we were doing in the Deep South didn't quite fit in.

Chapter 18
KNOCK ON WOOD (ENCORE)

Come the end of 1978 and disco has knocked some of us soul brothers and sisters out of the park. Almost everywhere you turn, almost every time you turn on the radio, you hear that beat. *Boom boom Boom boom.* It's changed so much now even from Johnnie Taylor and "Disco Lady." Ever since Donna Summer came on the scene, it's gotten more robotic. There are synthesizers now, and programmed drums instead of a real drummer. It's hard for us to get a look-in.

Earlier that year, I released a couple of singles on Mercury. It was an easy connection: Jud Phillips, the brother of Sun Records' founder Sam, has been running the label's office down in Memphis for years now. A lot of us from Stax were going over to him: William Bell, Con Funk Shun, the Bar-Kays . . . In fact, William's just had a number-one R&B hit on Mercury with "Tryin' to Love Two." Top 10 pop as well. Believe it or not, it's the only pop hit he's ever had, and this is the man who sung "Private Number" and "You Don't Miss Your Water." Anyways, I wrote all four songs with my wife, Sonja; she was there with me during the process, and it felt like crediting her was the right thing to do. One of them we called "Disco Summer," and although it didn't have a disco beat to it, didn't really sound nothing like disco to be honest, I still put the word in there—so maybe I was trying to go along with that whole movement. Not that it helped.

But then toward the end of the year, it happens, again. Someone calls me up and says, "Eddie, they've got a new record out on one of your songs." It's "Knock on Wood," again. I hear the intro, and this being the era of disco, it sounds right to me. But there's something else about that intro. It's different. Different than all the cover versions I've heard until now, and different from the other disco too. And then the way this woman started singing it was *definitely* different! The production was unique, and her voice was outstanding.

Turns out her name is Amii Stewart, and she's from D.C., my old home town, one of eleven children, born the same year the Falcons made their first record! She's a natural singer all right, but more than that, she's got a background in ballet. She'd been out on the road in a musical revue about the great Harlem musicians, *Bubbling Brown Sugar*, and it was when the musical hit London that she was spotted and signed, by a Brit called Barry Leng, to Hansa Records. The label was based out of a studio of the same name in Berlin, Germany. Boney M was on Hansa, so they knew about disco already. The first single they do with Amii is one of Barry's own songs, and it doesn't sell, so maybe

that's why they went down that tried and tested path of having
her do someone else's song, a song people knew well enough
but had never heard in a disco style. Why they chose "Knock on
Wood" I never discovered. They recorded it in London, at a tiny
little studio in Fulham called TW. The engineer was a young
guy called Alan Winstanley; Barry Leng was the producer.

Like I said already, Amii's voice was outstanding; you knew
the woman was coming to this with some serious soul. But she
had a fierce look to her, too—or at least she did by the time
the label got her dressed up! I saw someone recently describe it
as "Egyptian/Martian Disco Queen," which about sums it up!
Because Amii was a dancer, they could put her in a promotional
film, and people wanted to watch. So it was the whole package,
from the production to the look to the voice to the video. Oh,
and the song, as well. It's that thing about "Knock on Wood." It
works in any style.

Certainly worked as disco. Quickly got to the point I couldn't
turn on the radio without hearing my song. Soon enough, Amii
Stewart's "Knock on Wood" went up the charts in the UK, and
then it went up in the charts in the States, and then it went up the
charts all over the world. I couldn't keep track. Except for one
week, in April 1979, that I wouldn't forget in a hurry: that was
when "Knock on Wood" went to number one on the American
Hot 100. When you start out, you're always hoping something like
that will happen. You don't ever want to think it *won't*, especially
if you're not just a singer but, like me, a songwriter as well. Still,
when it does finally take place, it's a little hard to believe.

It was the time for it, of course. You look at all the other
number-one singles from the first half of 1979, and you can see
that the music business had gone disco crazy. The Bee Gees,
Gloria Gaynor, Donna Summer . . . even Blondie and Rod
Stewart had thrown their lot in with the disco sound. And just

a few weeks later, there was another number-one disco single, "Ring My Bell" by Anita Ward. It was written by my friend Frederic Knight and recorded at Malaco! You can't keep a good Stax man down!

Thanks to Amii Stewart, I knew my finances were going to be all right for a while. That was a good thing, given that I didn't have a record label to record with any more. But I wasn't dependent on handouts either. You know up top I said "almost" everywhere you turned by the end of 1978, it was disco? Well, if you turned on *Saturday Night Live,* you'd also see John Belushi and Dan Aykroyd dressed up like they were playing the R&B clubs back in the 1960s. They called themselves the Blues Brothers and what started out as a skit soon became a best-selling album, *Briefcase Full of Blues,* which they recorded on stage in Los Angeles. Their band was anchored by Steve Cropper and Donald "Duck" Dunn and the drummer Willie Hall, along with Matt "Guitar" Murphy, and Lou Marini and Tommy Malone on brass. And the set list included "Groove Me," "Soul Man," and "I Can't Turn You Loose." In 1980, it resulted in *that* movie: *The Blues Brothers.* I hope you've seen it. Directed by Jon Landis, funny as shit, and with some of the best musical performances and cameos you could ask for. Cropper and Dunn become film stars overnight! But not just them: *The Blues Brothers* movie goes a long way to bringing the sound and vision of Ray Charles, Aretha Franklin, and James Brown into the hearts and minds of a younger generation. I mean, Belushi and Aykroyd may have called themselves the Blues Brothers, but their first hit was with "Soul Man." So boom! we know right away they're doing soul music.

Meantime, disco is a double-edged sword. Sure, it's put "Knock on Wood" at number one. But in America especially, they didn't want to see the artists anymore, just wanted to hear your record in a club. So I went to London because they had both. They had all these ballrooms with the big old floors—the Decca Ballrooms and places like that—where they could put the lights in, have their dirty dancing or whatever you want to call it, and then they'd have an hour of soul music, and they'd bring an English band in or a band from the States. I found out there was space for me, in that area of time, where you don't know things are going to turn around until they do turn around. I stayed busy throughout, just never stopped.

Something else was going on over in England at the time too. I didn't totally get the punk/new wave thing, but out of it a younger generation had gone back to the 1960s and the whole "mod" scene that had produced not just the big British bands of the day, but the kids who bought American R&B singles and made them popular in the first place. There were some new bands on the scene introducing Motown and Stax singles into their live shows, and one of those groups, Secret Affair, had its own record label, I-Spy. They put out some records by one of the original Jamaican ska singers, Laurel Aitken. The only other artist to release something on I-Spy was Mr. Eddie Floyd.

It was Tim Whitsett who set up the deal for me. He was at Chrysalis Music in London by now, and he knew everyone over there. I'd been recording an album back home, at Malaco, with his brother Carson co-producing. Funny how time flies: Carson and I had been working together for ten years already! We used Andrew Love and the Memphis Horns, and when Tim talked about I-Spy, we tailored a couple of the cuts for that British sound. "The Beat Song" was about one of those records you used to dance and date to; the other side, "London," was my tribute to a city that had always done me proud. "We got soul in good old London town/ people come from miles and miles." We were hoping I-Spy would pick up the album too, but that didn't happen.

Still, I was getting bookings over in England. Lots of them. It was keeping me busy. I could jump from the discos to the live circuit and back again. And it was during that period, in September 1981, that I got asked to join a group called the Q-Tips at the Marquee Club on Wardour Street, in the middle of Soho. The Q-Tips were like a British M.G.'s or Mar-Keys. They had the horns, the rhythm section, they were playing our songs. And up front they had this singer who would go on to do major business on his own, Paul Young.

"The Q-Tips had a great name as a live act," says Paul. "If anything, we were too authentic, and people weren't really getting it; some people thought it was just an old record getting played on the radio when we were writing our own material."

At the time I met them, the Q-Tips were in the studio with Al Kooper, the same guy who signed Lynyrd Skynyrd about ten years earlier, when I was working with Alan Walden on our own company. The studio in question was on Wardour Street in Soho, out back of the Marquee Club. The Q-Tips were on Chrysalis at the time, so it was probably Tim Whitsett who suggested it would be good promo for all of us if I came down to join the group when they headlined the club that same week.

We arrived at doing "Raise Your Hand" and "'Knock on Wood.'" Now, for me, this is just business as usual; I sometimes forget that for younger people, those still on the way up and who know their history, it's business *un*usual!

"That was my first encounter with a hero," says Paul, though if he said that to me in person, I'd probably be looking around to see who he's talking about! "I don't think I'd ever met, let alone sang with anyone from the era that I loved so much. 'Love Is a Doggone Good Thing,' 'Things Get Better,' 'I've Never Found a Girl,' I love all those songs. So for us to meet Eddie and get to sing with him was great, so exciting. I remember we kept apologizing for the dressing rooms at the Marquee; they were terrible. My abiding memory is how scruffy the room looked, but then Eddie arrived in his stage outfit. So we had to do the whole of our set before he came on, and he was already in his stage clothes, and he had like a smoking jacket over the top."

When I finally got on stage, I could tell that Paul was nervous. So when it's his turn to sing, I let him know as much: "Come on, Paul!" "That was the great thing," Paul recalls now. "He was giving me a pointer to make sure that I knew that I had to come in on the second verse. So he was coaching me through it just in case I was getting too excited to realize I was coming up next. It was really nice when you're working with an artist who gives you these little pointers. Because I've worked with a lot of people where you say what you're going to do together, then you get on stage, and their aim is to upstage you. And that's not Eddie's way at all—Eddie's way is to make *you* look good."

For my part, I'm happy to sing the song, but I don't know there's a studio next door *recording* the song. I was surprised later on when I saw myself on an LP by the Q-Tips.

"I think we thought we would try and record the show," says Paul now, "and maybe use it for a single or an EP or something. But then we were dropped by the label! And they put out a live album anyway. It was all quite strange."

Still, that version of "Raise Your Hand" came out real good. "You can hear that I'm trying to curb my excitement on the vocal." says Paul. "I was so excited, I was singing in a key I don't normally sing in, and I hit notes on that record I will probably never hit again! There's a lot of volume there—Eddie definitely sings right from the diaphragm. That style of singing has died out, and everyone has gone over to this quiet style of singing that's taught by all the vocal coaches, where you don't push it too much. But Eddie was definitely of that era when it was all about posture and the voice being very big."

It was only a year or so after that that Paul Young went solo and had a big British number-one hit with his version of the old Marvin Gaye song, "Wherever I Lay My Hat (That's My Home)." And then only a year or so after that, he does the same thing in the States with "Every Time You Go Away," written by Daryl Hall, same guy who calls "I've Never Found a Girl" his favorite song in the world. For a while there, it's Paul Young who is the new blue-eyed boy of soul!

Many years later, we saw each other perform again when I was with Bill Wyman's Rhythm Kings. I told him, "Paul, I've been waiting twenty-five years to say to you, 'Congratulations on your success.'"

"In terms of being a person, he didn't let me down," says Paul, and again, I appreciate it. "He was solid, good, well-mannered, a gentleman. You want to be impressed by people you've admired, and I can probably quite truthfully say that when I've got up to sing with most other people, they haven't been half as accommodating as Eddie. They're all out for their own gain. But not Eddie."

Years later, I find myself working with Tim Whitsett again, and he understands the whole new digital and streaming market better than me, so we put out the album I recorded back at the time, the one with "London" and "The Beat Song." It's got me doing my own song "I Will Always Have Faith in You" for the first time and a whole heap of material that never saw release anywhere else: "Missing You," "It's So Easy," "You Must Have Been Dreaming." What I really like about the set is that the Memphis Horns played just like the horn sections over in the UK at the time, so you can't hear much difference between *them* and the section that fronted the Q-Tips. And you've got the evidence on that album, because we opened *Power* with the live version of "Raise Your Hand" from the Marquee. The album's from Jackson, Mississippi, but it's a London, England, record too. Both places feel like home.

Chapter 19
SOUL IS BACK AGAIN

By 1982, disco has run its course and the music business is in recession, but us soul singers are still out there working it. We haven't stopped. We *can't* stop. For those of us who've lived our whole lives in the music, this is who we are, this is what we do. We're soul men. And women. And because there's a lot of us still happily at it, then we know that if we team up together, the bookings will be that much better. This explains why my buddy John Abbey, the editor of *Blues & Soul* who also runs the Contempo label that put out my Malaco records in the UK, calls up about a tour he's looking to take around Europe. He wants me, Carla Thomas, Sam Moore, and Wilson Pickett.

Now Carla and I, as you know, are best of friends. Us going on the road together, couldn't be nothing more easy. Sam Moore, though, this will be his first time going out solo. After Atlantic took Sam & Dave back from Stax, their career took a dive. It was never as good for them as it had been when they had Hayes & Porter writing their songs and the M.G.'s backing them. Sam's been through some hard times since then, stuff he's talked about over the years, so it's no secret, but the good news is he's finally coming out the other side. He's ready to reclaim his name. He's gonna have to work twice as hard without a partner on stage, but he seems to be up for the challenge.

As for Pickett, things have not been going well for my old Falcons brother either. At the start of the 1970s, there may have been nobody bigger in all of southern soul: as well as gold singles and Top 10 hits galore, he was the headliner of the first ever R&B/soul package to travel to Africa. Then he signed to RCA for big bucks and went out to Vegas. But the label didn't know how to handle him; his records stopped selling, and the casino bookings dried up. Pickett tried his own hand at disco in the late '70s, recording an album with Rick Hall in Muscle Shoals, and it didn't do nothing. In '81 he got together with some of his old Atlantic Records brothers to revive this thing they had for five minutes in the 1960s, Solomon Burke's idea for a movement of musicians called the Soul Clan, and that didn't work out either. Now his wife's gone left him, and he's getting deep into some dark shit. Just to add to the problems, him and Sam got some beef between them.

I knew something was wrong with him on that tour right away 'cause Pickett reacted as soon as he saw Sam. It was when we got to the airport in New York; the flight wasn't leaving that night, and we had to check into the hotel at Kennedy. Now we are ready to go eat dinner, Pickett's downstairs eating first, and as

soon as Sam and his partner Joyce—now his wife—came through
the door, the brother went berserk. "That's it! Everybody leave!"
Pickett tells the people that's working for him that he wants to
have a meeting with everybody on the show. That's when the shit
hit the fan, 'cause who wants to have a goddamn meeting? *You*
ain't the promoter. But hey, Pickett was headlining the show—for
all his problems he was still the star attraction.

"Oh, fuck Pickett," says Carla.

"No, I'll go up, I wanna see what he's gonna say," I tell
her. So I go up there, and he starts telling these other people
working for him, "You find him yet?" and it's obvious he means
Sam, but they ain't really looking for him. They ain't doing that
shit. It was funny: "You got to go out in the hall . . . tear every
door down." They're not going to do that! Then he starts in on,
"I wanna know if everybody's with me or not."

He looks at me. Says, "I don't know about Eddie 'cause he
don't say nothing."

Eddie ain't said nothing 'cause if he *start* saying something,
then we got problems. I'm just looking at him, getting ready to
leave any damn way. I'm bored with all this. You're not paying
me! Same time, I'm trying to keep the peace.

"Eddie was like the sheriff on that whole tour," was how
John Abbey looks back on it. "I think Eddie kept Pickett out
of an awful lot of trouble, because Eddie's got that big brother
attitude towards everybody. On that particular tour, on the crazy
days with Pickett, I can't tell you how many times he helped me
out. Plus, Eddie looks as though he can look after himself. And I
get the feeling that Pickett knew that. I think if there was a fight,
Eddie would probably come out tops with most people."

Well, let me put it this way: I don't play. We'd have an
argument every time Pickett come up with something crazy,
and I'd just say, "Get out of my goddamn face, Wilson Pickett."

But, and I want you to know this as well, we ain't never *had* a fight. Never. It's like when Cropper says about "634–5789," that "they lunged across the room at each other." No, we *hollered* across the room at each other.

Still, the tour is trouble the whole way. We went to Finland, Norway, snow up your ass everywhere you turn, and every night I went to one of these gigs, it was like being in hell. Not for me or Carla onstage—we're both professionals—but with Pickett and Sam and whatever the problem is between them. Things get so bad that Sam and Joyce hire a bodyguard at the hotel in Portugal, and the guy looks like Shaft! They have him outside the door with a gun, so Pickett knows not to come after Sam no more!

Something bad has got to happen, because this tour is not blessed, no goddamn way. We get to Italy, and I'm in a room next to Pickett, and I got a cassette player, just narrating a whole lot of stuff just like a book for myself, and all of a sudden I hear someone holler. And then I hear Pickett say,

"Get his legs and throw him over the balcony."

We're eleven floors up; now how they gonna do *that?* And this was an old guy—his road manager.

Y' know, you always hear about this stuff in the music business, about someone being hung over a balcony by their ankles until they sign over their lives. I guess Pickett heard them old stories too! But you never think you're going to see it! Now this was one of those hotels where it's built around a courtyard, so everyone could see it for themselves! And when they do, someone calls the Italian police, and they take him off to jail. He's going down the hallway between them, looking back over and saying, "Have his motherfucking ass out of here by goddamn morning before I come back." He knows he's going to jail, and he don't give a fuck! And believe me, the next morning his road manager was *gone.*

That day we're on a flight to Paris. Pickett's causing so much commotion he starts knocking his own self out! He's hitting his own self in the chair! Mad. Talking shit. Pickett walks up the aisle, hammers on the captain's door, the captain comes out, looks at him, shuts the door again—and locks it! When we land, I know what's going to happen. Door opens up, and here come some big motherfucking gendarmes. They take him off first. When we walk into the terminal, Pickett's just sitting there—they didn't do nothing but walk him off the plane!

We're at the Olympia in Paris that night. Famous venue. Beautiful place. We know it's going to come down, though. Sure enough, Pickett goes on stage, sings about one goddamn song, gets the people excited—and then stops, comes back to the dressing room. They tore the seats out of that fucker! John Abbey ended the tour there and then, which we figured was what Pickett was after anyways. Either way, I never saw him again on that tour. There was only one flight going back to the States and Pickett didn't get on it. He went to Ghana, instead. Maybe he felt at home there after being greeted like a king back in 1971. But the tour was cut short by a whole week. The dates in England? Gone. The pay? Gone with it.

Now I tell you all of this because I know it's the kind of story you want to hear. But what I also want you to know is that Pickett was the kind of cat you couldn't really hold a grudge against. Years down the line he apologized for his behavior on that tour. And years further down the line from *that*, Pickett and I got to team up once more, and do it *right*. He's crazy, but at the end of the day, he's still my soul brother.

As the 1980s went on, a number of us soul singers who had been so prominent in the 1960s were struggling to find our place. The old hits were still getting some sales, sometimes getting rereleased even, and the compilations were starting to pile up. If you had a hand in writing them, like I did, then the royalties would help get you through the lean times. Because, although I'm one of the most positive guys you could hope to meet, they were now lean times. We'd just about held on during the early days of disco—and I'd done better than most thanks to Amii Stewart's "Knock on Wood"—but once disco collapsed, the industry collapsed with it, and the labels had no money to support older artists like ourselves. The new R&B street sound of the 1980s, electro and hip-hop, sounded nothing like soul music. It was mechanical, with drum machines, synthesizers and other new MIDI keyboards, and much of it had rapping on top. Sure, the DJs behind the rappers sampled James Brown left, right, and center, so James was still on the dance floor, but he wasn't getting paid for it. The Godfather of Soul couldn't even get a record deal. And if James Brown couldn't get a deal . . .

Then MTV came on the air, and attention switched from how you sounded on the radio to how you looked in a video. And MTV wanted you to look whiter than whitey. Was *years* before they broke down and started showing videos by black artists—and even then we're talking Michael Jackson and Prince. MTV didn't put hip-hop out there until the rock group Aerosmith teamed up with Run DMC. Most of us from the Stax era and around, we became *oldies* acts. Put us on a package tour like the one in 1982 and we could at least get out and do what we loved to do—which was get on stage and get paid for it. The down side? Having the likes of Pickett join us in the midst of his madness.

Me, I never stopped writing, and in the middle of the decade, I went down to New Orleans to do a duet with a singer called Tamiko Jones at the Sea-Saint Studio. That studio was a play on words—it was co-owned by the great producer Allen Toussaint, along with his partner, the all-rounder Marshall Sehorn. Allen was a true musical legend, though I never met him. Marshall we knew from up at Stax; he was always busy finding artists, making records, hustling deals. Down at Sea-Saint, we did the duet, and then, me being there and being an artist, I thought, *Well I got some songs, we're still in the studio,* and so we put a whole bunch of them down. Some was pure fun—"Looking for Girls" and "I'm So Funkful"—and some was deep, like "Our Love Will Survive" and "Look What Your Love Has Done to Me." Still, I leave. I got copies of all the songs we recorded, so hey, good enough for me. Far as I'm concerned, these are demos. A few years down the line, I'm in Japan when some girl hands me an album to sign. I look at it, and immediately I'm thinking, *What's this?*

There's a black-and-white picture of Eddie on the front, big Afro, three-piece cream-colored suit, wide collar, gold chain. I know that picture. I took it with a guy named Fred Toma in Memphis; he had me sitting at a desk, looking straight at myself in a mirror. I was using that picture as promotion. Now it's in front of me, on an LP sleeve, nine times over. The album's called *Try Me,* and I'm thinking, *Try me?* Like James Brown? Flip it over, it's on this New York label called Easy Street. When I ask around, Easy Street is a dance label, putting out all this electro and hip-hop, mostly singles, a lot of them in the new 12" format that had been around since Amii Stewart ran "Knock on Wood" a full six minutes on the dance floor. Easy Street could be the next Stax for all I know, but I still can't figure out what they're doing with an LP by Mr. Eddie Floyd.

That was Marshall for you though: he had a name for licensing stuff whether it was his to license or not. He'd brought in Wardell Quezerque to add strings and build it into a proper LP, and then I guess he'd sold it to whoever would buy it. I wasn't *unhappy* that *Try Me* came out, mind you. I wasn't really disappointed either, because I know things like that happen. My main thought when it finally caught up with me was, *I need to register these songs given that I wrote them all!* The other thought was, *I guess nobody really bought this record if I'm only hearing about it now. In Japan!* That kind of summed up the mid-1980s for me in the States.

I decided to spend more time in Europe instead and to base myself in London. The city that had always been good to me. There was a promoter interested in celebrating the 20th anniversary of the Stax/Volt Tour of Europe from 1967, so I told him to book me as many club dates as possible—pub dates if need be—and to put a band together for me. The catch was, it couldn't be a band that already existed. I didn't want to be up front of a group people already known as a local version of the M.G.'s or Q-Tips. I wanted a band of my own. To prove that I meant business, I rented myself a flat in London. All the way up in Wood Green, wrong side of the North Circular. I'd still go home to Montgomery, Alabama, and see my mom when we had time off, but it was good that you didn't have to jump on a flight every time you had a London gig. Of course, being that now I'm in Wood Green, I need a car to get around. So I bought a car. But I'm not used to driving on the left, and every time I turned the corner I'd hit the goddamn curb!

Part of the reason I ended up in Wood Green was because of the guy who became my band leader, the sax player Andy Dummett. He lived in the area, and early on in my visit, when I was still at the Columbia Hotel, he asked me round for dinner. It was the first time anyone from my UK bands had invited me to their house, and I appreciated it so much, I figured I might as well live near him. He introduced me to his father along the way, an Oxford professor who invited me to lunch up there as well, showed me round New College—I guess it was New when they built it 600 years earlier!—and their collection of rare books and manuscripts. Professor Michael Dummett was later knighted by the queen. All this was the start of a great relationship with a British group I kept for the next twenty-five to thirty years, would use them every time I came over to Europe: Chris Chesney, Gwyn Hood, Andy . . . I call them "the boys" though over that time they've grown into middle-aged men. They stuck with me through what was originally a hard climb back up. My first show was at a pub called the Sir George Robey. The place was right opposite the Rainbow Theater, where we'd publicly kicked off that 1967 tour with two high-profile, sold-out shows. No matter. I still deliver.

"We were playing small clubs," recalls Andy. "It was a struggle. The diary was by no means full. It wasn't the time when Eddie got the most recognition. We were doing places like the Half Moon in Putney, the Cricketers at Kennington Oval. It wasn't like we were playing the Jazz Café or Ronnie Scotts."

But hey, that's just the way it's got to be. If a man wants to work, he's got to understand that there will be times he's in demand, and maybe times when he's not. But if you don't keep working when you're not in demand, well, who's going to know you still exist? How's it ever going to come back around on you?

"Eddie was totally positive throughout," Andy recalls. "In performances, he always gives his all. No matter where, no matter what. He does it for the audience, and he just goes all out every single time. There are times when he might have a negative thing about the tour or the people he's working with, but that never affects what he does on a gig. Never, ever, ever. He's all out full on, on every gig, absolutely."

But that's the only way I know how to do it. I was working, I got me a good band, I got some shows coming through, I'm getting over to continental Europe and people like me. All depends how you look at it. Sure, I spent my fiftieth birthday having to acknowledge that I was no longer playing the same size venues I had done twenty years earlier, but I was grateful that I had a great band, a dedicated audience, a catalog of hit records, and I was still doing what I love doing. If I didn't, I could just have sat at home and collected on the publishing. But that would not have been me. I like to work. I love to stay busy.

We built up an hour-long show; there was easy enough hits for sixty minutes or more. And I taught my younger band a few of the ground rules. No drinks on stage. I don't just mean no alcohol, I mean, *no drinks*. No towels either. You're here to sweat, and when the sweat runs . . . well, you're welcome to have some of mine. I call it soul juice. Fact is, you *should* be feeling a certain amount of discomfort. The audience should know that you're working. As for telling the band how to play, I don't.

"His leadership is all by example," says Andy. "And by the occasional dropped hint. He doesn't say, 'Don't do this, do that.' That's not him. He just hopes that you pick up the signals."

That was the good thing about that UK band. They did pick up the signals. And when we got to Europe, it didn't feel that much different than 1967; the young people there seem to love me. We have this crazy situation in Holland where the crowd follows me back to the hotel, start chanting my name outside the window; I actually have to go out on the balcony and wave to them like I'm a member of the royal family! And in Italy, we get to appear on this live TV show *DOC*—the name had something to do with the wine in that country!—for five days straight, two songs a day direct to camera. Must have had an effect, because one day when we had some time off, we went to the Spanish Steps for some sight-seeing, and I got mobbed!

The reaction is enough for me to write a song about my positive feelings for the music and the culture that I came from. "Soul Is Back Again." It's a regeneration. When I return to the

States, I call up my good friend William Bell. After getting off Mercury and moving to Atlanta, he's started up his own company, Wilbe. It's a grassroots thing; he's mainly signing younger soul acts, filling what he saw as a "void in the industry."

William and I had often talked about working together and now seemed the perfect opportunity. I went down to Atlanta and stayed with William there. We recorded an album together at a local studio called the Sound Shop, with my songs, William producing, and a group I called the Soul Street Band, which was mainly musicians out of Memphis—some of them connected with the Hi Studio, behind me. There were some solid songs on there: "Soul Is Back Again," "From Your Head to Your Toes," and an attempt I made at a kind of electro-rap, called "She Likes the Soaps," about a woman who can't give up her television. We called the album *Flashback*, and it came out in '88. This time I *did* know about the release!

William, certainly, was happy with it. "I thought it was a very good album at the time," says William. "But Wilbe was just getting started, we didn't have all of our distribution set up the way that I wanted it to. So we had some success with it, but not as much as I would have liked, because we were still a fledgling young label at the time."

Flashback didn't make it out in the UK or Europe, which of course is where I was doing most of my work at the time. But as the first new album I'd had out in ten years that I was fully on board with, it was important that I made the statement. Soul is back again. And Eddie Floyd's not going away.

Chapter 20
EVERYBODY NEEDS SOMEBODY

"We're getting the band back together."

I'm with Steve Cropper in Toronto. We're participating in
a TV show about "legends," which is always a nice thing to
hear about yourself, though you'd be just as happy to know
you're still working toward being one. But that's not the reason
Cropper's comment got my attention. You're getting the band
back together? The M.G.'s?

No, he's talking about *the Blues Brothers Band*. It's a line from
the film. John Belushi as "Joliet" Jake and Dan Aykroyd as
"Elwood," they round up all the musicians from the group they
had going before Jake got sent down for a stretch. In real-life
names, that means not just Cropper and Dunn, but drummer

233

Willie Hall, guitarist Matt "Guitar" Murphy, and the brass section too: Tom "Bones" Malone, "Blue Lou" Marini, and "Mr. Fabulous" Alan Rubin. Every time they track down one of their former bandmates, that's Jake's line: "We're getting the band back together." Lord knows that movie and the records and tours it spun off served Cropper and Duck and the rest of the band well . . . but only until John Belushi died in 1982 from a cocaine overdose, and that was the end of that.

Or so it seemed. Now the band that backed Jake and Elwood in the movie and on stage—the Blues Brothers Band—is looking to reunite for real. And I'm being offered a gig I'll get to keep for just about the rest of my life!

The band hadn't played for a while until a surprise thirty-fifth birthday party for Dan Aykroyd in 1987. Matt "Guitar" Murphy had kept a band going in the meantime with this guy Larry Thurston on vocals, and his promoter started getting inquiries about the Blues Brothers Band doing some gigs. It was Cropper who suggested they get me in to headline alongside Larry Thurston.

Lou Marini sent me a video of Thurston fronting Matt Murphy's band. He looked good. That meant they already had someone who could handle a lot of the blues material. They clearly didn't need me for *that*. So I made it clear: I wasn't going to be a Blues Brother. I was going to be Eddie Floyd, special guest. If you change that title, we probably got problems. But there weren't none, and it was perfect. They were playing exactly what I wanted to hear, and I was still Eddie Floyd when I stepped on stage.

They'd open with the Blues Brothers set and do the hits they'd had with Belushi and Aykroyd, with Larry Thurston singing. And then they would bring me out, for what they called "the Stax show." Cropper and Dunn had recorded those hits as well, so they were on good ground to call it as much.

Larry Thurston may have been more of a blues singer, but as far as the up-tempo thing, that came in when I came in, 'cause I told him, "We got to be like Sam & Dave, my brother, let's go!' "After he did his set, and I did mine, we'd close out the show together, with "Everybody Needs Somebody to Love." There's one picture where you can see we was all way up in the sky, that's what we started doing. I'm in my fifties now, and I'm moving as much as I ever did!

My first tour—the "reunion" tour for the other guys—was a great success. No real surprise, when you look at the quality of the musicians, and consider the fact that they'd been away for five years or more, so people were hungry to see them and hear them. The next summer, in 1989, we get invited to play the Montreux Jazz Festival in Switzerland; the show is televised, and it results in an album: *The Blues Brothers Band Live in Montreux*, released on WEA Records (that's now Warner Elektra Atlantic; those labels kept folding in and merging in on each other) all across Europe and beyond. Got my two big crowd-pleasers on there: "Knock on Wood" and "Raise Your Hand." Demand increases, and we figure, hey, we enjoy this. Let's keep it going.

The core of the band stayed the same for as long as possible—that's the guys I mentioned up above from the movie. On keyboards, we started out with Paul Shaffer, who was known to the public as the late night talk show host David Letterman's musical director and sidekick. I'd first met Paul all the way back at Malaco. He was Canadian, so you can imagine that down in Jackson, Mississippi, his voice was very different. We knew then that he had to be into the music if he'd come that far from home for it! Still, with the Blues Brothers Band, Paul was often busy with Letterman, so we got Leon Pendarvis, who is still our number-one choice and played with us as recently as our 2017 reunion. But guess what? Leon is musical director for *Saturday Night Live*—yes, we got us *two* top TV late-night musical directors—and when we couldn't arrange the touring around Leon's season schedules either, we got Rusty Cloud, a great pianist in his own right. Same with the drums: no Willie Hall, then it's Steve Potts or Anton Fig. Serious musicians, all of them. But fun to hang with too. I'm having a blast. I'm playing to large audiences, the sound is good, the pay is fine, all that.

Fast forward a couple of years to 1992. We get to do a studio album together, *Red, White, & Blues*, and not only do I have the chance to revisit "I've Never Found a Girl" and "Big Bird," but Steve Cropper and Donald "Duck" Dunn get to record them for the first time. You have to remember, it was Booker who played those parts on the original Stax singles. Steve, being Steve, nailed the introduction to "Big Bird" like it was his all along! Now we take that song on the road with us, and ain't no looking back.

We'd do it at the end of the set, and especially at the end of a tour. I would always say, "I want to sing my good luck song; in the morning we're gonna be heading back to the USA." And we played that song like we were boarding the plane and taking off and flying. And then we'd introduce a section of musical turbulence, like when the plane's moving funny, and then it straightens out again. We took the people on that little trip. Alan Rubin would stretch out that initial guitar phrase on the trumpet, which was hard to play. It's harder to play eight times repeated. It's really hard twelve times—and sixteen times! We'd have to cut out and then come back in because it kills the trumpet player.

From this point on, we're busy as we choose to be, going all over the world, the far corners of Europe, to Japan, the Middle East even—and beyond. I'm not saying that every country we went to they knew me, but most of them did. And they knew the songs, so if they didn't know the artist, they knew *of* the artist, and all I got to do is get up there and do it—and *now* they know me.

On those first tours with the Blues Brothers, I got to promote some of the songs I'd done for *Flashback* on William Bell's label. Cropper always liked "She Loves the Soaps," and it stayed in the set for a while. One time in Sicily we were doing that song and there's a vamp at the end, and all of a sudden the power went off. The electricity has gone, but the horns are still playing and the drums are still playing and so, hey, Eddie's still singing. And the audience was singing the background, and they're clapping on the two and the four and they are *on it.* And they started even singing harmony, so we just kept playing for minutes until they got the sound back in and the band came back in. It was a magical moment—it was fantastic.

From my perspective, it was *all* good times. We never had no problems on the road. That was automatic. Everything was great, and it still is. We used to meet at the destination airport, pretty much all at the same time, the bus would be there to pick us all up, and it was very rare anyone missed. We had us a *ball.* But that doesn't mean you can't have an argument here and there. It just means you know well enough to move on from it.

"Part of the friction in the band at the time was down to our manager," recalls Lou Marini, who was about as close to a band leader as the Blues Brothers had. "He managed to make it so that nobody knew exactly what else was going on. And so that was part of the friction with Eddie and me, because the manager was hired by us, and I was the one who was dealing with him, and I wasn't really aware of all this shit, so I would bear the brunt of Eddie's ire, which was mostly about the manager. Over the years he and I had some intense fracases over a misunderstanding.

"One time in Japan I knew Eddie was bugged because he wanted to be playing more of his tunes. Or different tunes. But somehow in my effort to add tunes to the set, and in sound check saying, 'Let's rehearse this other song of yours,' thinking he'd be happy about it, he wasn't. Eddie's hands are mitts, y'know, and we're in the dressing room, and he's bugged, and I'm saying, 'Well, what the fuck, do you want to do another of your tunes or do you not?' And I'm trying to get the band to rehearse it so we had it together. And the next thing I know is that Eddie's fist goes up, I feel the breeze as it passes my head, and hits the door and punches through the wooden door. I mean, there was a hole in the door. All the guys in the band are like: *Holy shit!* I remember being oddly, totally calm, saying something like, 'Well, I can see that you are bugged!' But then the next day I went up to Eddie's room, we sat down and talked, and it was all totally cool. And I knew he loved me, and he knows I love him."

He's right on that. This stuff comes and goes. And to be clear, it wasn't just Lou, felt it at times. There was one time we were doing a gig with Aykroyd and Jim Belushi, John's brother. Now, the way Lou remembers it, is that "Jim is not as musical as he could be, so consequently he can fuck up tunes, leave parts out. Something happened where we were backstage, and he said something to Eddie, and it was . . . Jim came close to getting his clock rung. You could see it: 'You're way over the line and one more movement . . . '"

The Blues Brothers guys gave me the nickname the Alabama Slammer. There were a few incidents that inspired that. I was in London, there was this dude who was about 400 pounds, 6 feet 8 inches, drunk as a skunk. I'm getting ready to go on stage. I'm trying to stand next to this post so everyone can see the show. And this guy is trying to come past me and says, "Get out the way, man." I give him a look, but I still move a little, and then he says, "Get out the way!" And he jumps up and runs at me . . . and I slammed him. And as I slammed him, the sound man ran and grabbed me and said, "Don't do that, Eddie!" But at the same time, the band don't see it, and they're calling me on stage. It was perfect, 'cause they started off with "Big Bird," and the adrenalin is there, and that song "Big Bird" is building right from the beginning. And when I come off, all the people are saying, "We're sorry about that guy." But the whole time I was up on stage singing, guess what? The guy is back in his seat, nodding away to the music. He's just drunk!

There was another time we were at a festival in Switzerland. Our dressing room is a tent, which means it doesn't have a door to have a lock on it. I'm sitting in there waiting to go on, and somebody must have seen the band leave for the stage, figured there was no one left and that they could help themselves to some of what the musicians had left behind. But they didn't see *me*, so I'm just sitting there, and all of a sudden a hand comes up, not really up under the tent but through a little opening, this hand coming, and the bags are all sitting there, and this guy puts his hand around to find one of them, and I take it and I just grabbed him, and pulled him in. It was just an instant thing. Now I got him! He wasn't looking to run off with our bags after I let him go, I can assure you.

And somewhere in Italy—it was Parma or Rome—you've got an escalator going up to the club, and another one going down. I'm going up, and this guy grabs our briefcase with all our tickets and everything, and he's going down the wrong way, and I just turn around and go sliding down to try and catch up with him. We ended up outrunning him so he dropped the bag between some cars. Everything was in there!

We didn't always catch the thief though. And maybe the best way to tell you about the spirit in the Blues Brothers Band is from when were in Amsterdam. Leon had his bag with quite a bit of money in it, sitting right by his organ, and the only people back there is security, and they're trying to be real strict about that, and we're not liking them to begin with. And all of a sudden Leon's bag was gone. Now we approach them and say, "Nobody's been back there, and the way you security been, you wouldn't even let *us* back." And of course they say, 'We don't know anything.' And that's the first time Leon came out to Europe with us. How much did he lose? Thousands and thousands of dollars. And you know what? Everybody chipped in and gave him his money right back. Because it just was a family thing.

Around 1995, we're getting ready to tour again, when I get told Larry Thurston won't be there anymore. He's become a preacher. He was always reading the Bible on tour, and apparently one day, he quit drinking and went into preaching. Left the Blues Brothers Band *right* behind!

In comes a young guy, Tommy McDonnell, to take his place. For Tommy, it was an eye-opener. He had no idea just how big this thing had become. Like we'd go to Europe, places where English is not the first language, but they know the words to every one of the Blues Brothers songs. The Blues Brothers always attracted people from eight years old to eighty years old. Old-timers that remembered the movie from 1980 and their kids, then grandkids.

Everyone in the Blues Brothers Band got given a nickname, and Tommy's was "Pipes"—because he had one hell of a set of them. "But Eddie's was louder than mine," is how he recalls things. "And he was even more powerful than me on a microphone. Maybe it was from all the years when the technology wasn't up to snuff, and they didn't have monitors, because every performance I've ever seen him do, he was spot on. And it was different every night; it wasn't like the same boring thing. The energy was just ridiculous. When Eddie hit the stage it took it to a whole other level. He would start with 'Raise Your Hand' and people would be standing for the whole show, shouting and screaming. He is just so powerful on stage. I was in awe of his movements, the way he walks back and forth. He has a unique way of doing that. It kept the energy flowing. It's not like he ever stopped and then stood at the microphone. He held the microphone for the whole show."

"It's the real thing," says Lou of my delivery. "The combination of his energy and the way he moves onstage, constantly . . . The audience can't take their eyes off him because he's always moving. And then the way he's able to inspire the band, and the clarity of his leadership onstage. All those things."

Hey, I'm not looking for the compliments; I'm ready for people to say whatever they feel they need to about me, like when Lou talks about some of the run-ins we had. But you got to remember, I'm totally in shape from the era that I come from. I got the mind-set and the body. But still, with the Blues Brothers Band we became road dogs. Poland, Germany, Switzerland, England, Norward, Finland, France. In Italy, we played the main plaza in Turin, 14,000 people a night two nights running. Japan was constant, every winter we'd be there: Tokyo, Osaka . . . One year we went to Slovenia, Russia, Turkey, Lebanon . . . I mean, we saw the world. We had good times a-plenty. But believe me, we *worked*.

"When things get rough," recalls Lou, "and you have delayed flights, you have a fucked-up bus ride, and now you get to the gig and the backstage food is lame and people are sick and now you have to go onstage and there's thousands of people waiting for you to play, Eddie always used to say 'All right man, this is what we trained for,' and then you get up and you hit it. And that's one thing also that characterizes the Blues Brothers Band and always has: you could feel terrible, but you get onstage and the band starts playing, and there's so many guys that have so much energy, and so much honesty in their playing, that everybody is always lifted up."

"Back in those heydays, everyone was healthy, it was like a freight train," recalls "Pipes." "My thought was you don't ever want to come out before this band, and you don't ever want to come out after this band. You're going to be destroyed either way."

I started hearing of a *Blues Brothers* II round the time "Pipes" joined the group and, in 1997, it became official. John Landis would be directing again, and Jim Belushi, John's younger brother, would be playing the role of Dan Aykroyd's counterpart. But Jim pulled out just before pre-production started due to another commitment, and they got John Goodman in instead. Then Universal, which was financing the movie, insisted that the part of a kid, Buster, who was played by J. Evan Bonnifant, get written into the movie, like a third "Blues Brother," or a "Blues Nephew" perhaps.

None of this might have had anything to do with my story, except that Dan Aykroyd wrote in a part for me as well, as one of the musical cameos. This put me in the same camp as James Brown and Aretha Franklin, both invited back for an encore performance, and alongside Sam Moore, Erykah Badu, and Junior Wells. My scene had me singing "634–5789" as the owner of Ed's Love Exchange, a telephone sex hot line. I wrote the song with Cropper, as you well know—and Steve, along with Duck, was most certainly going to be a prominent part of this new movie like he was the first one. But as you also know, Cropper and I wrote it *for* Wilson Pickett. So John Landis and Dan Aykroyd figured, let's double our entertainment value. Let's bring in Wilson Pickett and have him and Eddie Floyd—the guy who sung it *and* the guy who wrote it—perform it together.

Now obviously I've seen Pickett since that crazy European tour he walked out on in 1982. We're bound to end up on the same show, or the same festival here and there. But really, there hasn't been a whole lot of interaction. I know Pickett's been in jail a couple of times, that he ran over an old guy in his New Jersey hometown while under the influence, that he was arrested for cocaine possession, and there was a story in the papers about him taking a drive, in the midnight hour, round his neighbor's lawn threatening to shoot the owner—who just happened to be the town mayor! So I don't know exactly what to expect when we meet in Toronto for the two days of filming.

The scene is set in this big warehouse with dozens of women in rollers and nightgowns answering the phones, pretending to be hot young girls; that's close to how it was back in the days when lonely men called those lines for a little bit of pretend female company. For the movie, the women have all got these precise dance moves to do; when the choreographer comes to work with me, it's simple steps, and I got it in one take, with John Goodman doing the same steps just behind me. But I don't see Pickett, and that part of it I don't particularly like. They said, "Well, he'll be here later." I knew what was happening with them. People like bullshit. They like to repeat bad shit; that's human nature. All those years and all the different things that have happened has reached all the way up. They didn't want to put me and Pickett together just in case!

I'm told I'm singing the first verse, Pickett the second. That didn't seem right to me. I'm saying, "Let Pickett sing it first, I don't give a shit." But Dan says, "No, it's *Ed's* Love Exchange, you got to sing it first." Finally, in rolls Pickett. Now they leave us together, and I figure Pickett's going to say, "Hey motherfucker it's *my* goddamn song." But he ain't in that same foul mood that he was all those goddamn years ago. Instead he says, "This is the greatest thing that could have happened to us." They were totally wrong about me and Pickett.

When it comes time to film together, I'm in a smart black suit with white necktie; Pickett is wearing brown leather jacket and matching leather pants. And dark shades! We're lip-synching when we film, because we'd already done the recording session with Paul Shaffer, except Pickett and I weren't there at the same time. Being that it's a movie, and they want all these special guests, they wheel the young blues guitarist Jonny Lang across the warehouse for a blazing solo and for him to sing the last verse too. The performance then ends with Pickett and me, surrounded by bikini-clad women with breast enlargements, being filmed by Johnny Lang for a pretend version of one of those cheap late-night commercials for the so-called Love Exchange—which then gets referenced in the final words of the song. Cut to the exterior of the building there in Toronto, with a big pink sign on it reading "Ed's" in giant letters leading up and off the roof. You know where that sign is now? In the cottage I keep full of mementos, that's where.

There are so many incredible musicians in *Blues Brothers 2000*. Look at the lineup of the band they put together for the film, which they called the Louisiana Gator Boys: Eric Clapton, B.B. King, Bo Diddley, Gary "US" Bonds, Dr. John, Billy Preston, Lou Rawls, Isaac Hayes, Clarence Clemons, Jeff "Skunk" Baxter, Charlie Musselwhite, Stevie Winwood . . . and more! Even my man from the Blues Brothers Band, Tommy McDonnell, got to be part of it.

So, I don't know if it's because there was just too many cooks in the kitchen; or whether it was because Jim Belushi pulled out and the kid stepped in; or whether *any* Blues Brothers movie was always going to struggle without John Belushi . . . but when the film comes out in 1998, it gets crucified by the critics and just about bombs at the box office too.

All the same, the soundtrack of *Blues Brothers 2000* holds up just fine: Cropper says he prefers it to the original movie's soundtrack. And why not? It features Aretha doing "R-E-S-P-E-C-T," Dr. John leading "Season of the Witch," a great all-star version of "Funky Nassau," and Junior Wells on "Cheaper to Keep Her." I was thrilled to be a part of it too, to get back with my man Pickett and have it all cool between us. I think our scene is just perfect the way it is. So what if I had to wait until I was in my sixties to appear in a proper movie? Maybe good things come to those who wait.

But that wasn't necessarily the best of it. To promote the film, they had us perform "634-5789" on David Letterman's show. Pickett and I hadn't sung next to each other in a live format in a long *long* time, and I think he was really looking to make a statement, to show that he was back in business and looking after himself after such a long time on the ropes. He was still Pickett though. I was looking forward to laughing and talking with him about the old days. But no, by the time he got to the studio, it's almost time for us to go on. And he's the one who lives in New York!

Wasn't time for nobody to tell us who's gonna sing what, or where. We just figure we'll do it like the movie: I'll take the first verse, he can take the second, and without Jonny Lang, we can share the third. We've got the whole Blues Brothers Band behind us, including Cropper and Dunn, we got Paul Shaffer and Leon Pendarvis sharing the keyboards, and we got John Goodman, Dan Aykroyd, and the little kid for back up! Everybody was loose and having fun. I mean, when you look at Matt "Guitar" Murphy, shit! I know if he's playing like that, it's going to be good.

When we get to that third verse, I know where I'm gonna stop and where he's gonna sing, but Pickett, he ain't thinking about that. Its ad-lib city! He's got that famous scream of his going full tilt, and it's driving me too. I found that all of a sudden I went much higher than where I would normally have went, 'cause I bounced off his note. Weren't nothing that we had talked about; we just let it flow.

Maybe it's hard for other styles of music to improvise like this. Maybe a lot of people just don't know how to do it. For us it seems natural, so I'm just glad that we came in at that time, that era, that style, where it will never be difficult to sing with each other, to perform like that.

All in all, this was one of my very best TV performances— and there have been a few! But Pickett, man, at the end, he puts his microphone back and walks off the stage before David Letterman can even get to shake his hand on camera! He didn't even go back to the dressing room, just went straight home! Even sobered up a little, the cat was still crazy.

Chapter 21
I GOT A REASON TO SMILE

Like I told you earlier, I made a decision very early in my career that I was going to leave politics well alone. So many things happening in politics, I wouldn't want to be part of that, no kind of way. Ain't really nothing more to say.

But if you ask me something about music, then I *know* what I'm talking about. So when I get a call in late 1988, just after President George H. W. Bush was elected, asking me if I'd like to play a concert that Lee Atwater is putting together as part of the Inaugural Celebrations, I say, "Okay, tell me more about it." I'm always spending time in D.C.—it's still one of my home cities—and yet in all these years, I've never really taken part in anything to do with the government there.

Lee Atwater calls me direct. His name's in the news a lot at this time because he was Bush's campaign chairman—and now they're about to make him chairman of the Republican National Committee. And he's still just thirty-seven years old. Lee's been accused of using racism in the Bush campaign, running negative ads against the Democratic candidate, Michael Dukakis, with the image of a black murderer to suggest that Dukakis is soft on crime. And that's as may be: a couple of years later, he did apologize for it. But when I get talking to Lee, it's obvious he doesn't just know our music like I know it, he *breathes* it, and he's determined to put on what he's calling a "Celebration of Blues & Soul" like the country has never seen. When I hear about some of the talent he's already brought on board, I know it's going to be for real. And when he tells me that they want to pay all of us properly, treat us right, give us free passes to all the other inaugural events, and that we'll be playing to the new president of the United States, then I'm in. As far as I'm concerned, this is an honor. It's also the chance to promote our music. You've got to remember, some of us are coming off a difficult decade. We *should* be celebrated for what we've done for this country! So my attitude is, I'll be involved as far as that you want me to sing. I don't go further than that.

When I get up to D.C., they have plenty of artists lined up, but they also have people dropping out through illness. After all, none of us are getting any younger. They say they still want more artists, so I say, "William Bell!" I jump on the phone and call him and say, "How would you like to play the inauguration? Five days of pure luxury!'"

Turns out Lee Atwater had already called William. In fact, the two of them went back a ways, to when Atwater was at college in South Carolina. "My band got stranded in a snow storm," William recalls. "He reminded me I had to use a college band for the concert, and he was the guitarist in that band. Still,

I've always been a Democrat, so I had some reservations about the concert. I hadn't yet agreed. But then Eddie called me and told me what it was about and said, 'Are *you* doing it?' We were always like that—and when I found out *he* was doing it I said I was in too. We had to look at the big picture. It was just an honor to do something for the head person of the country."

The "Celebration for Young Americans," as they called it publicly, was held at the Washington Convention Center, January 21, 1989, one day after George H. W. Bush officially became president. They'd hosted many of the major inaugural balls that previous night, so we had D.C. a little more to ourselves, but still, there's parties going on left, right, and center. We're just one of many. We knew the event was being filmed, because there had been talk of it going out as some kind of TV special, maybe on public broadcasting, but it didn't happen at the time. That doesn't matter; none of us are going to put any less effort in any which way.

Now you may have noticed I haven't mentioned the other musicians yet, apart from William, but that's because I want you to experience the event the way I did. It unfolded almost like a film of my life playing out in front of me. Is that Willie Dixon I see coming out on the stage early on in the evening, in his seventies now, singing the hit he wrote for Muddy Waters, "Hoochie Coochie Man?" Willie's the guy that produced—and played on—my first ever record, "Baby, That's It," with the Falcons, all the way back in 1956, remember. Without him taking a chance on that integrated vocal group back in the day, who knows what would have happened to me?

And there with the rectangular guitar, that can only be the great Bo Diddley, who engineered and played guitar on my very first solo single—"Will I Be the One" and "Set My Soul on Fire"—at his studio in D.C., in 1963. Bo's walking around telling everyone he discovered me, but that's okay; I appreciate his help too.

The next part of the show features a couple of my soul brothers from all the years down the line: Chuck Jackson, singing his big hits "I Don't Want to Cry" and "Any Day Now" from the early 1960s, back when the Falcons were just getting something going with Wilson Pickett; and Percy Sledge, who had what we often call the first Southern soul number-one single in 1966 with "When a Man Loves a Woman." That song was recorded at the studio in Muscle Shoals owned by Quin Ivy and engineered by Jimmy Johnson, and that's two other guys I've had major musical relationships with over the years. Chuck, Percy, and I have often appeared on the same bills over the years but never one like this.

And now we're moving into the Stax part of the night, and there's my man Steve Cropper stepping into the house band on guitar. Without all the hits I wrote with Steve—not just those I made famous as a singer like "Knock on Wood" and "Raise Your Hand" but the ones we gave over to Wilson Pickett, Otis Redding, and more—it would have been a different story for me, for sure. Without his guitar playing on my early Stax records, how would I have sounded? Same with Donald "Duck" Dunn, who's looking happy to be here too (like he ever looks *un*happy). That bass line on "Knock on Wood" is immortal, my brother!

Next, here's my soul brother William Bell, who I've been proud to call a friend since 1962, singing "Born under a Bad Sign," the hit he wrote with Booker for our fellow Stax artist at the time, Albert King. And then, up comes Carla Thomas, and she's the one I always give the credit to. Like I said back at the start of this book, if not for her taking on my songs, I may never have made it out of D.C. to Memphis and the world. Yet here we are tonight, back in D.C., just a mile or two from Howard University where she went to college, from the clubs we called home back in the day, and it has to be said, she is sounding sweet as ever. When Billy Preston, who's already been holding down double duties as master of ceremonies and Hammond organist, steps up to duet with her on "When Something Is Wrong with My Baby," she reaches the kind of vocal heights that give even the most experienced of us performers the shivers.

It's at this point that the new president walks in with his wife, Barbara Bush, and the band salutes him not with "Hail to the Chief" but with a blast from "Soul Finger." Hey, you're in our house right now! There's a brief interlude where President Bush takes the stage, and Lee Atwater gets to live out his fantasy, playing guitar on "High-Heeled Sneakers"—a song I covered back on my first solo album—with Percy Sledge, Sam Moore, Carla Thomas, and Chuck Jackson all out there in accompaniment, and Steve and Duck part of the band. Not me, though: I'm in the wings, getting ready for my own big moment. They all present the president with a guitar—an Epiphone, I think it was—which Bush straps on, and he pretends to play for a minute alongside Lee Atwater and Sam Moore while the media men go crazy with their cameras. Those shots will cover the next day's newspapers.

The first couple take their seats in the front row, and then, it's my turn. Most of us are only being asked to do but one or two songs—the biggest of our hits!—so I'll give you just a single guess as to which riff you hear when I count the band in. Well, I'm not even halfway through the first verse of "Knock on Wood" when I come straight down off the stage, past security and everybody, and reach for the first lady I saw. Well I didn't get the *first* lady I saw because that *was* the First Lady, if you see what I'm saying—and I couldn't very well put a hand on Barbara Bush! And then the later President Bush, George W., the son, he pushed my hand back, so I guess it wasn't going to be his wife either. And this girl is sitting there smiling, so I just grabbed her by the hand and took her way up on the stage, and we sang and we danced our way through "Knock on Wood." And she danced good. Didn't look afraid to be up there either. Find out later just why: it's Steffi Graf, the tennis champion! She'd won what they called the Golden Slam that year: all four major world titles. Undoubtedly she was number one! And she got right out of there and joined me.

"Knock on Wood" goes down a storm, and the rest of the night is one long party, from Sam Moore doing "Soul Man" through a whole Texas blues jam with Delbert McClinton, Jimmy Vaughan, Stevie Ray Vaughan, and Albert Collins. Oh yeah, and Ron Wood from the Rolling Stones is up there too. It was like Lee Atwater told the crowd at the start of the show: it was "pure American music in its best form." And the next day, Lee takes me personally on a tour of the White House; we have lunch there, and I get to visit the Oval Office. I've come a long way, and don't think I don't know it.

That wasn't the last time I got to visit the White House, though. So if you don't mind, I'm going to jump forward a quarter century—which is like jumping back to the start of my time at Stax!—all the way to April 9, 2013. President Barack Obama has just started his second term at the White House, and he's got a series of "In Performance" concerts happening in his D.C. home. One of them is dedicated to what they're calling "Memphis Soul," and of course, if you're going to have a concert with *that* title, you'd sure better be thinking of those of us from Stax.

Obama's done that all right. "The sound of Soulsville, U.S.A.," he says when he introduces the concert, is "a music that, at its core, is about the pain of being alone, the power of human connection, and the importance of treating each other right." Well, that's a part of it, but I prefer what he says next:

"These songs get us on the dance floor. They get stuck in our heads. We go back over them again and again. And they've played an important part in our history."

Just so you're aware, your Eddie Floyd of 2013 has grey hair now, and he's older in years than when Willie Dixon shuffled on stage at the D.C. Convention Center in 1989. But your Eddie Floyd of 2013 is still out there, still singing, and still giving it his all. Tonight it just happens to be the White House. And this time I've got Booker alongside as my bandleader, which is a good thing because like Cropper, who's a featured performer in his own right, this is someone I've written so many hits with that if I'm going to have a second chance to sing for a president of the United States, he should be there. There's some of the other surviving Stax artists on stage of course, and other people from Memphis music history, be they young, like Justin Timberlake—or not young, I guess, such as Charlie Musselwhite. Or me! And they've brought in other people to pay tribute to our music: Queen Latifah, Cyndi Lauper, and Alabama Shakes.

Now, tonight we're in the East Room of the White House, and it's intimate, so when I say that the First Family—Barack, Michelle, and their daughters, Malia and Sasha—is in the front row, I mean they're *right in front of me*. Like, I don't have to get off the stage to pull anyone out of their seats this time: I could just lean over and do so. But no, that's not the right way to play *this* event. So tonight, when we get to the bridge of "Knock on Wood," I've already got everyone clapping on the two and four, but as the horns break into that midsection, I look right at President Barack Obama and I lean over toward him and say, "Everybody give me a little soul clap," and he jumps out of the one rhythm, and into the other. I'm kind of messing, just like I messed on that other show. I already knew I was going to do that, but I didn't really know what *he* was going to do. We were looking each other in the eye, and he could still have stayed on the two and four, but I switched on him—and he switched right with me. Leaned his head sideways and got into the groove. He knew his soul music. Certainly knew his soul clap!

The way I look at that night, they got many people in that room who have been in politics for years, and there wasn't one of them not singing along to "Knock on Wood." Pretty much everyone except the Obamas is up on their feet too. And I had the feeling the First Family would like to have been! So what I'm saying is, they are just regular people; they went to college, they became who they are, and now they're in politics. And now you honor them a little different, a little more perhaps. But they're still people, like you or me. They still want to dance to soul music. People are just people.

But don't think that it isn't an honor to play for them. I've played at the Houses of Parliament (alongside Ben E. King and Dorothy Moore, in 1990, and got to sit in the Prime Minister's seat while being shown around). I've played for the Prince of Monaco. I could probably list you a few more. And *all* of it is a great honor. Is there any show that's been a greater honor than playing at the White House? If you want to put it in a sense of, you're singing for a person who runs the country, represents the country, then maybe not. That's got to be on top. But I don't think of it like that. I think of it that you're booked to do a show, and you give it your all, whoever you're singing for, wherever you be. If not, don't expect to get booked again.

Chapter 22
ED'S LOVE EXCHANGE

In 2002, I made my first album of all-new material in about fifteen years, *To the Bone*. And for the very first time in my career, I recorded part of it in sweet home Alabama, right here in Montgomery, in The Woods, as I call it. I had Danny Jones from William Bell's old studio as my producer and engineer, Mike Stewart from that same setup (he'd engineered *Flashback* on William's label all those years earlier) playing guitars and keyboards, and my friends from the Blues Brothers Band backing me. I'd been carrying some of these songs around for years, waiting for the right time to put them down, but I guess the recent years of touring had rubbed off on me, because when you listen to it, they're certainly in more of a blues style than you might think you know me for. You can sense as much from the titles: "Piece of You," "Maintenance Man," "Trouble in Our Home," and so on. I'd been in the studio with the guys from the Blues Brothers a few times by now, but it was wonderful to do it under my own name; to have Duck back in with me once more on bass, almost forty years on from when we first recorded together; plus Steve Potts on drums, and the horn section of Lou, Alan, and, on trombone now, Birch "Slide" Johnson. I also recorded a few other songs up in Georgia with Danny and Mike providing most of the backing, bringing in a great Nashville guitarist, Pat Buchanan, for a soaring solo on "I Heard It Through the Walls." And on two of these other new songs I bring in one of my sons, Anthony Floyd, to duet with me.

Anthony, if you recall, is from my first marriage back in Detroit, where he still lives, and he's been singing all his life. Sounds just like me, got that deep voice! I had figured this was a great chance to give him a little promotion, a push to show the world what he's capable of. Like I wrote on the sleeve, "It's said that every man wants his son to walk in his footsteps, and Anthony does that and more." All the same, he hasn't shown quite that hunger I had all my life, that determination to get out and do it for myself. It's something I've talked over with him.

I don't bag up nothing when I talk to my kids; I just talk to them straight on. Like I try to tell Anthony, we both have a very similar voice, and I know when I'm out, and I got to do certain things and I'm speaking with people, I have to speak different, in different tones even. And I try to tell him you got to get upbeat when you around other people. It's okay to have that deep voice. But say it upbeat!

The way I communicate is I sort of just listen to the tempo of the person I meet. When I get the tempo of him, I match his tempo. I start when he wants to start, I stop when he wants to stop. It works that way. Another thing is, when you hear me speak, I don't think I intimidate people, but I think my kids feel they've been intimidated a lot of times when I speak to them. They shouldn't be! I'm only just telling you what you should be knowing. I'm not hollering at you. I'm just speaking like an entertainer would speak—and they never heard it like that, and I guess that might intimidate them a bit.

Well, that's as may be. Another few years down the line, I'd write and produce a whole album of new songs for Anthony, and put it out on my own label, Doo Wop Soul. Meantime, *To the Bone* comes out on Rock House, which is a blues label run by my friend, guitarist and singer Roy Roberts out of North Carolina. You'll remember my saying I never really had expectations when I set off on my own in the 1960s. Nothing's really changed with me—but with the business it has. I know round this time, in the early 2000s, people have stopped buying CDs and they're just copying them off their friends' instead; they're starting to find the music that they want online, and they don't feel the need to pay for it anymore. But that doesn't really make a difference to me. I'm never going to stop writing songs, never going to stop recording them, and when I'm happy with those recordings, then as long as I find a way to do so, I'm never going to stop releasing them. Anything good happens from there, it's a bonus.

After all, the demand for me as a performer only gathered steam in the twenty-first century. In March 2004, the Blues Brothers Band is at the San Remo Song Festival, one of the longest running song contests in the world, a big annual TV production over there. We're not actually competing in the festival; we're backing an Italian singer. Well, the boys are backing her; I'm along because we've booked a concert in Morgana Bay to make the most of the trip.

When we walk into our hotel, Steve Cropper immediately recognizes Bill Wyman, the former bass player from the Rolling

Stones. Turns out he's over with his long-standing guitarist and friend Terry Taylor; they're backing the singer who's on the TV show after us. Bill knows all about me, even though we've never met.

Turns out he's been a big fan of Booker T. and the M.G.'s all the way from the early 1960s. Donald "Duck" Dunn was his favorite bass player "and a good mate as well," says Bill.

Bill and Terry came to see us at the Victory Club on the Bay the next night, and Bill got up and joined us on bass for three songs. Duck wasn't with us on that show, so it wasn't like Bill was kicking his friend off the stage or nothing! The next night, we did the TV show again, and then, "We just hung out all night at the hotel, all sitting round, all getting a bit sloshed," as Bill recalls it. "There was about eight or ten of us, and we did a dozen bottles or so of red wine! They ran out of wine in our hotel, and our roadie had to go down the road to the next hotel and cop a few more bottles for us! It was that evening that I got all the information from Eddie and asked if he'd be interested in playing with us."

"Us" turned out to be Bill Wyman's Rhythm Kings. He'd put that group together after quitting the Rolling Stones in 1993 in pursuit of a simpler life. He didn't want to tour anymore, especially not on the level of the Stones. He and Terry Taylor, who he'd been close friends with since they worked on an album together in the 1960s, went back to basics. "At first we were just going to cut some tracks on acoustic guitars, some blues stuff," remembers Terry. "But then it was, let's add a drummer, then you add more instruments, and the next we know, we've got a full band album with Georgia Fame, Gary Brooker, Albert Lee, and others."

"The Stones were living in France from 1971 onwards, and we never mixed with other people musically," recalls Bill. "Or very rarely. I did some solo stuff myself, recording with Howlin' Wolf and performing with people like Buddy Guy. But the Stones never jammed with other people. In those days we never had people come on stage to jam with us or us jam with them; we were unsociable!"

I guess Bill soon made up for lost time. When he put out his first studio album, *Struttin' Our Stuff*, the record company wanted gigs, so they had the band go to Europe. And *only* Europe, because Bill doesn't fly. Even for Europe, he takes boats. By the time I meet up with Bill, the Rhythm Kings have put out a whole number of studio albums and toured with all manner of musicians and singers. When Bill asks if I'd like to join them for some upcoming shows, I say the same as I did with Cropper about the Blues Brothers Band: put me on as a "special guest," and we're good to go.

And go we did. That October we toured the UK, did about twenty dates or so. I'd sing "634–5789," "Knock on Wood," "Raise Your Hand," and "Soul Man." Bill wanted me to do "Big Bird," but I saved that for the Blues Brothers Band. The projects were similar in a few ways, although Bill played a lot of older, faster, rock 'n' roll songs as well as the blues stuff. He'd do Johnny Burnette's "Tear It Up" at double tempo. He'd do something from way back like "I Put a Spell on You" but also more mellow songs like the Lovin' Spoonful's "Daydream." And he and Terry always wrote a lot together, and some of those songs would be in the set as well.

Bill attracted an amazing amount of talent for his Rhythm Kings. When I played with them at the Albert Hall in London in 2006, the group included Georgia Fame, Andy Fairweather Low, and Albert Lee, as well as Terry, the group's resident singer Beverley Skeete, and a fine set of musicians all across the board. Every time I went out with them, there were people of that level.

Sometimes though, I had to be clear about what was in and out of bounds. There was a time they had Mary Wilson from the Supremes on with then. We were doing a festival in Monaco and Terry and Bill say, "Get up for the encore, Eddie." I had to say, "No. She's singing Tamla." They were saying, "So?" And I had to explain "It's like oil and water don't mix. Stax and Motown don't mix." You don't compromise on your soul music. Well, I don't, at any rate.

I toured the UK with the Rhythm Kings again in September 2007 and finally, some more dates in Europe in late 2009. I was in my seventies by then, so I'd be making a point of the fact I was still around: "It's 2005, and I'm still alive!" "It's 2007, and I ain't yet in heaven!" I couldn't exactly complain about the touring schedule though: Bill's a year older than me, he spent decades in the biggest rock 'n' roll group in the world, and here he was, traveling in the same bus with the rest of us.

It might be because I know how to balance myself that I've never had a bad run of health. Nothing more than a hernia from jumping around. And that's important, because not everyone else in my world has been able to teach themselves to calm down. If that's the case, it can catch up on you.

Case in point: in January 2006, I was over in Amsterdam with the Rhythm Kings when I got the news at breakfast that Wilson Pickett had passed. Even though I knew he'd lived hard, I can't say I'd totally expected it. We had done a couple of shows together maybe two or three years before that when the Blues Brothers were playing Cannes with Sam Moore, Solomon Burke, and Wilson Pickett. But I get to the show, and Pickett's already been on and gone. I'm wondering, "What's that all about? He didn't even wait for me?" But then I hear from other people that he isn't feeling well, so it's understandable—but it means we don't even get to speak.

He was only sixty-four when he passed. I guess his body just gave out on him. Our lives had been thrown together several times over the decades, from our time together in the Falcons to "634–5789" to the various shows and tours and festivals we appeared on together, and finally with *Blues Brothers 2000*. It's tougher than tough watching my old soul brothers pass away, one by one. Don't think it isn't; there's a price to pay for living into old, old age. The Rhythm Kings saw me cry that morning in Amsterdam, and I ain't afraid to admit as much.

By a coincidence, I'd been booked in for a TV show to do a jazz version of "Knock on Wood" that day in Amsterdam. My head is in jazz from all the way back, so it's fine by me. I go to the studio, and I do the vocal in one take—and the pianist said, "I don't know how you would have known all the little breaks we were getting ready to do, 'cause none of those chords are like the original 'Knock on Wood.'" I said, "I know music!" But because I'd just heard that Wilson had passed, I wasn't really even feeling like going through *nothing*. I just told him to play it, and I decided instantly not to sing it all the way up, I went all the way down with the bass. I was feeling low that day, believe me.

Chapter 23
EDDIE LOVES YOU SO

In 2008, at the humble age of seventy-two, I put out my first album on Stax in over thirty-five years, *Eddie Loves You So*. Stax? I hear you ask. Didn't the label go bust back in 1975? Didn't the "family" split up? Yes, and yes. Let me give you the shortest of history lessons.

The building on East McLemore was officially padlocked, and they were instructed to cease business in January of 1976. Al Bell continued to seek funding to get the label back in business, but that summer, when a judge in bankruptcy court gave Al one more week to raise half a million and he couldn't do so, the creditors started a mass sell-off.

Al had plenty on his mind right then. That same time, July 1976, he went up in court on those fourteen counts of conspiracy, to the tune of $18,000,000, against Union Planters. We all went to the trial to support him. And the guy from Union Planters that had been making all these loans, Joe Harwell, he comes in waving at everyone, like "What's up!" The prosecutors say to him, "Mr. Harwell, you have $18,000,000 of embezzlement here with different companies and so-called companies. You and Mr. Bell would have gotten together." Joe Harwell said: "It was me and only me." They had put him in the federal pen in Missouri, and they brought him down to make him so-called testify on Al Bell. And he blew that whole thing apart! He stood at the back door when the sheriffs were taking him out, said something to everyone in the court, he didn't give a fuck!

He may have been found innocent, but they destroyed my brother Al. He's a nice man, he went to university, well educated, if we want somebody to speak about Stax, it might as well be him. But once he went through all of that about Stax . . . He's still standing, but I know him, and he's not quite right.

Al admits as much. "A lot of my memory is lost from 1975–76," he says today. "That's when they really came to destroy me. I didn't realize I was disrupting the industry. I was just doing what we were doing."

Still, Al ended up doing all right in the end. Years later, he went off to head up Motown for Berry Gordy and helped oversee its successful sale to MCA. Then he started his own label and put out that song "Whoomp! (There It Is)" if a song is what you want to call it. Thing sold over four million copies. One of the last of the big blockbusters. Al could always smell a hit!

But all that was in the future when they started selling off Stax. Early in 1977 the publishing companies—including all of my copyrights from my years at Stax—went to the highest cash bidder, which was a guy called Al Bennett, who had founded Liberty Records some twenty years earlier. Bennett got East Memphis and Birdees for a $250,000 down payment on $1.8 million; five years later, after paying off the last of those installments, he sold the companies for at least twice as much to Rondor Music. It's hard to put a price on what that catalog was truly worth, but if you've got just an inkling of how often Stax songs get into movies, commercials, TV shows, how often they're played on the radio, how many times a year they get covered by other artists, you'll know that a quarter of a million up front was a steal.

Bennett tried to buy the Stax master tapes and the name as well, but this time the installment plan didn't carry enough weight with the court; they went for a lump payment of $1.3 million from a liquidation company that specialized in exactly this kind of transaction. Sure enough, before the year was out, that company had sold it on to a middleman company who quickly sold it on to Fantasy Records out in Berkeley, California. You know that both those companies extracted a significant profit, or they wouldn't have done the deal.

Fantasy, at least, was a proper music company, actively engaged in the business of making, promoting, and hopefully selling records. And it was a good sign when they hired David Porter—the first African American on the Stax payroll back in the 1960s, remember—to revive the company's fortunes. But there was only so much David could achieve; the label's name had been soured by its collapse, and although he signed some good artists, he was dealing with a company that was just a shell of its former self. It was too soon, and Stax shut up shop—again—within eighteen months.

Fantasy focused on the back catalog instead, marketing it—some might say milking it—for all it was worth. Felt like

I had more records out in the '80s and '90s, certainly on more compilations, than I ever had during the 1960s and '70s! In 2005 Fantasy was sold to Concord Records for a cool $80 million; you've got to believe our catalog played a significant part in those valuations. Concord then set about once again reviving the good name of Stax as an active record label; it re-signed Booker T. Jones, Isaac Hayes—and yours truly.

It was all much the same story with the Stax building on East McLemore. The bank, which had taken possession of the premises, sold it to a church in 1981. No installments needed for this deal: the church got it for ten bucks, on condition it be used for a nonprofit enterprise. It tells you how bad real estate had got in Memphis by then that the bank had to give the building away.

Bad times may also explain why the church in question couldn't come up with the funds to put anything in its place. Instead, in 1989, they tore the building down. Sure, we protested. Stax was history, man! That building, that old cinema where all the magic happened on the sloping studio floor, it was like tearing down Motown, or Sun Records. Should never have happened!

Well, as William Bell sang it all the way back in 1961, you don't miss your water until your well runs dry. Only when the building came down and the lot stood empty for year after year after year, did the Memphis musical community get together with the city's civic leaders to figure an alternative. As we turned the corner into the 2000s, a Stax Academy opened on the empty lot, providing an after-school education for local kids. Plans to rebuild an exact replica of Stax as a Museum of American Soul Music came to fruition in 2003. And I've got to say, it was impressive from the get-go. They rebuilt the structure to its original plans; they put the logo out front; got some of the M.G.'s precious equipment, down to the Hammond M3 on which Booker recorded "Green

Onions," to put behind glass in the sloping studio; tracked down the original recording equipment, including the giant mono recorder that Jim had his sister Estelle mortgage her house for; put a souvenir store—with records, of course—where Estelle's Satellite shop used to be; and made the rest of the premises a proper celebration of black American music, with multimedia history exhibitions going back to the spirituals sung in the cotton fields and the hallelujahs of the gospel church. You won't find anything like it anywhere else in America—and you certainly won't find Isaac Hayes's gold-plated Cadillac nowhere else!

I'm recognized within that museum with my own display, and so is everyone else. And that's as it should be. We all had a part to play; we all get the acknowledgment. Occasionally I go up there to take part in an event or just to stop by; it always freaks out the tourists, many of them from Europe, when they see a real, live Stax artist walking through the premises! And the story gets better: in 2005, a Soulsville Charter School was set up right next door. It takes struggling neighborhood elementary students and gives them a musical education right on up to high school graduation, with music as the central academic focus. These kids can play like nothing you've heard. If you go back to the start of my life story, you'll know how far we've all traveled that a kid can now be encouraged to focus on his soul music at school rather than be punished for it!

The Stax Museum has helped reinvigorate Memphis as a tourist music destination, one that includes Sun Studios, the Rock 'n' Soul Museum, a Walk of Fame on Beale Street and, at the Lorraine Motel where Dr. Martin Luther King Jr. was assassinated—but where "Knock on Wood" and so many other great Stax songs were written—the National Civil Rights Museum.

But I'm getting ahead of myself. For my album with Stax, *Eddie Loves You So*, I was hooked up with a couple of young musicians and producers out of Boston: Michael Dinallo and Ducky Carlisle, who went by the production name of the Tremolo Twins. The love that these guys had for my music was evident when they came over to London to meet me and brought a demo of an old Falcons song, "Since You've Been Gone," begging me to record it. Turned out we'd done the song back in 1960, just with piano, and it had been stored away with all the rest of my Uncle Robert West's recordings; Michael and Ducky found it on a Falcons compilation.

Well, with that kind of dedication from them, I knew we could get on just great, so we discussed doing the kind of album that I'd explored with *Back to the Roots*, but this time, especially as backed by Stax, doing it properly. We'd record a whole variety of songs I'd written over the years for other people, songs that people might know but might not know *me* for them. Like "I'll Always Have Faith in You," a hit for Carla Thomas and later covered by Billy Eckstine; "You Don't Know What You Mean to Me," which Cropper and I wrote for Sam & Dave; "Till My Back Ain't Got No Bone," which William Bell had recorded in 1971, though I also loved Esther Phillips's version from 1974; and "I Don't Want to Be with Nobody but You" from Dorothy Moore's million-selling album *Misty Blue*. (Dorothy's version was a cover of "I Don't Want to Be with Nobody but My Baby" from *Soul Street*, but she slowed it down, made it such a sweet ballad, that it was *her* recording I wanted to take on for myself!) We also did "Never Get Enough of Your Love," one of my solo singles on Safice from 1964, and I welcomed the chance to sing lead on "You're So Fine," the Falcons breakout song from 1959.

"You're So Fine" was one of just two songs from *Eddie Loves You So* that I'd also recorded for *Back to the Roots*. The other was "Consider Me," the only cut on the new album that had enjoyed success under my own name. But that was mostly in other countries, flipped over from the B-side, and along the way, I've come to believe that "Consider Me" is one of the better tracks I've written or recorded. Although there's no way of improving upon Booker's original production, with that heavenly Hammond part, I like to push the song out again, remind people it's there. As much as anything, I just love singing it in the studio to a new arrangement.

What I really liked about *Eddie Loves You So*, was that Ducky and Michael's recording and production was all of a groove. This felt like a real album, like it had all been recorded by the same musicians in the same studio at much the same time. And that's how it was. We had a solid rhythm section, we got B3 and piano, a brass section and some strings too. The result was true country soul, falling in that sweet spot I really enjoy, where the tempo slows down, and the singer's allowed to unfold his story. Nothing here runs away with itself; it all sounds authentic. I saw one review say that "it could have come out in 1967," and I realized it was meant as a compliment.

Eddie Loves You So got good reviews all around. The fact that I included a couple of new songs, and that many listeners couldn't tell as much, suggested to me that I still write well. As for my voice, the worst that was written about it was that it was a "trifle less brassy than forty years ago." And the biggest inaccuracy was that I sounded good for a man in his seventh decade. Hey, I was in my eighth already! But I'll take it! The only comment *I* may have had about the record was whether the keys that the Tremolo Twins laid the tracks down in were the ones best suited for my voice, but I guess that's what you get for coming in to sing once they've already been recorded.

I went back to the clubs to tour behind *Eddie Loves You So*. But all of us had to pause and reflect when Isaac Hayes left us that summer, just two days before I was meant to play with him in Philadelphia. What can I say about Isaac that

you don't already know? He'd gone through bankruptcy after
Stax collapsed; he'd badly needed those unpaid royalties to
keep up with his lifestyle. But he'd forced his way back and
found a whole other career as the voice of Chef on *South Park*.
Younger people might know him from that, and those of a
certain generation as Black Moses, the archetype of that deep,
deep voice, of the story-telling soul man and the composer
behind *Shaft*. And then others still know him as the dedicated
songwriter and producer who would show up every day at
East McLemore in the 1960s and contribute something to the
musical magic, whether it be writing "Soul Man" or "Hold On,
I'm Comin'" with David Porter for Sam & Dave, or walking
into my session for "Knock on Wood" and conjuring up that
middle eight out of nowhere. Isaac lived several lives, and every
one of them was worthy of praise.

One of the great tragedies of Isaac passing when he did was
that he had just provided a new recording for the movie *Soul
Men*, starring Samuel L. Jackson and Bernie Mac. They were
playing a duo getting back together after all these years, which
might remind you of Sam & Dave. The soundtrack also came out
through the new Stax setup with Concord and included Isaac's
new take on "Never Can Say Goodbye," John Legend singing
"I'm Your Puppet," and then no less than three songs of mine.
On top of my own recording of "I've Never Found a Girl," there
was Meshell Ndegeocello interpreting "Water," and Sharon Leal,
the female star of the movie, taking on my favorite, "Comfort
Me." What should have been a celebration—the movie played
well, did all right at the box office—was marred not just by the
passing of Isaac but, the very day before, and three months ahead
of the movie's release, that of its co-star Bernie Mac. I had five
years on Isaac already, some twenty on Bernie Mac. It was a
reminder that you never know when your number might be up.

Maybe that helps explain why, at some point in the 1990s, I had made the decision to truly come back to my roots. After all those years living elsewhere, in Detroit, D.C., Memphis, London—even had a flat in Paris for a while—plus all the time spent living out of a suitcase, I felt the call of sweet home Alabama like never before. Of course, I was never far from it anyway, with all the recording we did in Muscle Shoals, and with my ma and grandma being down here. But there comes a time when you start thinking, home is where I want to be. I like the slow pace down in Alabama. I can deal with the heat in summer, and the storms that they bring. I like the space we got down here. And I appreciate the way people show you respect— whatever you may think from what you've seen and read over the years. No one refers to me as Eddie Floyd down here. It's a funny thing about the South. Country people, they gonna call you by your first name. But if I'm older than you, I'm a Mister, period. Mister Eddie. To the kids, it's Uncle Eddie. And to some adults, all of the family of the kids, they say "I heard about your Uncle." And we call a woman of a certain age "Miss" or "Mrs.," depending. Nothing wrong with politeness in this world.

Besides, my second wife, Sonja, and I had grown apart, as couples often do, and we decided to move on with our lives. We've remained good friends all the way down the line. Never been no fighting wherever we be. A lot of people can't do it like that; they just got to be fighting. But we ain't got no problem with each other, and I know all along I'm gonna take care of my baby girl Nicolle. She grew up to become a lawyer in Atlanta; her own kids are now moving on to college. I got that bond with all my kids. And same with their moms; no problem with any of them.

So I found myself a decent plot of land easy driving distance from Montgomery, on a public road, not too big or flashy, but large enough that I could build myself a homestead and have myself some privacy. It was all woods when I bought it, and I cleared the land myself. And when I say I cleared the land myself, I don't mean I hired someone to do it. I mean, I got me a tractor and pulled out the trees with my own damn hands! I was involved in every part of the building, too, right down to excavating and filling a couple of ponds out front. I call it "The Farm." Not that I'm actually farming out there, but it gives you a sense of the place. And I've built it up over the years: got myself a separate building with all my mementos; an indoor shrine to my team, the Dallas Cowboys; a room for the beds that belonged to my mother and grandmother; and plenty of space for guests when the family comes down. From Montgomery, I can drive up to Memphis in a few hours, over to Jackson in less than that, up to Macon. It's a longer drive to the Dallas Cowboys games, but I can't help myself. A man's got to have his team. It was like Bill Wyman with his Crystal Palace, the soccer club; you couldn't keep him away from them!

Funny thing is, though, this is my home city, and I must have played it but only a handful of times in all my life. I got to perform at the Laicos Club on Holt Street way back in the 1960s, when I was on Stax; a few years ago, a student came to interview me and brought by a picture he'd found. And every now and then there's been a special event that I've been asked to pitch in for. But Montgomery, for all its musical history, is not really a big music town.

Course that's not true of Alabama as a whole. These days, aren't too many people don't know about FAME Studios in Muscle Shoals, about the Swampers who built their own place across town, about Rick Hall and Quin Ivy, and how some of the greatest songs in the world—and not just soul music— were recorded up there. No surprise then that when they got to building an Alabama Music Hall of Fame they located it in

Tuscumbia, one of four municipalities—along with Sheffield, Florence, and Muscle Shoals itself—that forms the city of Muscle Shoals. The induction awards started in 1985 and run every other year. You won't be surprised to know the first inductees were people like Nat King Cole, Hank Williams, Rick Hall, Buddy Killen, Sam Phillips, W. C. Handy, and the Muscle Shoals Rhythm Section. You might not know all the other great music people to come out of Alabama: Dinah Washington, Tammy Wynette, Jimmie Rodgers, the Commodores, Martha Reeves, so many members of the Temptations, Dan Penn and Spooner Oldham, the groups Alabama and Styx, even Sun Ra. And that's not counting the rich tradition of us solo soul singers: Percy Sledge, Clarence Carter, Candi Staton, and of course Wilson Pickett and yours truly. Some of us had to leave the state behind to find ourselves, but all of us took Alabama along for the ride. I was inducted in 2003, alongside Clarence Carter and Emmylou Harris.

Montgomery is changing now, with younger people moving in, the city embracing its history rather than hiding from it, and a Mayor, Todd Strange, who seems to want to do some good things. I met him a couple of times, at the Alabama Music Hall of Fame. He asked me, "Would you consider maybe having a big studio in downtown Montgomery?" I said, "Well, maybe a *little* studio." I'm not really interested in no studio, I'm happy being off in the woods. I don't advertise myself. I've never done that. And I like that people leave me alone when I come into town; most of them got no idea who I am. Just maybe see that I dress all right and that I'm polite to people. That's enough for an old man. But I also like the notion of being recognized in my hometown for what I've *achieved*, so I leave that door open.

Something else the mayor's talking about is putting together a permanent exhibit to Montgomery's musicians at the airport.

It's a tiny airport, nothing like one of those big city hubs; you can park up and be on board your plane within about ten minutes, and that's at Montgomery pace! Still, if you've been through the airports at Cleveland—or even Philly—you'll know what I'm talking about. A city *should* celebrate its music culture.

Listen, I'm always happy to give something back. I just don't feel the need to make a big song and dance about it. In 2017, I met this guy at the Governor's Awards in Montgomery where I was honored. He's from Mount Meigs; he's a school teacher there; he knows that I come from there. He meets me, and he tells me who he is and what he does. That sent me right off because all through these years, I never stopped thinking about where I come from, and I never stopped thinking about the kids. Look, I was there sixty years ago, and I know things must have changed. From what he's saying, the kids at Mount Meigs now, they're the real undesirables, they don't know where they wanna go in the world.

He invites me down there to see what these kids do. They write poems, and every year somebody gathers a book on them. Not only that school, but other ones like it across the state. He sent the book up to me, and I looked at the poems, and the first one hit me, period. It said "Tiny three walls, tiny windows, all that I have to see. Sour milk and sloppy joes is what I have to eat." Sixty-five years earlier that's what I saw—and powdered milk is what I had to drink. Now if that wasn't all the way close! This is 2017. Sour milk and sloppy joes? Mine was "powdered milk and gingerbread," that's what *we* were getting at night. Never was a dinner. It just sounded like the exact same way it was back then.

So during the next few weeks, I went up to Memphis, four times in all, and I put musical tracks together. I read the poems, and I put the right stuff behind them. If he was a person who was brutalized out on the street and he's talking death, I knew what music I wanted to put behind that. And if he was a motivated speaker who wanted to rule the world, I gave him that kind of music. I sent it to the man I'd met to play for the kids. I'm told they're all really excited about me coming down and playing it all for them.

And then a week before it takes place, I'm told the director will have to speak, and someone else will have to speak, and maybe I could sing a little and say a few words to them, because they only have an hour. But they got years! Man, they got eleven hours before the next day!

I wrote and told the man, "I can see that your hands are tied. Congratulations on your kids, but I decline on coming." I wouldn't want to do it that way. I definitely wouldn't have went and sung a song—and then turned around and chastised 'em. They know who they are. My theory was, if I did go out and show them everything I've been doing, that's like telling the person they can make it too, just because I did. But life is not that simple. I'm willing to go out, tell the whole damn world, *I want to live*, period. That should be enough.

Chapter 24
EDDIE'S GOING SHAGGING

I think I'm complete. I've always felt that way, all through my life. The blessing part of it is, I think I'm complete, and then boom! Something else starts. So here we go, we're writing a book! There's many other things happening right now, in my eighties, that I'm going to get a chance to do if I'm lucky.

I have no regrets. I think I've had the opportunity to play with almost everybody. Or at least almost everybody who's been alive for me to play with. (I still wish I could have sung with Johnny Ace!) But really, I'm a fan of them all. I see a guy, and he's playing the guitar the way he's playing. We have no jealousy. We never have any problem with music.

I'm happy that I'm still playing with Steve—and every now and then, with Booker too. We had the Royal Albert Hall shows celebrating Stax in 2017, and then at the end of the year, we played up in New York to celebrate the release of another Blues Brothers Band album, *The Last Shade of Blue Before Black*. Only the second studio album we'd ever done and the first in a quarter century, and I got a couple of my own songs on there, including a new number: "Don't Forget About James Brown." You know by now that I don't never stop writing, and I also give credit where credit is due. But other than that show, I retired from the Blues Brothers Band a fair few years ago. Just a little too much traveling and touring; it was time to slow down. I knew I'd found the right moment to leave when they brought in a new vocalist, Bobby Harden, and he was everything I'd been when I was younger. Every time I see him, I tell him, "I saw you, my man, and I said, 'That's it! I can go back to the house and rest!'" It's wonderful when you can find someone younger who gets what it is you're doing. Sometimes I play with the younger people, and they be nice, but the music doesn't always quite lock in. We went through a period where the new guys, nine times out of ten, they would say, "That's *all* you want me to play on it?" I'd said, "Don't play no more, that's for sure!" I mean, listen to Duck's bass line on "Knock on Wood." It's all you need.

I miss Duck so much. He died in Tokyo, in 2012, in his bed, after five nights of double shows at the Blue Note, playing alongside Cropper and me and Steve Potts. We'd had us a blast; had no idea that this was going to be the end of the road for him. You can imagine how we felt when we heard he wasn't going to be joining us for breakfast, not for the flight home, not for nothing ever again. I guess if you have to go, and we all do, then maybe being on tour, playing the music you love with the people you love, is about the best way for it to happen. But look, if you'd met Duck, you would have had the same reaction that everyone else had. He was a very genuine person. Love him with all my heart, and I miss him, all the time. Never seen him frown. There was just always a smile; that's the way he was.

I'm proud to say that I've never had a manager—not in the sense of someone who controls your career. Nobody's ever led me anywhere. It's not like I had someone who got me to a record deal, recorded an album on me, and now we're gonna book you all over the country. I've seen some artists like that, out on the road, tired, be out there for months, getting ready to go home, the phone rings: "You've got to go do a show in LA." "Huh? But I'm *tired*." People with managers will be trying to get you fifteen interviews, where one interview might be totally sufficient.

I have people saying to me, "If you got this guy here, you could be doing twenty television shows." But that don't faze me. I think you'll find I did me some TV shows down the years, do you understand? I mean, I did play the White House!

These people keep saying, "But you could be . . . but you could be . . ." and I say, I'm fine, man, what are you talking about? I got a badass Lincoln I bought with cash. But I ain't driven it in eight years because I like to drive a truck! And people say, "Yeah but you could be more." And I always ask them, "What is 'more'?" It's a common thing for human beings to feel that way. But I'm happy with exactly what I've got. Satisfied with it.

People say to me, "Hey, Eddie, you could sell your publishing rights for ten million dollars, you know?" But I'm in my eighties: I don't need ten million dollars. Maybe I'm happy to just keep working with the same company that's done right by me all along. Getting greedy doesn't often work out in the long run. Besides, all money ain't for you, remember?

The way it works is this: I just stay within that circuit, where I've been for all these years, and that means people know how to find me. So, I receive a telephone call and they say, "Can we book you?" I say, "Okay, what is it, when is it?" You tell me the price, and I say "Okay," if I can do it for that. You pay for my flight. And I'll be there. And I don't ever miss a show. A lot of people don't have that reputation.

I've been blessed that it's been just enough. I'm just trying to be there, just keep doing something, and hope it comes to you as a result. So maybe you get one very, very big gig—like the Albert Hall—and the next one is not so big, but it's a gig, so how can I fight it?

If I look back over the last ten years, a period most people would have spent in retirement already, I figure I've ticked off several more boxes. In 2013, I made another studio album, *Down by the Sea*. Like you might guess from that title, it's my beach music record. "Eddie's Going Shagging." And I know what some of my British fans are going to think, but that just means *you* don't know how to shag like they do in the Carolinas! Come on over to my place and see it for yourself. Better yet, give it a listen.

The year before that, I made a Christmas album: *I'll Be Your Santa Claus*. You got this far in the story; you'll know how much I love Christmas. Always wanted to make me a Christmas record. So I did. Wrote all the songs too, from "Doo Wop Christmas" to "Santa and the Boys." Bobby Manuel showed up to play guitar for me. And I'm looking dapper as ever on the front cover. Did I expect it to sell? That wasn't the point. Not at this stage. I'm doing this stuff for me, for my family, for my friends, and for whoever else is interested. Fact is, I'm fortunate enough that I can do these things.

Maybe one idea I have left is to do a duets album. I'd love to get together with Miss Carla, Mavis Staples, Dorothy Moore maybe—I wrote a couple of songs for her most recent album—and do it in the studio together this time. And no second takes!

Maybe that will happen, maybe it won't, but at the same time, it's not like I can help myself.

For example, I've got this thing about trains. Always have, ever since I used to make that journey from Montgomery to Detroit with my mother. I've got model trains in the same guest house where I keep my souvenirs. We've all got our hobbies, right? Just so happens that some of the best train journeys you can still take in the States are up in the Carolinas, where I still go perform on that beach circuit. Recently, I went up there, had me a lovely little time on the old stream trains, made sure to get lots of pictures. And when I came home, I recorded a song for the train guys, put a video to it from all the stills from that last journey, and brought it on up as a souvenir, a little gesture of thanks to the folks who keep the old lines alive.

I get a lot of opportunities to revisit my past nowadays. I'm at the age where they start giving you these awards whether you want them or not. Maybe they figure they want to give you something now so you can show up on stage to collect in person; it's not much of an awards show if everyone's passed on already! I've even been to England for the *Mojo Magazine Awards*. In 2016, I get a brass note on Beale Street in Memphis—it's like the city's equivalent of the Hollywood Walk of Fame—and in November 2018, I finally get inducted into the Memphis Music Hall of Fame too. See what I mean? Every time I feel complete, something else comes along. Every few months, one of my songs shows up on another movie, another TV show. We had a song cut on Carla that was lost in the Stax vaults all the way into the 1990s, "It Ain't No Easy Thing." Sweet song too; in 2018 it got used on a new movie *White Boy Rick*. The following year they rerelease the Soul Explosion on vinyl after a half century, and another forgotten song I wrote for Carla, "Book of Love," is finally available once more.

Miss Thomas was there for my induction into the Memphis Music Hall of Fame. In fact, she gave the induction speech which makes sense, because without her, as you well know by now . . . She and William Bell then shared "634–5789," leaving me to try and match them by performing "Knock on Wood" just *one more time*. It was a beautiful evening. Jerry Lee Lewis, who's got two years on me, was there, played "Great Balls of Fire" to honor its own award. The Box Tops, who started out in Memphis covering a lot of Stax soul music, they got inducted too. And so did Aretha Franklin, who came from Memphis even if her music did not; the Queen of Soul had passed away earlier in the year. That's what I mean: they got to get you on stage while they still can!

Just a few years back, they had a Radio Caroline boat cruise in the seas around Britain. Emperor Rosko was on board; he's still going strong. The Rhythm Kings came for the ride too. Not Bill Wyman—it wasn't his thing—but Terry was there with everyone else. We had us a ball hanging with the people who were in the audience each night, many of them who'd bought the records back in the '60s. The same people who put me in the British charts—and, like Rosco said back in '67, "not only at number one, but also at number two."

The day that cruise ended though, I received bad news. My aunt Kathleen West had fallen and broken her hip. You didn't think she'd still be around, did you? Sadly, she wasn't for much longer, I'm sorry to say. When I got back and saw her in the hospital, she didn't actually really know me. But she made it to ninety-nine—and a half.

People say we got some good genes in our family. That may be true, and some of us do have a habit of sticking around, but the genes from my generation is just about gone. We still have little saplings all over the place; they'll take over. And that's all how it should be.

Of all the things I've done in my life, I particularly like to revisit what we did with the Falcons, the world's first soul group. It's still so hard to believe some of it took place over sixty years ago! A few years back, we were told we'd be receiving a gold disc and that it would be presented in Detroit. Mack Rice was in a residential home by then, suffering from Alzheimer's disease, but we were hoping he'd be able to join us. When Mack went back to Detroit after he was done with all the music, he took the money he'd earned from all his songwriting and started an asphalt company. Ended up with all manner of trucks, a massive business! I figure he must have laid down half the roads in Motor City this last twenty-five years. Sadly, he passed away in the summer of 2016. I went up for the funeral, of course, and then a couple of months later, went back up and reunited with Willie Schofield, Ben Knight, and Lance Finney for the awards show. I told people there, all the family and friends, my favorite singer in the Falcons was Joe Stubbs; it's no insult on Pickett to say that, just tells you how good the competition was back there, back then. But Joe, too, he's long gone, passed away back in 1998, just fifty-five years old.

Having made it through my eightieth birthday and thrown that big party, I figured well, let's keep going strong. So for my eighty-first, I went back up to Detroit for a week to have a birthday with the kids up there. And then me and Willie Schofield went on a walk around Detroit. All the neighborhoods, all the places we'd been and where we started the music. That's something I'd never done before. My uncle's real estate office, the bar on the corner, the school out the back of me—most of the places aren't there anymore, though United Sounds Systems recording studios got a historical marker in 2017. And, of course, Hitsville U.S.A. never got torn down like Stax did. Motown always made money. I guess Berry Gordy learned a lot from watching my Uncle Robert West back in the day, what he did with all his little labels and with us, the Falcons.

That's why I have a slogan: The only thing new is you. No matter who it be, whenever it be. Because the music's coming from way back, and you're not coming up with nothing new but you. It's about you, how you present it, what you bring to it, how you live it. I'm singing just like I did my whole life and whenever I achieve something, that's a plus. But I'm not thinking, *If I just go do this, I can get that.* 'Cause if you think like that you won't get anything. No, just stay straight. Just work at it. That's all you do. I love the music; I write the music, and if then I realize the people love the music . . . I'm good to go.

ACKNOWLEDGMENTS

I first met Eddie Floyd in the spring of 2015, in his home city of Montgomery, Alabama, as I concluded a weeks-long road trip researching a Wilson Pickett biography. My journey had taken me from New York to Detroit, Memphis, and Muscle Shoals— all cities that, coincidentally, have loomed large in Eddie's own musical voyage.

I had contacted Eddie by sending an email to the address listed on his website and then leaving a message on the published phone number. Eddie called me back personally. I have often dealt directly with musicians, but this was, I believe, the first time I'd found a proven hit-maker, and in this case a true soul music legend, giving out his direct line, online.

We met at Montgomery's smartest hotel. Eddie, his silver hair the only true sign of old age on a honed body that men half his age would covet, was dressed to the nines, sporting a stylish two-tone suit as if ready to step on stage at a moment's notice. After conducting our interview in the hotel bar, Eddie offered to stand lunch as thanks for traveling to his neck of the woods. Such behavior is not entirely unknown, but it is certainly uncommon; most musicians assume respect (and gratuities) to flow towards them as a matter of course. To my rather sheepish protestations that the hotel restaurant didn't cater to my diet, Eddie suggested we cross the road into Montgomery's passably busy downtown, where his fashion sense certainly caught the eye, even if his face did not elicit immediate recognition. At the end of our meal at a popular pasta restaurant, during which Eddie enjoyed another glass of red wine as he reminisced about his decades-long relationship with fellow Montgomery native, the "Wicked" Pickett, he paid by pulling an old-fashioned bank roll from his pants pocket and peeling off the requisite notes. I then walked with him to his vehicle, a large pick-up with a "STAX" license plate, commemorating the Memphis record label with which he made his name as a solo musician. I came away under no illusions that I had just spent several hours with the living embodiment of the Soul Man.

Two years later, after the Wilson Pickett biography was published, it struck me that too many of his and Eddie Floyd's generation—those who hit their creative and commercial peaks in the mid-to-late 1960s, during which time "soul" became the byword for black American popular music to the extent that it replaced R&B as the name of the *Billboard* chart—had passed away without telling their stories. Sure, some of Detroit's Motown legends had published autobiographies, but with the exception of forerunners like James Brown and Ray Charles, none of those singers who had committed to a grittier version of soul music had ever seemingly put pen to paper—or even voice to tape—to record their life stories for posterity.

To some extent, the lack of first-hand accounts reflects the commercial reality check of a music that is greatly loved and internationally revered, but one in which the individual singers rarely receive due respect as artists, only as interchangeable front men for what's often presumed to be other peoples' songs. I therefore approached Eddie Floyd with a view to righting that wrong.

As you might conclude, given that you're holding his book in your hands, Eddie welcomed my suggestion, and in the summer of 2017, I stayed at his homestead just outside Montgomery, where only a couple of weeks earlier he had hosted a vast crowd of family and friends to celebrate his eightieth birthday. Over the course of several days, he not only put me up in his house, but he sat for hours of interviews, dug out dozens of photographs, took me on guided tours of his childhood haunts—and, as when I'd met him two years earlier, refused to let me pay for a thing. We met for further interviews and observations on three more occasions: in London in September 2017 for the BBC Proms "Stax Records: 50 Years of Soul" two-nighter at the Royal Albert Hall, in New York City at the end of that November for rehearsals and then a long-awaited reunion of the Blues Brothers Band, and in Memphis in June 2018. I would like to take this opportunity to thank Mr. Eddie Floyd not only for agreeing to tell his story in the first place, and for having faith in me as his conduit for doing so, but for his sincere hospitality and generosity throughout the process, as evidenced above.

With Eddie's full encouragement, I set about conducting further interviews to make his autobiography the richest that it could be. My gratitude to Steve Cropper in Nashville, David Porter in Memphis, and Alvertis Isbell in Little Rock for welcoming me on a road trip I took in November 2017. Thanks are also due the Stax legends (albeit for different reasons) William Bell and Deanie Parker and Eddie's former business partners Alan Walden and Tim Whitsett, for talking extensively by phone when we couldn't connect physically. My gratitude to Lou "Blue" Marini, founding member of the Blues Brothers Band for taking me into his home to talk, to Tommy McDonnell from the Blues Brothers Band for his interview, to Bobby Harden from the same band for his enthusiasm and friendship, and to Eddie's UK bandleader Andy Dummett for long-distance conversation and correspondence.

It's a mark of the reverence with which Eddie Floyd is held by those outside his immediate musical community that Bruce Springsteen agreed to an interview upon receipt of just a single email; I thank him for taking time out from his busy Broadway schedule to call me. Ditto Paul Young for his memories. Bill Wyman jumped at the chance to talk about his occasional Rhythm Kings front man, inviting me to call him in the South of France. My thanks to Terry Taylor, Bill's long-time musical comrade and Rhythm Kings guitarist, for sitting with me in London and facilitating that interview with Bill. Additional gratitude to Willie Schofield for welcoming me into his Detroit home in 2015 to discuss the Falcons, to Brett Fleming of WEVL Memphis's "Soul Stew" for permission to use his 2017 interview with Eddie and Ms. Carla Thomas, and to former *Blues & Soul* editor, tour promoter, and Contempo label head John Abbey for his assistance past and present.

Thank you to Scott B. Bomar at BMG Books for jumping at the opportunity to publish Eddie's autobiography and for patiently shepherding it through to publication, to Kate Hyman for introducing us, and to the Author's Guild for its assistance with contracts, a valuable benefit of membership.

Almost everyone I spoke to throughout this process, from the superstars to the session musicians, from the businessmen to the backroom staff, talked enthusiastically about Eddie's considerable skill sets: an unyielding work ethic, a commitment to his craft as singer and writer alike, a uniquely powerful voice and commanding stage presence, a hands-on but bullshit-free approach to business, and a deeply personal connection with his audience. These attributes are manifested by the fact that Eddie has remained untainted by scandal throughout his six-decade career, and could still be found conducting his own business affairs in the late 2010s. I believe it's fair to say Eddie understands that while his career has involved not just its considerable highs but also its inevitable lows, he has never wavered in his own gratitude for an incredibly fulfilling life, in which he has taken his childhood dreams of a musical career further than such dreams might once have allowed. I hope his story serves as inspiration.

—Tony Fletcher, Kingston NY, November 2019.

INDEX